Pure Water

The Science of Water, Waves, Water Pollution,
Water Treatment, Water Therapy
and Water Ecology

Casey Adams, Ph.D.

Pure Water: The Science of Water, Waves, Water Pollution,
    Water Treatment, Water Therapy and Water Ecology
Copyright © 2010 Casey Adams
SACRED EARTH PUBLISHING
Wilmington, Delaware
http://www.sacredearthpublishers.com
All rights reserved.
Printed in USA
Original cover painting ("Rays") by Patrick Parker
Original back cover image by Ilco
Interior drawings by Virginia Callow

Publishers Cataloging in Publication Data
Adams, Casey
Pure Water: The Science of Water, Waves, Water Pollution,
    Water Treatment, Water Therapy and Water Ecology
First Edition
1. Science. 2. Health
    Bibliography and References; Index

Library of Congress Control Number: 2010920973

ISBN 978-1-936251-04-9

For those who seek the humility of water
as it seeks the lowest point

Table of Contents

Introduction

All of us are attracted to the beauty and rhythms of water. Think about it. Higher-priced houses are typically near or on ocean fronts, lake fronts or river sides. Among those houses near the water, those houses with water views are the most expensive. For those houses not near the water, we often add artificial bodies of water such as ponds, fountains, and pools.

We yearn to connect with the rhythm of water. When we go on vacation, we typically travel to water. We go to the lake, the ocean, the river, or the waterfalls. Again, we seek to connect with this flowing medium. Why?

The dimension of water is one of motion, flexibility, sound, and diffusion. Water stimulates relaxation, letting our body energies harmonize with the flow and rhythms of its movement. Once within water, we can flow with its tides and currents; surf its waves and eddies; and synchronize with its motion. Into water we can dive, piercing the surface like a knife into butter; sliding into its depths. In water our bodies can soak, feeling the water pressure embracing our skin and filling our pores.

There is an inexhaustibly beautiful nature about water. It has a harmonic quality: an orchestration of motion, power, color and grace. Water moves in waves, and in order to synchronize with it, one must cooperate with this movement. This means harmonizing, somehow to the wave motion of water. A surfer accomplishes this by taking off at the crest and cruising along the wall of the wave, between the crest and the trough. Utilizing the power that balances at this wall, a surfer can gain incredible speeds, rendering power and maneuverability.

This power can be extended to all aspects of water. Water provides instant hydration, nutrition, and therapy to every organ in the body. Every cell bathes in water, and an ionic balance is achieved on each side of the cell membrane. Our bodies also maintain such a balance, as we bathe and drink water each and every day. Without water for only a few days, our body will cease function. This is the equivalent nature of water: Without it, life on this planet will cease.

Our search, then, is for pure water. We need water in nature's pureness. Polluted water is toxic to our bodies. Our bodies become sick immediately from water filled with disease-causing microorganisms or chemical toxins. Without purity, our water will make us sick. Without purity, our water is practically useless.

For thousands of years prior to this past century, humans were intimately connected to nature. We lived with the tides, the rivers, the oceans, the streams and the lakes. We drank water by dipping our hands in and slurping it up. We bathed by taking a big dive into clear waters. Our waters were pure, and those living among natural surroundings had little fear of cholera, dengue fever and other waterborne diseases. This all before the advent of chlorinated water treatment systems.

What has changed? Why is pure water so hard to find today? Why is it even a country home now needs an expensive filtration system to avoid disease? Why is it that millions are dying from waterborne diseases from drinking the waters that their ancestors drank from for thousands of years?

This book sets out to answer these questions. Along the way, we answer some of the critical questions regarding the best types of water to drink, the best filter systems, and in general, how to use water to keep the body healthier.

—Casey Adams, January, 2010 *cadams@realnaturalhealth.com*

~ One ~

What is Water?

Water is the most abundant molecule on the planet. It is also the planet's most useful and effective molecule. What makes water so special?

In strictly chemistry terms, water is composed of two hydrogen atoms and one oxygen atom, bound together with covalent orbital bonding. This means the oxygen atom and the two hydrogen ions theoretically share two of electrons amongst themselves.

This 'sharing' oxygen atom has eight electron orbitals among two shells. The first shell is complete with two electrons, so there isn't any sharing in this shell. The second shell is complete when there are eight electrons. Oxygen, however, only has six electrons in that second shell. This means it needs two more electrons to become *stable*. This is where hydrogen comes in.

The hydrogen ion, on the hand, only has one electron in its first shell, and it needs two to fill out this shell. So oxygen shares one electron from each of two hydrogens to fill out its shell, while the sharing also fills out the hydrogen shells. This gives the entire molecule equilibrium. It is now water, with a molecular formula of H_2O.

Water's molecular arrangement, called covalence, creates two "ears" or hydrogen bonds on one side of the oxygen atom. This sharing of electrons creates a rather unique bond angle between the oxygen and two hydrogen atoms. While many assume the geometric 109-degree tetrahedral structure, water's two oxygen-hydrogen bonds orient at 104.5-degree angles from each other.

Chemists and physicists theorize this mysterious bond angle is due to weak polar repulsion-attraction forces that exist between the two hydrogens. Whatever the reason, this is but one of many mysteries that plague water from a scientific perspective.

We often hear the phrase "water is water" as the discussion of hydration comes up. While all water contains H_2O, there are many different forms of water, depending upon where the water has been, what temperature it is and what is in it. The compounds water mixes with, and the chemicals that dissolve in it also depend upon its temperature and elemental state. These in turn relate to water's ionic properties, mineral content, pollutants, dissolved solids and microorganism content. These in turn affect water's magnetic polarity, taste, smell and usefulness as a hydrating compound.

The terms 'soft water' and 'hard water' are thrown around rather loosely in the commercial water biz. Water's total dissolved solid level or number of calcium carbonate ions are typically used to measure 'hardness.' Over 150 parts per million (ppm) of dissolved solids is usually considered 'hard.' In other words, the measurement is based upon the water's mineral content. Calcium and iron deposits are usually the big deterrent. Soft water is generated by adding sodium chloride to the water. As we will discuss in depth later, this 'soft' water might be good for the pipes in our house, but it is not so good for our body's 'pipes.'

The mineral levels in water directly affect the polarity and pH of our water. Higher mineral levels create more alkalinity. Calcium and magnesium are the minerals most often found in natural waters, but numerous trace elements are also found in natural spring and well waters. These natural minerals or dissolved solids also directly relate to water's surface tension and adhesion ability, which in turn affects its ability to be assimilated and utilized efficiently. This in turn directly affects water's ability to adequately hydrate the body. Certainly, the phrase "water is water" simply doesn't register.

Water circulates through all living organisms as a vital fluid. In humans, 70-90% of our blood is water and about 75% of our muscle tissue is water, depending upon our age and health. At the cellular level, some 60% of the body's water is intracellular while about 40% is extracellular.

Meanwhile, over two-thirds (about 71%) of the earth's surface is water. Geologists estimate that about 96.6% of the earth's water lies on the earth's surface in the form of oceans, rivers, and lakes. Another 1.75% is estimated to be in the form of ice, and about 1.7% of the earth's waters are thought to be underground in the form of aquifers and underground rivers. Water is also held in soil moisture, in the atmosphere, and within living organisms. Still, these combined are minute compared with the other waters of the planet. Some estimates are that there are about 332,500,000 cubic miles of water on the planet.

Over 96% of the earth's water is salt water. Of the remaining fresh water, more than 68% lies within glaciers and ice. Thirty percent of fresh water is under ground, leaving just under 1% of fresh water (which is 3% of the earth's total water) on the surface. Rivers only account for about 2% of this surface water, or $1/700^{th}$ of 1% of the total water. Thus, useable fresh surface water is only about $3/10^{th}$ of 1% of the total water on earth. This means that over 99% of the earth's waters are not readily useable by humans. Ground water pumping increases that only slightly, as does the current capacity to convert salt water to fresh water with desalination.

Very little of the water in our environment is drinkable. Surface water supplies about 90% of the water moving into vapor, and organism transpiration provides the other 10%. The sun's radiation breaks the water's inter-bonding, leading to vaporization. This process will occur until the air is saturated with vapor, leading to a relative humidity of 100%. Most of this water vapor stays over the oceans, while about 10% moves over land where it can fall into fresh water reserves. Water vapor moves towards colder regions. As the saturated air is cooled, condensation occurs. In this form water vapor changes into liquid water, retained within cloud formations. While water droplets are not exclusively held in clouds (fog and air also contains water droplets), clouds provide the majority of traveling water.

Because the atmospheric pressure is less at greater altitudes, the air temperature is also cooler. Cooler air allows the water droplets to be retained within the clouds as they move about the atmosphere. This cooler air (below dew point) accompanies condensation levels higher than evaporation levels, causing clouds to form. Because air rises, and the air below a cloud is denser than the cloud itself, clouds float.

Cloud water constantly evaporates and condenses as clouds gyrate and temperatures change. There are two general theories of what causes rain. Some believe that precipitation requires the water droplets to condense upon particles of dust or salt. An accumulation of water droplets colliding with these particulates are thought to produce precipitation. Other scientists believe that ice crystals form in clouds as temperatures cool—referred to as the *Bergeron-Findeisen process*. This causes the ice to fall out due to increased weight. If the temperature near land is higher, the ice crystals melt. If the ground temperature is less, they drop as snow or ice rain.

In the 1980s, David Sands, PhD—a professor of plant sciences at the University of Montana—and a team of researchers found that certain bacteria seemed to be present in most precipitation and ice events, leading them to propose an effect called *bio-precipitation* (Caple *et al.* 1986). In 2008, further evidence has uncovered that these bacteria may play a critical role in forming the ice that eventually falls to the earth as either rain or snow.

Once rain or snow falls, the surface water gathers into streams, some of which filter into the ground and become part of underwater aquifers. These aquifers form pockets of water storage. Their waters also flow out to lakes and oceans—just as surface rivers do. This outflow of fresh waters through surface and underground rivers complete the water cycle. The circulation process around the earth is very precise. For this reason, we can almost predict within a few inches how much annual rainfall each particular region around the planet will receive.

As water moves, it has considerably more energy than when it is stagnant. While moving within a living system, water brings together various minerals and nutrients, sparking enzymatic reactions that create a host of byproducts.

The composition of ocean water and the composition of human blood are very similar. Both contain similar levels of electrolytes, including magnesium (3.7% by weight in ocean, 4.8% by weight in blood); sodium (30.6% vs. 34.8% respectively); potassium (1.9% vs. 1.1%); calcium (2.1% vs. 1.2%); sulfide (7.7% vs. 10.9%) and chloride (55.2% vs. 40.1%). We can thus say with certainty that not only are the earth and the human organism both made up of about 70% water, but the content of much of that water is also extremely similar. We note that other living organisms vary slightly in their water content from humans as well.

Within living organisms, water travels via channels of current. Within the earth, we see this same movement of water: in the form of channels of rivers, streams, and springs. Within the oceans, we also see channels of tides, eddies, currents and streams of differentiated water. We also see these same circulatory effects as we follow fluids circulating through our body via blood vessels, capillaries and the lymphatic system. Within the basal membranes, we also see extracellular water moving in channel diffusion, and we see streams of water flowing in and out of the cell through ion channels embedded within cell membranes.

Because water belongs to the chemical family of hydrides, its melting and boiling points should correspond with the rest of the family—regulated theoretically by its molecular weight. However, this is not the case with water. If water were aligned with the characteristics of other compounds in the hydride family it would not be in liquid form at the temperatures of living systems—notably on the earth and in the body. It would evaporate and exist as vapor at these temperatures. Water is a unique substance to say the least.

The extraordinary stability of the covalent bonding between two hydrogens and oxygen renders water the unique ability to have a higher boiling point than expected and a lower melting point than expected, as well as an abnormal amount of surface tension. Surface tension is created by the weak hydrogen bonds that occur between separate water molecules. These weak bonds pull molecules together, creating a surface area and adhesion. Water's surface tension allows it to retain its shape and structure throughout its travels. Without surface tension, water would simply seep into its surrounding environment and disappear.

Water's surface tension also translates and refracts light together with other radiation. As the visible light spectrum collides with water, part of the light will refract through the water and part of the light will reflect off the water's surface. Its refractive strength is also evident when we see an upside down reflection of a scene on the other side of a lake. We also notice this effect when we hear and see sonic waves transmitting through the medium of water. Many species of life, such as whales and dolphins, utilize sonic waves to communicate.

Water's surface tension renders it the ability to form a sort of thin membrane enabling it to resist entry to various substances and objects. This aspect gives water the ability to support and protect living organisms.

Water's inward surface tension combined with its unique angular orbital bonding renders raindrops, dewdrops, and bubbles almost perfectly spherical in shape. With this convex inward surface tension we also find, as D'Arcy Wentworth Thompson pointed out almost a century ago, that the surface tension of water is also at least partially responsible for the appearance of rainbows through water vapor.

The Liquid Element

Just about every ancient, traditional, and modern scientific technology recognizes the elemental layer of liquid matter. As opposed to the slower oscillations of the solid layer, the water or liquid elemental state oscillates with a greater amount of speed and variability. We also know from chemical analysis that liquids have quite different electronic characteristics than solids. Rather than providing stability, rigidity, and structure, liquids will conform to the shape of the solids they surround or are contained within. We can easily observe these effects. Liquid molecules contain weaker electronic bonds between each other due to proximity, allowing the ability to move around each other without rigid sequencing. However, this does not mean liquids are any less organized. The magnetic moments of molecules within water display a great amount of organized polarity and consistency. Hence, they consistently display the same characteristics; including surface tension, vapor points, and solubility. Liquids also display an amazing ability to convey and even conduct radiation and electricity.

For thousands of years, natural scientists and philosophers intently analyzed nature's elements. The Greek philosophers, the Egyptians, the ancient Chinese and the Vedic texts of the Indus valley all subscribed to the concept of the layering of matter into basic elements. This elemental view of the world has influenced scientific reasoning ever since. Today, modern western science assumes this stratification of elements as fundamental to the understanding of chemistry, physics, astronomy, physiology, and biology.

Unmistakably the elemental layering of the elements by these ancient and modern technologies has many similarities. While the Vedic methodology discussed the gross elements as earth, water, fire air, and ether, the Chinese science discussed these similarly as earth, water, fire, metal and wood. The Greeks embraced the Vedic version, as did the Arabs, Romans and Eastern Europeans. As western science matured through the European alchemists of the middle ages and the scientist-philosophers of the Renaissance, the characteristics of solids, liquids, gases, heat and space (or the aether) were gradually expanded upon.

Similar elemental derivatives have also played a key role in the Egyptian, North American Indian, Japanese, Mayan, and Polynesian cultures. In the North American Indian tradition, for example, the elements of nature are related as Brother Sun, Mother Earth, Grandmother Moon, the Four Brothers of the wind and the Four Directions. The Japanese *godai,* meaning "five great," also reflects five physical elements, namely *chi* (earth), *sui* (water), *kaze* (wind), *ka* (fire) and ku (sky). In analyzing and applying these traditions to modern science's observational schema, it seems apparent that earth relates to solid matter, water relates to liquid matter, fire relates to thermal radiation, wind or air relates to gas, and ether, space, metal, void or sky relates to the medium of the electromagnetic. As Dr. Rudolph Ballentine (1996) observed, the ancient references to metal and wood from Chinese tradition appear to parallel the references of air/wind and ether/sky, respectively, from the ancient Vedic tradition.

In the traditional schema, each of the elements was connected to a personification or consciousness. Many were also connected to particular body organs and their pathways. In both Ayurvedic and Chinese therapies, for example, each element moves through the body within specific channel systems. These channel systems are called *meridians* in Chinese medicine, and *nadis* and *chakras* in Ayurvedic medicine.

The solids of the physical world translate energy into structured and layered compositions of different elements. The densest solid elements are made of stratified, crystallized, or latticed structures, which exhibit slower waveforms. This element makes up the structural components of the body including the skin, tissues, and boney network. It also comprises the planet's structures in the form of soil, sand, rocks and crystals.

The less dense liquid element circulates through the cytoplasm, blood, tissues, and lymph systems of our body. The liquid element also circulates through the rivers, streams, aquifers, and oceans of the planet in the form of water, magma, petroleum and other compounds.

The more subtle gas element circulates molecules via diffusion and effusion. Our planet has a vast atmosphere of gas, through which travel vaporized fluids, odors and wind. Gas also travels easily through most biological organisms. Gases exchanged through our lungs include oxygen, carbon dioxide and nitrogen. Chambers around the body such as the inner ear and nasal cavities also harbor the gas element. The distance between molecules within a gas produces the illusion of invisibility because our retinal cells and neurons are designed to matriculate objects with greater densities.

The planet and body also circulate the less dense thermal element, via currents of infrared radiation—which regulates and stimulates many of the body's and planet's metabolic processes.

Finally, pure electromagnetic waveforms circulate through the body's nervous systems and more subtle energy networks. The electromagnetic medium has gone through a number of descriptions over the centuries, from "sky" to "aether" to "space" the most current description as "plasma." Plasma was first described as a particular type of electromagnetic ion medium, but over recent years its definition has been expanded into an elemental state.

Each elemental state of matter provides a medium through which particular types of waveforms move. Solids provide a medium for seismic waves. Liquids provide a medium for the classic fluid surface and tortional waves. Gases provide a medium for pressure waves. Thermals provide a medium for infrared waves. Space/plasma provides a medium for the higher frequency electromagnetic waveforms of various spectra.

As the elements interact, they produce activity and progression. For example, as water interacts with the more structured solid layers, we find that some molecules dissolve while others precipitate. When a substance is dissolved into a liquid, the properties of the liquid will typically change—it may taste different, have a different boiling point, and may look quite different. This is because the bonds between liquid molecules are substantially weaker than in solids, allowing a greater level of bonding penetration and change following exposure to a new substance. This is also the strength of the liquid medium: Being able to absorb and adjust with a minimum of character change. This is especially the case for water. Water's strength lies in its flexibility.

The type of molecular activity produced within liquids relate to solubility, surface tension, fluid pressure and osmotic differentials. This contrasts with the lattice-driven molecular foundation. We can see water's interactions with the other elements when we observe the motion of ocean waves, moving rivers and pressurized springs.

Different fluid compositions have different interactions with the other elements. This is due to differentials in surface tension, density, polarity, chemical composition and other characteristics. We can also see this as different fluids interact. This is most obviously seen in the case of petroleum mixed with water. Oil will separate from water because oil is *hydrophobic*. The molecular structure of oil is made of hydrocarbons and the molecular structure of water is an oxygen-hydrogen bonding structure. Water's bonding structure creates a polar molecule. This means water molecules tend to attract each other magnetically. Oil molecules, on the other hand, do not have a distinct polarity because of the complexity of the various atoms and bonding structures. However, like water, oil molecules still will have significant surface tension. Oil's molecules are consistently attracted to each other. The two liquids are thus out of phase with each other. Oil's bonding patterns create a variance of magnetic fields, which repel water's magnetic fields.

However, an *emulsifier* like liquid soap will attract both oil and water. One side of soap's molecule will attract water and the other side will attract the oil molecules. This polar separation is why dish soap is useful for cleaning up oily dishes.

The bonding interference patterns in both petroleum and water molecules have more stability and strength at their surfaces. This effect again is referred to as surface tension: A blend of *cohesive* and *adhesive forces*, balancing each other to create a polarity barrier at the surface. This is a rather simplistic explanation, however. What we are observing with surface tension is the cohesive interaction of standing wave interference patterns. Their cohesiveness is another way of saying their molecules are interacting together *in phase* with each other.

Careful observation of large bodies of water will unveil smaller streams moving within the waters at various directions. The ability liquids have in forming streams or channels relates to migratory polar forces driven by tidal, temperature and other environmental influences. This characteristic of the liquid elemental state is called *capillary action*. Capillary action allows living organisms to move fluids around in conveyor motion. This action allows nutrient circulation and detoxification—both processes linked to the dissolving and converting mechanisms of fluids. Capillary action is closely related to surface tension, as polar barriers are formed at the edges of the capillary stream.

Fluids are perfect mediums for transmitting a wide range of waveforms. While solids absorb and transmit longer waveforms, their rigidity makes them less able to respond to shorter oscillations without a considerable amount of alteration. Solids will provide negative interference for shorter waveforms with higher frequency. For this reason, we see light transmitting through liquids while solids tend to block light. At the same time, we find liquids will often create the same kind of prism effects that crystals and glass may create as light refracts and diffracts through them. However, liquids will provide a variance of refraction or diffraction, as its molecular bonds move and readjust.

Liquids also radiate through other elemental states. As water moves through the atmosphere of air, it becomes altered by the various pressure and movements of air. Pressurized air in the form of wind interacts with water in the open ocean to form the waves that eventually hit the beach. Water also moves over various rocks, soil, and sediment, changing the structure and appearance of those solids. After a heavy rain, water will create channels into soils and hillsides, leaching nutrients. This effect is not unlike refraction. Just as light refracts through water as it is altered by those waveform interactions, water is channeled through rocks and soils.

Liquids also have element interaction characteristics. Different liquids will have unique *boiling points* and *freezing points*. When a solid interacts with a fluid, the rate of interaction can be measured as *solubility*. Many liquids also become solids with particular temperature changes. This conversion is precise: Every liquid has a specific freezing point, with little variance for that substance outside of other environmental factors such as atmospheric pressure. We observe this tendency between water and ice. Pure water will always freeze at 32 degrees Fahrenheit or 0 degrees Celsius. This same precision governs a liquid's boiling point as well.

What is the molecular difference between a liquid and its respective solid version? Not too much when considering only chemical composition. However, the substances have quite different structures and different waveform functions. We can drive a car onto a frozen lake during the winter, but the car would quickly sink if we tried that during the summer. The inter-molecular bonds of frozen water are latticed and crystallized. When the temperature increases, the inter-molecular bonds of water molecules become weak hydrogen bonds.

The type of inter-molecular bonds also relates to *viscosity*, and *density*. Density is the weight-volume relationship, while viscosity is a motion-speed calculation. Each of these characteristics translates to the bonding between different molecules of chemicals, which in turn relates to the electromagnetic waveform interaction between the atoms of those molecules. The difference in density or viscosity will also translate to a different interaction between that fluid and other compounds.

The atomic bonding within molecules create polarity potentials that interact with the polarity of other molecules. Within the liquid element, atomic bonds create magnetic field differences. Solubility, motion, surface tension, adhesion and cohesion are behaviors that essentially relate to electromagnetism: Physicists and chemists today classify these properties more precisely as quantum characteristics of spin, angular momentum and so on.

The Fluid Atom

When most of us look around, we see *objects*. When we look at water, we see something a bit different: We see fluidity. Are these two types of elements so different? Objects like rocks, mountains, desks, and buildings seemingly stand still. Over time, however, dramatic changes to their appearance attest to molecular fluidity. If we were to take two snapshots of any stationary object a hundred years apart, we would likely see some change in the object, but nowhere near the amount of change that occurred to its molecular structure. Did the object move? Seemingly not, but a great exchange of molecular matter has taken place. Most of the atoms have been recycled and replaced by new ones. The object might look similar, but its molecular makeup is brand new.

We can also see this molecular fluidity over time as buildings collapse, desks rust, and mountains are worn away by the elements. These seeming "solids" are actually fluid in essence. Their fluid motion is simply moving more slowly than fluids we are used to.

To better understand the liquid element of matter from a scientific perspective, we should probably review humankind's process of gradual discovery of subatomic matter.

This story started thousands of years ago.

The ancient Greek philosophers proposed that the synergies between the pulses of nature and mathematical logic were tied to a common bond with elements of a transcendent nature. This greatly influenced the progression of natural science for many centuries to come. The scientific contributions of Hippocrates, Pythagoras, Socrates, Plato, Aristotle, Copernicus, and others established the groundwork for centuries of progressive scientific endeavor and a reverence for mathematical modeling. The view that nature could be measured using relationships of numbers and mathematical formulae set into motion a codification of the elements.

Using mathematics, early scientists began to divide time and motion into smaller and smaller increments. They split nature's rhythms into smaller and smaller fractions of periodicity. As instrumentation developed to access smaller and deeper views of nature, precise measurements of nature's elements became increasingly possible. The early microscopes of Zacharias and father Hans Janssen, and later Anthony Leeuwenhoek come to mind.

Dalton's atomic theory, put forth by British John Dalton in the early nineteenth century, proposed that the tiniest indivisible pieces of matter could be assigned the unit he called the *atom*. He concluded that matter must be made up of these indivisible units. Furthermore, he suggested that the indivisible atoms of different elements must each have a unique atomic weight, and compounds were made up of different combinations of these indivisible units he called atoms.

While others had previously envisioned the existence of the atom—from the Sir Isaac Newton to the Greeks and even the ancient Vedic philosophers thousands of years earlier—Dalton's theories—with his notions of subatomic electrons—brought a mathematical basis to the aspect of these minute structures.

The characterization of elemental atoms, such as weight and atomic number, gave rise to an atom's ability to marry atoms to form molecular compounds. This perspective envisioned molecular compounds being composed of atoms brought together by a need to become stable.

In the late nineteenth century, Russian Dimitri Mendeleev and German Lothar Meyer each independently sorted the known atoms into a table by mass and atomic number. It is said that Mendeleev's configuration dawned upon him as he awoke from a dream. The table was based upon the notion that sorting the basic elements by number also grouped their relative chemical and physical properties. Atomic mass was used as the vertical basis for the chart, with atomic numbers providing the sequence. Their reactivity with hydrogen and oxygen provided the basis for their horizontal arrangement.

The Classic Periodic Table

As the atomic makeup of different compounds was compared, it became apparent that an atom's bonding propensity was somehow connected to its mass and atomic number. As instrumentation further developed—due in part to the pioneering work of T.W. Richards, most known for his work in standardizing thermometers and the radioactive transformation of lead, which he called "radiolead"— the reactivity of atoms was linked to undetermined subatomic elements within the atom. The atomic number was soon expanded into the concept of subatomic particles, which included electrons and protons. These provided a semblance of balance and a rationale for the combination atoms, at least for the moment.

The subatomic particle theory proposed that each atom is composed of a nucleus containing protons and neutrons, encircled by electrons. It was proposed that the atomic number of an element is equivalent to the number of protons within the atom. The mass was calculated as the count of protons plus neutrons within the nucleus. This proposal allowed each atomic element a unique atomic number, yet the balance between the atom's electron count and proton count could change, depending on the circumstance. In other words, the stability of an atom and its propensity to combine with others, would vary with its balance of subatomic particles.

The somewhat crude periodic table design of Mendeleev and Meyer created a standard still used and still relevant to chemists. Its arrangement has proved useful, as numerous new atomic elements discovered since have all fit nicely within the same table. Furthermore, holes in the table have predicted elements found later. Today the table hosts 117 elements. Mendeleev's table had 60 elements.

Of the 117 elements in today's table, 94 are commonly found in nature, and the rest are theoretical elements produced in mass accelerator research. The table sorts the alkali metals into the first column and the alkaline earth metals into the second column. As successive columns move right, transition metals give way to metalloids, halogen gases, and finally noble gases in the last and eighteenth column. As the characters of each element are closely reviewed, it becomes obvious that as the leftmost columns provide a greater tendency of attracting electrons from other elements. This characteristic renders it easier for rightmost class to becoming negative ions (as in the case of oxygen) and the more leftmost columns to become positive ions, or *cations* (as in the case of hydrogen).

If the elements' mass, number and these ionizing characteristics were graphed on an X and Y-axis, the periodic table would take the form of a circular spiral. This is illustrated by the famed *Mayan periodic table*, in which the elements are sorted in circular shape with the smallest elements in the center.

As we step back and consider not only the circumstances for the periodic table's discovery, but elements falling into place among the table by atomic number and ionic characteristics, it is not difficult to notice nature's symphony of synchrony. It is quite amazing that over a decade before subatomic electromagnetic properties became apparent, the table was conceived by Mendeleev and Meyer. The fact that its arrangement ties into subatomic orbital shells and valence, as we will discuss, is further testament for nature's congruity. Furthermore, within this periodic arrangement we find an unquestionable cyclic (i.e., "periodic") rhythm between the different elements and their properties. This combination of microcosm and macrocosm has been driving our continued research and profound curiosity.

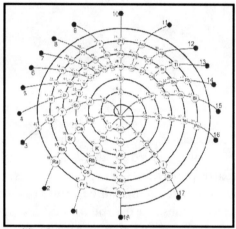

The Spiral Periodic Table (Jan Scholten)

Dalton's early nineteenth century atomic theory began to unfold a range of theories on the properties of matter. These included Frenchman Joseph Proust's eighteenth century *law of definite proportion;* Antoine Lavoisier's eighteenth century *law of mass conservation;* and Dalton's own *law of multiple proportions.* These "laws" became the guidebook early theoretical physicists used to develop the notion of the particle universe.

In 1897, English scientist Sir Joseph Thomson (also known as Lord Kelvin)—who won the 1906 Nobel Prize for Physics—passed cathode rays through a slit within a vacuum tube. Using magnetic fields, Thomson was able to bend the rays. This indicated to Sir Thomson that elemental matter must have inherent electronic and magnetic characteristics. Sir Thomson went on to visualize atoms surrounded by subatomic electron units. He compared them to plums sitting in plum pudding. This theory became the *plum pudding model*, eventually abandoned in favor of the visualization of Japanese physicist Hantaro Nagaoka referred to as the *Saturnian model*. This of course visualized electrons moving around the nucleus much as the rings of Saturn encircle that planet. Nagoaka's imagery evolved into the *Rutherford-Bohr model*, which utilized the progressive work of Niels Bohr and Ernest Rutherford to visualize electrons orbiting the nucleus in multiple orbit projections.

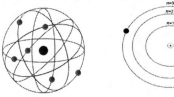

The Rutherford Atom   **The Bohr Model**

Continued research in the early twentieth century gradually eliminated the Bohr-Rutherford model as an acceptable description of subatomic particle motion. The problem was that these subatomic particles did not seem to maintain rules of normal "particle" behavior. As a result, these neat orbital paths simply could not be confirmed. Through the progressive research and proposals of Paul Dirac, John von Neumann, Max Planck, Louis de Broglie, Max Born, Niels Bohr, and Erwin Schrödinger, statistical probability and electromagnetic behavior led to revised mathematical models using *wave mechanics*.

In the late nineteenth century, Swiss Nobel Lauriat Alfred Werner suggested a mathematical model for the coordination between subatomic particle in atoms that came together to form molecules. Werner proposed a *coordination number*, or the number of direct associations between atoms within a molecule. The German chemist Richard Abegg had already noticed that the number *eight* came up consistently in molecular combinations. This combined with the observation that oxidation states between elements also tended to differ by eight provided the grist for Dr. Abegg to suggest *Abegg's rule of eight.*

This led the American chemist Gilbert Lewis to provide the calculations to formulate the *octet rule*. This suggested that electron pairs are shared to the extent of the capacity of their *orbital shells:* As these 'shells' fill up they ultimately establish their most stable state—that of a noble gas. Later this combination recipe became known as the *valence bond theory,* and the *rule of eighteen* became the model of metal stability.

Many of these atomic theories were the result of bombarding atomic elements with various types of radiation—scattering their subatomic particles and recording the results. This process led to continued correlations between subatomic particles and electromagnetic waves. When an atom seemingly garnered enough electrons to fill up its outer shell or valence number, more stability resulted. Should stable atoms and molecules be bombarded with radiation, energy was released, creating ions with less stability.

From these *mass accelerator* experiments came relationships between the subatomic particles and their stability within respective orbits. This became known as the *electron shell model*. In this model, subatomic orbits of atoms and ions were classified by the number of electron particles in their *orbit shell*. When an orbit shell had a certain number of electrons, it was found to be more stable. This stable state is called *valence*. These stable energy states were found to have an order based on the formula $(2xN)^2$ where N is the orbit number. This translates to a state of stability with two electrons in the first orbital shell, eight in the second, eighteen in the third and so on.

Sir J.J. Thomson proposed the fundamental reason for this is that each atomic element has a unique *ground state,* where it has a balanced number of electrons, protons and neutrons. Thomson shot beams of atomic ions through magnetic fields, revealing variances of subatomic electromagnetic character. His research and other mass accelerator research eventually determined that when an element had an imbalance between electrons and protons it became unstable, and needed stability. This is called an *ion*. When the element becomes unstable due to a variance between neutrons and protons in the nucleus, it can created instability and *decay* among its environment. These imbalanced elements eventually coined *isotopes*. Some isotopes are considered stable, however. This relates to their balance with protons and the combinations they can make in nature.

In our discussion about water, we are most concerned about ions. An *ion* is an atom or molecule that does not have a complete valence, or stability among its electron shells. This ion seeks to arrive at back at its particular balanced ground state by combining with other elements. In this combination, the ion theoretically "borrows" electrons from another atom or molecule to complete its valence. This "sharing" brings into view a disconnect with regard to particle physics: Electron particles have never been found.

As electron microscope images of molecular orbits were brought into the equation, electron orbit characteristics began to become evident. The concept of individual orbiting paths soon became irrelevant. These valence shells or orbits were observed as regions where electrons had a greater probability of existing. These were referred to as *electron clouds*. These 'clouds' were consistent with specific energy emissions following bombardment in mass accelerator research and the valence quantifications. They just were not consistent with the notion of an individual particle called the electron.

Using the valence shell model for the water molecule, there is a sharing of electron valence, or a *covalence* existing between the two hydrogen atoms and the oxygen atom. The hydrogen atoms each have one electron within their (first) outer shells, while the oxygen has six electrons within its (second) outer shell. Since the first shell is balanced with two electrons, and oxygen's outer shell is balanced with eight electrons, the three atoms "share" their respective electrons to each become more balanced as they commingle.

At the turn of the twentieth century, the realities of electromagnetic oscillation within the atom began to unfold. Physicists could not help but correlate atomic theory with the same energies being emitted by light and observed within alternating electrical currents. Using mass spectrometers, mass accelerators and electron microscopes, electromagnetic radiation became the fundamental element of the atom.

Combining observations with calculations, Max Planck characterized the smallest unit of energy absorbed or emitted at the atomic level was characteristic of light emission. He captured this within a fundamental unit called the *quantum*. Dr. Planck's ground-breaking quantum theory proposed that every atom radiated a number of distinct energy components. He labeled these energy components *"quanta"* (Latin for "measurable unit") because he thought each subatomic particle should have a measurable and quantifiable amount of energy. Dr. Planck also devised a formula that determined a fundamental numerical value for each quantum. This was called *Planck's constant*.

This constant proved important because it allowed Niels Bohr to arrive at an expanded *quantum theory*. Bohr's theory focused upon the notion that the electron's orbit was electromagnetic in character. Dr. Bohr's proposal was founded upon an atom's ability to release radiation or absorb radiation. This release or absorption of energy, he proposed, occurred as electrons were bumped up or down in their orbits, or were released. His work confirmed that each atom had a natural *grounded energy state*, where its energy level was balanced. He suggested that chemical reactions occurred because electrons became excited to higher quantum states or reduced to lower quantum states. Bohr's quantum model did not completely abandon Dr. Lewis' orbital shell model however. Valence or stability is reached when atoms shared energy states to fill out their potential. Dr. Bohr received the Nobel Prize in physics in 1922 for these theories.

In 1924, Louis de Broglie wrote a doctoral dissertation that stunned the physics world: He proposed that all subatomic matter was better described as composed of waves rather than orbiting particles. Using subatomic momentum and velocity measurements, de Broglie created a formula that calculated the wavelength of an electron.

The wavelength of an electron? This was hard to perceive using a particle view of matter. Despite the dramatic research of physicists over the previous decades, the Newtonian model of the electron particle orbiting the nucleus was still firmly implanted into the perception of both the scientific community and the media. Quite simply, it was (and still is) hard to lose the visualization of little electron balls floating around a nucleus. The particle view also fit so nicely with the atomic numbers of the periodic table, and the combining of atoms into molecules.

Yet de Broglie's hypothesis became the only reasonable explanation for the evolving mass accelerator observations. Research using diffraction among sodium chloride crystals cinched de Broglie's hypothesis. His *wave mechanics theory* of subatomic matter stubbornly rose to scientific acceptance.

As particle accelerator instrumentation developed, physicists accumulated an array of characteristics linking subatomic activity with wave mechanics. While experiences with polarity, and conductivity awoke nineteenth century physicists to the tie between electricity and magnetism, radiation bombardment awoke twentieth century physicists to energy emission. As physicists like Bohr, Einstein, Planck, and de Broglie unraveled subatomic units with waveform mechanics, the perception of particle electrons became increasingly blurry. The electron became a waveform probability rather than an object. The orbit of the electron expanded from a single line to an electron radiation cloud:

The orientation of electron clouds within a molecule relates to the relative polarity (or magnetic orientation) between the atoms that make up that molecule. The relative polarities between electron clouds in a molecule create precise angles of interaction. Some molecules display cloud angles of 90 degrees. Others form 120-degree angles, 45-degree angles, or even the odd 104.5-degree angle, as in the case of water. While the cloud formation can be mathematically broken down into valence numbers, only polarity explains the duplicating precision of their architecture.

These polar clouds also create beautiful the crystalline or lattice structures that provide the architecture for the illusion of a three-dimensional 'solid' world. This illusion of solidity is evidenced by the foolhardy impression that ice, snowflakes and glaciers offer a solid platform. The melted snowman, our rapidly retreating glaciers, and a fall through the ice into cold water can quickly dispel such illusions. The Newtonian-Dalton view of matter as made up of tiny solids encircling bigger solids simply does not fit the science any longer.

This wave quantum view of the atom developed further in the mid 1920s with the work of Werner Heisenberg, Dr. Max Born and Pascual Jordan. Their efforts resulted in the *matrix mechanics* version of the quantum theory. This matrix version approached wave-based elements as time-dependent operators within a rotating reference frame. This was also called the *Heisenberg picture*, eventually rejected in favor of the *Schrödinger picture*, which assumed a system evolving with time-independent operators. Dr. Erwin Schrödinger proposed this new wave mechanic vision by unveiling the now-famous *Schrödinger equation*. His vision seemed to provide the solution to the mechanical problems then existing within the quantum perspective. The wave and the particle could exist simultaneously, Schrödinger hypothesized.

Professor Heisenberg then unleashed a little bomb that got physicists thinking about the problems of quantum perception. Heisenberg illustrated the mathematical impossibility of simultaneously determining the position and the momentum of a subatomic particle. This famous proposition was termed the *Uncertainty Principle*. The principle was later ascribed as the new problem of the major quantum numbers—driven by the electron's apparent duality of having wave and particle character simultaneously.

The uncertainty principle became a call to reason for the new wave-particle theory. It was mathematically inconceivable to use the quantum theory to locate the particle, and it was inconceivable to attempt to measure the various energy components of subatomic particles using classical mechanics. The quantum theory was likened to the opening of a new dimension of matter very unlike the "solid" physical world.

The lingering premise for the continued view of matter as waves and particles simultaneously leans on Thomas Young's famous double-slit experiment. The diagram below illustrates his experiment. Electrons acted like waves when they were shot through the two-gap opening. Their waveforms collide and refract with each other, forming reflected images similar to how ocean waves might move through two side-by-side canal openings. The confusing thing occurs as the reflecting screen is analyzed for pulse count. Here the basis for the particle is upheld.

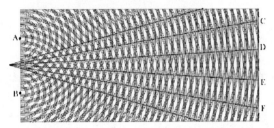

In mass accelerator research, subatomic behavior has continued this incongruence: bombardments imply both particle and wave characteristics. The obvious characteristics of subatomic waves—interference, diffraction, and refraction—are unavoidable. But so are the particle characteristics.

Although this wave-particle theory has been described by physicists as inconceivable, it has become the accepted theory for subatomic matter over the last half-century. Curiously, some physicists have also explained this inconceivability with a twist of further incomprehensibility: Subatomic elements can be *particles sometimes and waves at other times*.

The proposal submitted by Dr. David Bohm in the early 1950s was that the particle is simply *guided* by wave motion. This required, he theorized, a hidden *local effect* at work within the electron. Alternatively, he figured this also required a *non-local effect* guiding all electron motion throughout the universe.

This possibly supposedly resolved the inconceivability of the quantum wave-particle theory proposed decades earlier. The four basic quantum numbers proposed a unit baseline for particle existence. The first quantum number is the *principal quantum,* described as the subatomic *singular* quality. Without first defining an electron or other subatomic particles as distinct units with singularity, no further quantum characteristics could be possible. While this singularity is given wave qualities, the first quantum supplants the particle aspect. The second quantum number is based upon the orbital qualities of the particle-wave, notably its *angular momentum.* This is also sometimes referred to as the second subshell quantum. The third quantum number is the *magnetic projection of that angular momentum*. The magnetic field projects perpendicular to the electron motion. The fourth principle quantum number is the *spin quantum*.

These primary quantum numbers provided a mechanical picture to the waveform characteristics consistent with the oscillating, orbital, rotational, magnetic, and radiating electron.

As mass accelerator research progressed into the 1960s, Caltech physicist Dr. Murray Gell-Mann proposed the existence of several even smaller quanta contained within protons and neutrons. He supposed that if protons and neutrons could be quantified as particles, their scattering upon collision should reveal their subcomponents. These tiny particle parts were successively labeled *quarks, leptons, gluons, bosons,* and *antiquarks*. These characterizations were expanded with other qualities such as *charm, upness, downness, strangeness, top, bottom, hyperchange,* and of course, *flavor*.

Using linear accelerator collisions and subsequent formulae, it was initially proposed that quarks were thoroughly disconnected from each other. They apparently contained no charge. This circumstance presented a problem, however. Since quarks were conceived as elemental units without charge, they should also be able to separate from the proton quite easily. What force was keeping these theoretical units connected yet separated?

It was later proposed the quarks must be confined within the *hadon* (a proton or neutron). This meant another force must exist that keeps the quarks inside the hadon separated. Otherwise, there would be a loss of singularity. This proposed force was called the *strong force:* A field holding the protons and neutrons together. This strong force had to be mediated, it was supposed. The *gluon* was proposed as the mediator or transfer agent for this strong force within the hadon. It was subsequently proposed that quarks could be *colored* (or given these strong charges) by these gluons.

The puzzle this presented was a picture where quarks are moving around freely yet contained within the proton. There must be another, weaker force keeping these quarks confined, these physicists figured. This force was labeled the *weak force*. It was suggested that these weak forces were mediated by the existence of yet another subatomic unit, the *boson*. Bosons were assigned activities such as nuclear decay and neutrino function. Instead of exerting *color* as in the case of the gluon, bosons theoretically transfer *flavor* to these subatomic parts—by passing on weak forces.

Through this effort to quantify wave-like behavior using abstract and primarily symbolic unit representation, physicists have constructed a theoretical basis for measuring and predicting various nuclear activities. Whether these units actually exist is presumably besides the point. Regardless of not being directly observed, these quantifying virtual objects fit observation—allowing physicists to quantify previously undefined forces of nature. The quantification of quarks, gluons, gravitons and even photons and electrons allow a semblance of congruity for theoretical physicists. We might conclude that quantum mechanics is essentially an attempt to physically explain something beyond our comprehension.

In the early days of quantum mechanic formulation, there was heady disagreement between theoretical physicists on how atomic quantum characteristics were cast, especially in describing particle-waves with inconceivable characteristics. One of the most famous arguments set forth in a 1935 paper presented by Einstein, Boris Podolsky, and Nathan Rosen as the *"EPF Paradox."* This position (also characterized by Einstein as *"God doesn't play dice."*) argued that either the theory of quantum mechanics was missing critical elements (termed *"local hidden variables"*) or there was a broader *"non-local effect"* allowing particles to act and respond consistently—even at great distances from the observer. A non-local effect was presumed to be a force acting outside of the system. A local hidden variable was an unknown cause-and-effect consideration playing upon the situation.

This argument was embraced by Irish physicist Dr. John Bell in the early 1960s, who attempted to explain the existence of a non-local effect pragmatically. The basic assumption of the now-famous *Bell's Theorem* states that the gap between the probabilities of quantum mechanics and reality could not be due to local hidden variables. As this theorem was tested, *Bell's inequalities* were applied to two particles splitting off from each other. While these two particles may be independently tested to show no local hidden variables, they also may end up either neutralizing each other or otherwise reflecting each other. This implied their relationship continued beyond any effect of quantum mechanics. This led to the possibility that particles are able to instantaneously exchange information. This is often referred to as the *Bohm Interpretation,* and sometimes as the *seamless whole.*

This discussion illustrates that science has arrived at the conclusion that physical matter is inseparable from the wave mechanics of electromagnetism. The illusion of matter being solid is due to increased electromagnetic density centered around points of leverage that create structure and function. With this, we can provide a clearer representation of a water molecule:

The Quantum Water Molecule

This understanding also allows us to apply the characteristics of matter to waveform language: Atomic weight is a function of the element's frequency. The electron shells or orbitals are frequency levels. The reason we perceive particular valences among the shells within an atom is because the waveform frequencies within a stable atom or molecule resonate to a particular harmonic: In other words, they have a basic underlying integral frequency multiple. This provides a tuning or balance with the environment. Atoms or molecules with frequency levels outside of these valence shell multiples are imbalanced: They are ions, seeking balance among nature's sea of harmonic waveforms.

In other words, the objects we see around us are not so solid after all. An electron microscope journey through smallness reveals "solid" objects are made up of rhythmically gyrating quanta aligned structurally in spatial blocks of resonating polarity. This polarity of different aspects provides differentiation: They each spin, gyrate, tumble, and orient in different formats with particular frequencies and magnetic orientations.

Water illustrates these characteristics of matter most effectively. While solids move too slow for our eyes to perceive their motion, gases are moving so fast that we cannot perceive them with the naked eye. Water and fluids, on the other hand, provide a window into the flow and motion of the physical universe. Fluids illustrate how molecules and atoms flow with current, polarity and positioning—rendering temporary surface areas and structures that evolve as their atomic elements change hands.

Indeed, we can also see in fluids that matter is not moving chaotically. Watching waves of water rhythmically lift up and pound the beaches and reefs with precise power, efficiency and beauty will dispel any doubt of chaos. As we witness water's orderly conversion from liquid into vapor, only to be redelivered with cyclic rainfalls that nourish land and organisms with orderly seasonal routine, we capture a glimpse of the rhythmicity of molecular matter.

Mysteries of the Seas

The earth's surface is more water than earth, prompting Arthur Clarke to once state, *"How inappropriate to call this planet Earth, when clearly it is ocean."* The earth's surface contains a volume of about 3 million cubic miles of water, averaging a depth of two miles deep. While the saline content of our bodies stays at about 0.8%, the saline content of the earth's oceans maintains a steady level of about 3.4% sodium chloride, or salt.

The mystery of salt water was illustrated in 2007 when amateur inventor John Kanzius developed a radio wave frequency generator able to ignite salt water. This effect, corroborated by University of Pittsburgh scientists, astounded the scientific world. As seemingly harmless radio waves collide with saltwater, they can ignite a flame of over 1500 degrees Fahrenheit. How could saltwater become so flammable when hit with simple radio waves?

We might also wonder: How does the ocean so consistently maintain its 3.4% salt levels despite the dumping of salt from land and constantly changing environmental conditions?

About 540 megatons of salt are flushed down from rivers and land erosion. If the volume over the period of this dumping is calculated, the earth could only be about 60 million years old. Meanwhile, archeological evidence has put the earth's age at about

4,500 million years. Furthermore, the ocean's salinity has not been increasing over years of measurement. The ocean's salt content is being maintained by a mysterious mechanism of equilibrium.

This is not the only elemental maintenance occurring within the ocean's waters. Many other minerals, including magnesium and sulfate, are being conveyed between the land, air and ocean floor, while the ocean somehow maintains an equilibrium that consistently supports at least half the life populating the planet.

Consider the sulfate mystery. Nature somehow dumps hundreds of millions more tons of sulfur into the oceans than the land or atmosphere have the capacity to provide, according to geological calculations. Somehow, sulfur is being delivered into the water at an incredible rate. The sulfur conveyer then deposits tremendous volumes of sulfur onto the ocean floor, where it migrates into the earth's crust and becomes part of the magma circuit.

The mineral conveyor mystery does not stop with salt and sulfur. Similar mysteries have been found among magnesium, mercury, iodine and other ionic minerals important to all life processes.

After much research, the only reasonable solution to this mystery is a conversion process known only to biological organisms: Methylation.

Methylation is the process of combining methyl groups with particular ions, from which they can be transported through different elemental states. The human organism and most other living organisms conduct methylation to attain homeostasis and detoxification within the body. The liver, for example, stimulates methylation using B vitamins and other minerals to detoxify the bloodstream.

Within the ocean's mineral ion conveyor system, we find varying degrees of methylation involving methyl-iodide, methyl-mercury, dimethyl-sulfide and even methyl-chloride. These methyl groups can move between gas, liquid and solid states to provide balance and equilibrium to the ocean's mineral content. The question becomes: What is the governor factor for this process?

Positive and Negative Ions

The electromagnetic interaction between water and the atmosphere produces a similar process of equilibrium. Atmospheric ions are suspended in the atmosphere, producing a stabilization of the interface between water, land and air.

Atmospheric ions are created when a element becomes unstable, and acts upon molecules in the air, creating ions. A decayed radioactive atom produces 50,000 to 500,000 positive and negative ions. Airborne radon produces in the neighborhood of 250,000 ion pairings per radon atom. Cosmic rays also produce ions, as does water in motion.

Outdoor ion counts in rural areas in good weather conditions can range from 200 to 4,000 negative ions, and 250 to 1500 positive ions per cubic centimeter. Positive ion count can increase to over five thousand ions per cubic centimeter ahead of an incoming storm front. This is due to the sudden increase in humidity within the storm front. Once the storm front hits, the level of positive ions falls quickly, and negative ion levels dramatically rise.

Ion pollutants dramatically reduce total ion count. This is thought to be because both positive and negative ions will attach to unstable pollutant particles.

Natural settings containing moisture can contain dramatically more ions. For example, a waterfall might have as much as 100,000 negative ions per cubic centimeter. Ion levels around crowded freeways tend to be quite low, often below 100 negative ions per cubic centimeter.

Numerous trials have indicated that indoor ion levels are slightly lower than outdoor levels. This is thought to be because outdoor ions tend to interact with greater levels of moisture, and thus last longer than do their indoor cousins. This also correlates with the existence of the various electromagnetic fields existing within the home due to the use of various electronic appliances.

Negative ions can form easily. One pass of the comb through the hair can create from 1000 to 10,000 ions per cubic centimeter. The living organism is a tremendous ion producer. Assuming adequate grounding onto the earth or a grounding metal, a typical human exhalation will contain from 20,000 to 50,000 ions per cubic centimeter. This correlates with the fluid levels in the body.

Positive ions are typically generated with a decrease of atmospheric pressure; an increase in wind and temperature; a decrease in humidity and a decrease in elevation. This is particularly noticeable in Foehn winds—warm winds that descend from mountainous areas down to areas of lower elevation. Wind patterns considered Foehn include the dry southerly wind (meaning it comes from the south) blowing through the Alps, Switzerland and across southern Germany. The Sharav or Hamsin winds blowing though the desert of the Middle East are Foehns. The Sirocco that blows through Italy and the Mistral that blows through southern France are both considered Foehns. The Chinook winds of western Canada and NW United States, and the Santa Ana winds that blow through southern California from time to time are also considered Foehns. Foehn winds have also been occasionally spotted around various mountain ranges such as the Colorado Rocky Mountains and Tennessee's Smokey Mountains. Foehn winds tend to funnel between mountain ridges, which accelerate their gusting speeds to an excess of 50 miles per hour. Anther notable characteristic of a Foehn wind is that it usually accompanies dramatic increase in air temperature.

Foehn winds are also known for their ultralow humidity and propensity to cause erratic fires. They also can cause a number of negative physical and emotional effects in both humans and animals. For these various reasons, the Foehn is often referred culturally as an 'ill wind.' While some have disputed the effects of Foehn winds, both research and observation has indicated otherwise. Research performed by Sulman (*et al.* 1973-1980) indicated these winds are associated with headaches, heat stress, and irritability. Others have documented an increase in allergies and sinus ailments during Foehn winds.

Positive ions also correlate with these immediate changes in temperature, pressure, and humidity. Because positive ions are also linked to Foehn winds, it is safe to assume that the various effects related to positive ions are also connected with the environmental effects of Foehn winds.

Not surprisingly, negative ions' effects upon health and behavior have been the subject of intense study for the past eighty years. This began in 1926, when Russian scientist Alexander Chizhevsky cruelly exposed animals to ionized air with negative ions and/or positive ions. In these studies, he found—as other studies have concluded such as Krueger and Reed (1976)—that while living in

positive ion conditions produces more illness and shorter life duration than those living in negative ion conditions.

Negative ions have also been linked to health benefits among
humans in a number of studies. Increased negative ions were associated with higher levels of cognition and memory by Delyukov and
Didyk (1999), and by Baron (1987). Negative ions were linked with
lower levels of aggression by Baron as well. A lower incidence of
asthma was observed by Ben-Dou (1983). Lower levels of irritability and higher serotonin levels were also linked with negative ions in
two studies by Sulman (1984; 1980).

In Sulman's 1980 study, daily urine samples were taken from
1,000 volunteers one to two days before a storm's arrival during
Feohn winds, and during normal weather conditions. The samples
were analyzed for neurotransmitter and hormone levels, including
serotonin, adrenaline, noradrenaline, histamine, and thyroxine metabolites. The results concluded that during positive ion conditions,
an overproduction of serotonin levels resulted in irritability. In positive ion conditions, Sulman discovered adrenal deficiency and early
exhaustion. Positive ions were also associated with hyperthyroidism
and subclinical "apathetic" thyroid symptoms.

As Niels Jonassen points out, the effects linked with negative
ions may not be as simple as the presence or abundance of these
ions. Certain atmospheric conditions appear to create pathways
through which flow ion currents. Where these layered currents flow,
their ion effects are observed. This is compared to the current of a
river, or the current created within the body by electric shock. It
might also be compared with the pathway of *qi* created by an acu-
puncturist's needle.

The evolution of the study of ions in the atmosphere leads us
to an understanding of mechanical waves and currents moving
though the atmosphere. We might have a clear notion of how currents move through the solid mediums of wires and metals, or even
the ability of fluids to transmit currents. Currents moving through
the atmosphere are beyond our vision, however. This does not
mean we cannot understand their presence and motion through
empirical research and measurement. While we might imagine the
atmosphere is made up of an unorganized chaotic collection of gas
and water particles bumping around, the organized effects of

weather fronts and pressurized ion currents winding through the atmosphere indicate organized motion.

Organized atmospheric currents are driven by humidity, temperature and pressure. These in turn are driven by ionization. Current flows of ionized pairings created by the electromagnetic forces of radiation give us reason to believe there is a non-local effect at work. As we can observe through the effects of human-propagated radio waves, specific types of 'receptor' antennas, or receptors within nature, react to specific types of ionization signals. This perspective provides the clearest explanation for Sulman's and others' observations that changing weather patterns (with apparent ion changes) affect some people physically while not affecting others. Ionizing radiation is organized and moving within currents that drive particular physiological pathways conducted by water.

Water Clustering

Water's surface tension and unique structured fluidity is due to the existence of *weak hydrogen bonds* existing between different water molecules. These weak electromagnetic forces contain a dipolar element that draws the water molecules together into structured formations. When water freezes, we observe rigid formations as crystal lattices. While in the liquid form, this rigidity is lost. At the same time, water's weak hydrogen intermolecular bonding creates a unique activity known as *water clustering*.

Over the past four decades, chemists and physicists have been observing these organized yet weak-hydrogen-bond clusters forming and breaking up within water, seemingly on a spontaneous basis. Initially it was supposed that these structures were simply randomly forming these complex structures.

However, upon further observation it became evident that once a cluster broke apart another cluster would form in its place. Many of the new clusters often replicated the shape of the previous clusters. Many of these clusters took on symmetrical geometric shapes, such as icosahedrals.

The first observations of water clustering were presented to the scientific community in the 1950s. X-ray diffraction techniques illustrated water molecules clumping into groupings, sometimes only for short periods. The clusters seemed at first to be flickering and random. Over the years, observations with diffraction as well as nuclear magnetic resonance have established that these weak dipole interactions between hydrogen bonds create periodic clustering of groups of water molecules in a variety of situations. Clusters from 25 to 90 water molecules have been observed, forming a number of distinct geometric structures.

One of the more recognized researchers in this area of water clustering was Dr. Mu Shik Jhon, who from the 1950s until his death in 2004 investigated and participated in more than 280 research papers over a distinguished career in science. As a former president of the Association of Academies of Sciences in Asia and president of the Korean Academy of Science and Technology, and an assistant professor at the University of Virginia, Dr. Jhon's research into the molecular structure and properties of water are well established and documented. Dr. Jhon's research indicated that although cluster sizes can vary greatly, there appears to be more frequent structuring of water within five or six molecule groups. Seemingly because resonating electron-wave orbits are positioned at particular angles, the resulting clusters observed in his research had either pentagonal (five-sided) or hexagonal (six-sided) structures. Dr. Jhon's research also indicated that hexagonal water clusters appeared to have more stability in the presence of calcium and sodium—key macrominerals regulating metabolism.

Hexagonal clusters appear to produce lower surface tension because of their stability. Pentagonal water clusters bond together in larger strings, increasing higher surface tension. For example, research by Professor Martin Chaplin of London South Bank University reported that water could form complex icosohedral clusters. His clustering research observed up to twenty 14-molecule tetrahedrals, totaling 280 H_2O molecules weakly bonded together.

Physicists Giuliano Preparata and Emilio Del Giudice mathematically calculated a polarity-clustering model in a 1991 *Physical Review Letters* paper. They called the clusters of water molecules *"coherent domains."* This paper followed an experiment where the radiation fields of water were tested before and after additives were added. They reported that the electric dipoles in water molecules interact with coherence. They described a type of *"collective dynamic"* existed in water, because the resulting polarity fields were consistent with the polarization of the additive.

At 32 degrees Fahrenheit or 0 degrees Celsius, pure water will crystallize rapidly into lattice form. This provides another type of coherence, as the dipolar and electromagnetic resonance are retained within the solid lattice structure. During the process of forming this lattice, crystallization occurs. As a result, partially frozen water will form into beautiful crystal shapes, many resembling delicate snowflakes. Each snowflake, in fact, is unique. Famously, no two snowflakes are exactly alike.

We thus see a wide variety of crystal shapes form as water becomes frozen. Researchers have observed these crystal structures taking on various sizes and dimensions. The clustering structures undoubtedly play a significant role in this crystalline formation.

Controlled laboratory research has concluded that catalytic enzyme activity will vary greatly, depending upon the nature of the organic solvents in the solution (Zaks and Klibanox 1988; Lee and Dordick 2002). Different solvents have been shown to specifically affect the clustering structures in water. Mineralized water, for example, creates more hexagonal structures. This in turn affects the surface tension of the water and the water's reactive ability. Reactions take place through an interactive process between the electromagnetic bonding forces inherent between the reactive species and the solvent. Water is the universal solvent. The solute components facilitate the structure of the water to buffer or promote a particular reaction.

This is illustrated by *allosteric regulation*. Here, water molecule structures further or slow particular reactions. These mechanics illustrate water as a conductor and sometimes buffer of reactivity with its ever-changing clustered structures.

These clusters form and disappear quickly. They are thus often described as *fleeting*. While these fleeting clusters of H_2O molecules are not well understood, their existence has stood up to scientific scrutiny. Questions remain regarding water clusters. What causes them to appear and why do they disappear so quickly? Why do they often reform with the same geometric design? Could this be the result of a type of memory system?

Water Memory

Consider the ability of an iron-oxide tape to memorize data or sounds through electromagnetic field manipulation. Our ability to tape-record a song or speech onto a magnetic tape occurs simply by impinging a magnetic charge upon the iron oxide surface with a magnetized head. This occurs as a result of being able to affect the polarity of the iron oxide molecules. Later, when the reader head travels over the previously magnetically charged iron oxide tape, the polarity effects made earlier will be translated back into electronic pulses. These are converted by the electronics into speaker pulses and back into the sounds recorded. Today, this magnetic polarization technology provides the foundation for the information age.

When we press a magnet upon any magnetizable metal, we can change the polarity of most of the molecules making up that metal. The polarity is changed through a repositioning of the electron orbital orientation, rendering one side 'electron-heavy' and the other side 'proton-heavy.' This polarization causes an effective means for memorization. After removing the magnet, some molecules will revert to their original polarity. Others will remain in the same direction. In either case, there is a recollection of positioning and orientation long after the magnet encounter.

Water portrays similar polarity characteristics. Water is certainly no metal, but because of its molecular orientation, it has the ability to shift in polarity, depending upon what has been dissolved in it. As the universal solvent, water has the ability to fully or weakly bond with molecules of various substances. This often results in a pH change in the water. In this case, the water is obviously 'remembering' the solute.

Things get more interesting upon further dilution. When a solution is diluted many times with regular water, leaving theoretically few if any molecules or ions of the solute in the remaining solution, this diluted solution seems to 'remember' the character of the former solution. This astounding fact has been presented and proven in peer-reviewed scientific research over the past three decades. It has also become evident during 250 years of homeopathic "provings." Still, there are doubters among the scientific community. Let's review the evidence.

In 1982, a physics research team led by Professor Alain Aspect from the University of Paris determined that following separation, subatomic particles exhibited activities that indicated an invisible mechanism of mutual communication or guidance despite being separated by long distances. This supported *Bell's theorem*, which promoted non-local hidden variables (independent from perception and direct influences) within the quantum mechanics view of the universe. Einstein and others, remember, had issues with non-local influences.

When two particles split from each other and continue the same waveform character though separated and exposed to external environmental influences, each molecule must be influenced identically from a distant force. This 'ghostly action' was seen to be acting at a distance because of the great separation between their trajectories. Dr. Aspect continues as a professor at Ecole Polytechnique University and is the Research Director at the French National Center for Scientific Research (CNRS). In 2005 was awarded the Gold Medal by the CNRS for his research.

The proposal of a memory (or 'ghostly action') existing within a solution long after a substance is diluted away has been clinically applied over the last 250 years of homeopathic medicine. Homeopaths and researchers have observed clinical success with dilution factors well-beyond one million parts to one: A level at which no molecule of the substance could theoretically remain. Homeopathy and Bach flower remedies such as the *rescue remedy* have documented successful clinical applications with diluted substances with deep and lasting healing response.

After millions of case histories and hundreds of clinical trials illustrating the effectiveness of diluted homeopathic dosing, conventional researchers have entered the controversy to settle the case. Hundreds of studies provide clear evidence of efficaciousness of homeopathy, while some have brought it into question. Whether the positive study results are due to what homeopaths describe as molecular memory or something else is yet to be ascertained. Research on the subject continues to be controversial.

Some rather bold evidence for molecular memory has come from well-respected researchers with no prior acceptance of homeopathy. One of these was a well-known French medical doctor and researcher named Jacques Benveniste, M.D. At one time Dr. Benveniste was the research director at the French National Institute for Health and Medical Research (INSERM). Dr. Benveniste's career was very distinguished, having been credited with the discovery of the platelet-activating factor. Whilst performing research on the immune system—notably the action of basophils—Dr. Benveniste and his research technician Elisabeth Davenas inadvertently observed that basophil activity continued despite extremely low dilution levels: Dilution levels so low it was doubtful any molecules of the biochemical remained in the solution.

Over a four-year period of continual trials, showing repeated confirmation with increasing controls, Dr. Benveniste and his research team concluded some sort of memory effect was taking place within a former solution following thorough dilution. It was suspected that water might have some faculty to retain and transmit an antibody's biological activity long after the basophil was diluted out of the solution.

Furthermore, as Dr. Benveniste and his team initially diluted a substance, the activity of the substance decreased, as would be expected. At least until the ninth dilution. After the ninth dilution, the activity of the substance began to increase with successive dilutions—as has been observed during 250 years of clinical homeopathic application.

Dr. Benvienste's research effort was joined by five other research labs in four countries. All of these labs were able to independently replicate Dr. Benvienste's results. After conducting no less than 300 trials, the results were published in 1988 in *Nature* magazine, authored by thirteen of the researchers. The authors eventually concluded that, *"transmission of the biological information could be related to the molecular organization of water"* (Davenas *et al.* 1988).

The research became controversial to say the least. This *memory of water* conclusion had vast implications in the study of medicine and our knowledge of physics. The result of the research was to inadvertently provide the evidence for the premise of homeopathy—which Dr. Benveniste had previously not agreed with.

The research challenged others too. *Nature* magazine's editor apparently assembled a team of outspoken 'verifiers' who challenged Benvienste's results and protocol. Initially they observed while the lab confirmed the results. The 'verifiers' then modified the protocols to remove bias. With the change in protocol, the team could not duplicate the results. Dr. Benvienste and his associates responded to deaf ears by explaining that the protocol changes themselves eradicated the results. Until his demise in 2004, Dr. Benveniste and other researchers repeatedly confirmed his findings (Bastide *et al.* 1987; Youbicier-Simo *et al.* 1993; Endler *et al.* 1994; Smith 1994; Pongratz *et al.* 1995; Benveniste *et al.* 1992).

Ironically, the controversy revolved around the premise of whether a chemical molecule must be present within the water in order to provoke a particular biochemical action. This reminds us of the debate regarding the local versus the non-local effects in the quantum theory.

Determining with certainty whether there are any molecules of the original substance left in the water is calculated using probability. Theoretically, the former substance should be completely displaced by water molecules after so many dilutions. Because this is difficult to prove with observation, mathematical probability provides the best estimate. Certainly after thousands of dilutions, most scientists believe, the original substance should be gone.

Viewing the liquid content's molecules and atoms as combinations of interfering radiation creates a new paradigm. If matter is composed of waveform energy and water's radiating waveforms interfere with a solute's waveforms, the interference patterns between them should create a residual memory. This might be compared with a pond's ripples reflecting a rock tossed into the pond long after the rock was tossed in.

Over the past decade and partially in response to the controversial nature of Benveniste's research, the scientific basis for homeopathy has undergone a flurry of research. Most of this research has occurred in Europe, where homeopathy is often practiced by conventional physicians. Hundreds of controlled and randomized studies assessing homeopathic treatments have now been accumulated. Over the past few years, four major independent meta-studies have analyzed this volume of research. Three of the reviews concluded that the effects of homeopathy were more significant than the effects of a placebo, while one concluded homeopathy's effects were consistent with the effects of a placebo.

However, this latter review was also highly criticized for its elimination of studies (Jonas 2003; Chast 2005; Merrell and Shalts 2002).

The implication is simple: Chemical reactions do not require particles to physically touch. We can easily surmise this as chemical reactions are created simply by exposing substances to radiation. There is virtually no difference between a reaction caused by radiation and a reaction between two chemical substances. In the latter, each substance is composed of radiating quanta that create an interference pattern as the two are mixed.

The inability of the 'verifiers' to duplicate Dr. Benveniste's laboratory results is easily explained. Dr. Benveniste's and his associates' research included a particular solution mixing protocol. This protocol created the interactivity between the substance and the substrate. In their attempts to remove "bias" the 'verifiers' did not apply this mixing procedure.

In an interview shortly before his death in 2004, Dr. Benveniste explained his and the other labs' process of dilution, mixing and testing. He described agitating the diluted solution for twenty seconds with a spinning motion, creating a spiral or funnel shape inside the beaker. He called this motion a *vortex*. As Dr. Benveniste explained it, *"Only then do you get the transmission of the information."*

Succussing has been standard practice of homeopathy since the father of modern homeopathy Dr. Samuel Hahnemann began his clinical provings. (*Ayurvedic* doctors also practiced a form of homeopathy for many centuries before Hahnemann.) The process of homeopathic dilution as described by Dr. Hahnemann also required this process of succussion, which was a swirling and knocking of the substance upon the heel of the hand in order to mix the memory components. This practice of succussion is still widely practiced amongst homeopathic manufacturers and homeopathic physicians conducting clinical dilutions for patients. This succussion process is quite consistent with the process of vortex mixing documented in Dr. Benveniste's research.

This implies that at least part of water's memory capacity is retained and accessed through its waveform nature. Succession stimulates a coherent interference between the dissolved substance's molecular waveforms and the water's molecular waveforms. This type of interference would logically imbed a sustained 'fingerprint' of sorts upon the waveform structure of the remaining water molecules. This of course takes place on a polar electromagnetic level.

Water's memory capacity is quite easily observed as we watch a rock being dropped into a pond. For minutes or even hours afterward, the resulting waves traveling away from the entrance point of the rock specifically reflect the size of the rock, its velocity, and even its shape to some degree. A small rock will create a different rippling than a large rock might. A flat rock will create a different waveform than a round rock might. The size and shape of the ripples will also reflect the velocity of the toss into the water. A harder toss will be reflected quite differently than a light lob might. The resulting ripples will reflect the information about the rock and the throw for some time. They will also affect other surface events occurring within the pond.

Water memory is not really that fantastic. We all know that when water is heated and cooled, it will retain a 'recollection' of that temperature input for a period of time. The hotter the initial flame, the longer the water will remain hot. An electric stove will heat water at a different degree than a gas stove might. Thermal heat from the sun creates still another temperature range.

As water is cooled, again it reflects the cooling source. Water cooled with ice will cool differently than water cooled in a refrigerator or even freezer. Though we might expect the result to be proportionate to the temperature the water is exposed to, in reality, different sources have different effects. The radiative interactions will also dramatically change the water's characteristics for hours or even days following the changes. Although this 'thermal memory' appears resident among most substances, the presence of water hastens the radiative conduction and retention process, which makes water an efficient thermal conductor. For this reason, food is most efficiently cooked in water.

Water is also used in various other radiative conducting mechanisms such as heated floors, steam baths, and so on. When in need of an instant cooling mechanism, water is also sought after for its ability to immediately conduct cooler temperatures. Water quite easily 'remembers' the temperature of its immediate surroundings, easily transporting that memory to 'external' substances.

Water's memory is also observed with regard to water's solubility and surface tension characteristics. When we dissolve a substance into water, the water's specific gravity and surface tension will change, reflecting the properties of the added substance. This solvent will also change the water's boiling and melting points. As the solute is precipitated out of the water, the water will often retain a variance in these characteristics as compared to the original water source. This variance may be caused by the presence of additional hydrogen ions in the water, or by the formation of particular types of water clusters.

Intentional Water

As researchers have come to understand the placebo effect over the past century, double-blind studies have become the norm to isolate a treatment's success from various biases, notably expectations affecting the results. Following the results of thousands of trials, it has been commonly accepted that the placebo effect may skew results by as much as 33%. In other words, up to 33% of the test subjects will improve simply because they expected improvement from the therapy, or their doctors expected improvement. When we consider this is one-third of the population being tested, a placebo-range result has quite an influence on healing. What causes the placebo-result? Expectations.

Expectations are no more than conscious intentions for a particular result. These intentions can affect research results in either a positive or negative way. In medical research, it would be considered positive if the placebo effect increased the efficacy of the treatment. Perhaps the treatment required some personal interaction between the researcher or clinician and the patient. Perhaps this created a placebo effect and increased the positive results of the therapy. Should we then say that clinicians should not have personal interaction with patients so we do not create any additional opportunities for healing? Certainly not.

The viability of the *non-local effects* and *local effects* of personal consciousness, clinician consciousness and group consciousness has significant implications toward healing. Certainly the placebo effect illustrates the non-local effect conscious expectations have upon healing. If consciousness can have up to a 33% positive effect upon treatment and the health of the body, then we must accept the notion that consciousness can somehow be retained, memorized, and transmitted within the radiative waveforms exchanged during these studies (Leder 2005).

Whether or not we relate the clinical results of homeopathy to the effects of water memory, we can illustrate through the placebo effect that intention can influence physical results through expectation. Therefore, should a substance be diluted down to the infinitesimal solute state by a therapist who intends a particular therapeutic effect, the resulting solution should contain some molecular memory of the substance. This will be accompanied by the effects of the conscious intentions of the healer. The combination of these two effects occurs in homeopathy just as it occurs in pharmaceutical research.

In fact, these intentional effects from the physician is precisely why the gold standard of research is the *double-blind* method: Both the patient and the physician must not know which treatment is the one being tested. This is because research has shown that somehow, when a physician knows which of the treatments is the medicine; the medicine will somehow have better results among the patients. Science has yet to explain this anomaly.

We see this effect everyday: When we give a gift to someone, they might look upon and treasure the gift decades later. As they look upon the gift in the future, there will be a retrieval of the conscious intent of its giver. Does the gift itself physically contain that consciousness? Possibly not, but the physical gift connects the receiver to the memory of the intention of its giver. The gift becomes a vehicle for the transmission of the consciousness of the giver.

How did it arrive at that point? A connection between the giver's intent and the gift had to take place at some point—perhaps when the giver picked out the gift. Therefore, we would say that the gift *reflects* the consciousness of the giver. As soon as the giver interacted with the gift by taking possession of it, the gift has taken on a new character for its receiver: It is now irrevocably tied to the consciousness of the giver.

Does the gift physically contain the consciousness of the giver? By perception it certainly does. Perhaps it simply serves as a reminder or a trigger for the memory. In either case, the perceived effect is the same. The gift triggers the memory of the original conscious intent.

In the 1990s, Masaru Emoto and an assistant began taking photographs illustrating water crystal formation under different circumstances and influences. He first published these findings in 1999. Emoto's photographic images implied that water crystal formation varied not only to water sources, but also to interactions with music, spoken words and even written words. Water exposed to different types of music formed different crystals: classical music created full symmetrical crystal shapes while hard rock created unsymmetrical and disoriented shapes. Water exposed to different types of words or phrases apparently formed different crystals: uplifting words created full, symmetrical crystals while words of hatred or anger created disoriented shapes (Emoto 2004).

This research became well publicized yet controversial among the scientific community. Some researchers decried Emoto's reports as lacking the rigor acceptable for peer-review. While the photos themselves create little doubt regarding the variability of ice crystal formation, the question of his research boils down to the extent controls were applied to the process of choosing photographs for publication. Because we now understand that the same water can form a variety of ice crystals shapes, Emoto chose a photo to represent each scenario. Was there any bias in the selection of the photo crystals to publish? This concern has yet to be adequately resolved. Therefore, although Emoto's crystal photograph research is intriguing, and may indicate water's ability to reflect consciousness, the research falls short as controlled evidence linking intention with water.

There are still a number of undeniable characteristics about water that confirm water's ability to reflect intention. These are found as we continue to sniff the trail of evidence concerning water's capacity for memory.

As we have touched upon earlier, water's ability to retain memory has been clinically examined through the medical science of homeopathy, beginning with Dr. Samuel Hahnemann's original research with dilutions two centuries ago. While the *'like cures like'* portion of homeopathy is well accepted by modern medicine (the basis for vaccination) the notion that water will retain a distant memory of a substance diluted to the point of theoretically diluting every molecule of the substance away is not acceptable to some in the scientific community.

As we discussed earlier, research on water memory was advanced greatly by Dr. Jacques Benveniste and his esteemed research associates from a number of respected research institutions. Dr. Benveniste, a successful French medical doctor, discovered accidentally in 1984 that white blood cells responded to an allergen in a solution despite there theoretically being no remaining antibody molecules in the solution. This led to hundreds of studies among Dr. Benveniste's team and other research labs, which mostly replicated these results. These results confirm that a water-based solution somehow retains memory after full dilution. Over 300 trials were performed confirming these results.

In 1991, Benveniste developed a system of amplifying molecular signals through sensitive electromagnetic microcoils and transducers. After a few years of application, the process was refined to the point where his research team was able to record molecular emissions into digital form. The molecular signal associated with the digital recordings indicated frequencies in the 0-22 KHz range. Incredibly, the digital recordings could be played back through an amplified transducer in the presence of a particular reactive organ, such as cholinergic activity among (cruelly harvested) pig hearts. His digital playback resulted in the same physiological result the biochemical hormone might have—without the physical biochemical present. Dr. Benveniste demonstrated this effect emphatically when he was able to send disks or email recordings to labs in remote locations. In these cases, the playback of the recordings would have the same effect (Benvienste 1997).

As Dr. Benvienste continued his research, he discovered that the effective transmission of the signal had some dependency on the mixing system employed. Without the proper mixing process, the diluted mixture's ability to affect the same result was substantially decreased. On the other hand, proper mixing resulted in a significantly greater effect (22.6 versus 3.2 coronary flow changes in an acetylcholine dilute, for example) when compared to the solution *prior to mixing* (Benvienste 1999).

The ability of water molecules to retain particular electromagnetic waveform interference patterns is illustrated using these data. As we established earlier, a waveform basis for matter is supported by a century's worth of physics research. We might compare this with voice vibration. In order for voice vibration to be instructive, there must be a precise manipulation of waveforms striking the eardrum, which contain the message of the speaker.

The transmission of sound and visual signals via radio waves parallels this fundamental process. It also provides an illustration for the ability water has to conduct radiative information.

In the same way, we can connect the size and shape of a wave breaking on the beach to a myriad of atmospheric and tidal events occurring far out to sea. There may have been a large windstorm thousands of miles away. There may have been a hurricane storm front. These may be combined with a large tidal change due to the moon's orbit around the earth. Talk about non-local events.

This holds true for sonar wave composition. Intelligent transmissions of dolphins and whales can travel for thousands of miles. Whales have been known to communicate amongst themselves between remote locations. If we take the net radiative effect of all the living organisms within the ocean, we have the basis for a medium of consciousness conduction.

If we were to design an instrument to pick these subtle waves of consciousness being conducted by water, that instrument would likely resemble the ear of a whale or dolphin. Certainly we have attempted to duplicate this technology with the use of sonar devices, allowing us to "see" objects in the distance under water.

As far as connecting consciousness to seemingly random activity, we are reminded of the random event research led initially by Dr. Helmut Schmidt, and later by Princeton's Dr. Robert Jahn and Dr. Robert Nelson.

The central issue with this research was whether accidents truly exist. If accidents exist, then at least we could assume that physical events are random rather than the results of consciousness. One way to test an assumption of accidental behavior within our microcosm is to isolate one particular event we already assume is a random event, and test it for ultimate randomness. If an isolated event can be random, then we could at least accept the notion that accidents do exist.

For at least hundreds of years, researchers and philosophers have counted flipped coins, dice throws, and card deals in an attempt to reveal the underlying principles of random events. It was assumed that these events were ultimately random because there seemed no way to influence them. Each event seemed to be thoroughly disconnected and isolated from the other. Each throw of the dice appeared to be affected only by the potential options on each die. The previous throw seemed thoroughly disconnected from the current throw. And so it was with coin tosses.

Hundreds of coin tosses would indicate a growing trend toward a 50/50 split of the tosses. At least until the numbers started getting larger. As the coin tosses increased into the thousands, the differential between the theoretical 50/50 remained intact and even sometimes grew larger. For some reason, the tosses were not conclusively arriving at what most thought would be the random result: That as the number of tosses increased, the percentage of heads and the percentage of tails would increasingly approach 50/50.

In an attempt to resolve this seeming riddle of nature, Dr. Helmut Schmidt—then a physicist at Boeing—invented a machine called the *random event generator* in 1969. This device utilized a mechanical basis to produce a theoretically random flashing of one of four lights, using the decay emissions from the strontium-90 isotope. This produced a theoretically natural random event, as this decay was considered ultimately chaotic. The light system was set up to enable an observer to predict which light would come on by pressing a button under one of the lights. With a choice of four selections, the statistical average over a large number of guesses should be no more than 25%. However, large trial numbers resulted in levels closer to 27%, indicating some sort of inherent human ability to either predict or influence the result existed (Schmidt 1969, Palmer 1997).

The research became somewhat controversial due to this unknown: Were the observers predicting the results or affecting the results? In an attempt to isolate these two factors, Dr. Schmidt refined the methodology and instrumentation to reflect the early coin toss experiments. His new random number generator (RNG) performed random calculations to produce odd of even numbers. Using computer programming, large numbers of results could be compiled quickly and accurately. Today the terms random event generator (REG) and random number generator (RNG) are often used interchangeably.

Dr. Schmidt's series of studies with the RNG resulted in the same curious results as the earlier coin toss research: As the numbers got increasingly higher, significant variances between 50/50 remained, typically within the 1-4% range. These seemed to be somehow influenced by the observer of the RNG machine. Can a person consciously will a coin to land on the heads or tails side? How about throughout a large range of tosses?

Enter Princeton professors Dr. Robert Jahn and later Dr. Roger Nelson, who refined the random number generator research within a project called the Princeton Engineering Anomalies Research (PEAR). Dr. Jahn improved upon the machine and increased the number of controls in the protocol. Dr. Nelson expanded the scope of the research. Like Dr. Schmidt's machine, Dr. Jahn's machines would randomly produce either a one or a zero in a random sequence. Dr. Jahn's software was careful to remove any possible source of bias. Additionally, Dr. Jahn's software could be run on smaller personal computers, while Dr. Schmidt's programs required a computer the size of an office to run (and earlier technology).

As hundreds of REG studies were conducted and compiled by Dr. Jahn and other researchers, a consistent result again emerged. RNG variances from 50/50 continued with larger runs. Trying to find association, Dr. Jahn began investigating outside events or environmental conditions to find a possible correlation with these variances. One of the first relationships Dr. Jahn discovered was related to the personnel attending or observing the REG runs. Variances trended differently for female observers than for male observers, for example. Seeing a possible human influence, Dr. Jahn's trials began to ask observers to wish for one result or another. This nearly always resulted in larger variances: While some results trended towards the wished result, some trended in the opposite direction, depending upon the person.

In other words, some observers could influence the REG results more than others. Some influenced the results positively, and some influenced the results negatively. Note that observers were not physically able to affect the results. They were merely observing the results—primarily from within the room or near the room where the equipment was located.

After exhaustive testing, REG results were found to be connected not only to human influence: Seemingly unrelated global events taking place thousands of miles away also influenced REG results. These included earthquakes and other large natural disasters. They also included large sporting events and international events such as Princess Diana's funeral (Jahn and Dunne 2007; Dunne and Jahn 2005; Jahn and Dunn, 1987; Jahn *et al.* 2007; Dunne *et al.* 1983).

While the REG research initially focused on the ability of humans to influence theoretically random events, another conclusion began to become evident: A theoretically random event—supposedly isolated and thus unattached to any other event—appears to be connected to seemingly unrelated events, after isolating all known forms of bias.

The REG protocol scientifically isolated seemingly random and controlled events. Yet even these events appear to be connected with and influenced by other events. If even the most theoretically isolated random event cannot be shown to occur randomly, then our assumption of even a partially chaotic world would prove to be erroneous.

The ability of nature's seemingly random events to be driven by intention and consciousness opens up the logical nexus that the elements provide a medium for the conduction of intention: This of course includes water.

A number of researchers have confirmed water's ability to retain or reflect the intentions of a therapeutic practitioner in peer-reviewed research. Dr. Edward Brame, Dr. Douglas Dean, Dr. Bernard Grad, and others have either led or co-authored studies—some confirmed by infrared spectroscopy analysis—that healer-touched water maintained molecular changes. In more than one of these, the molecular bond angles had slightly shifted. In others, decreased surface tension of the water confirmed a subtle molecular change. In some of these, the rate of seed sprouting and plant growth was affected by applying water that had been touched by healers applying intention (Dean 1983; Dean *et al.* 1974; Grad 1964, Grad *et al.* 1984; Schwartz *et al.* 1987).

The effects of emission bombardment have been well established by physicists in mass accelerator and spectrometry research. Because each electron orbit has particular waveform or quantum characteristics, bombarding an atom with radiation of the right frequency will boost certain electrons into lower or higher energy levels. This typically also affects spin or angular momentum, and sometimes produces an ion or an isotope that goes on to create other effects in the local and non-local environment. This of course can create effects within water or whatever medium exposed. The affected medium then 'conducts' this change throughout.

We are again reminded of the rock being tossed into the pond: The entire pond is affected by the toss. The pond reverberates with ripples for some time, indicating the character of the rock and the toss. Certainly a stone tossed with the intention of really stirring up the pond will produce that effect. The pond will thus 'remember' the intention with a flurry of steep and prolonged waves.

Perhaps we should look more closely at waves.

~ Two ~

A World of Waves

Our universe is pulsing with rhythm. Throughout nature, we see repeating rhythmic occurrences. Each day we observe the sun's rise and set, establishing a cycle that is repetitious, adjusting slightly with every cycle. Seasonal changes with the rotation of the earth in respect to its orbit are apparent. We see this seasonal rhythmic rise and fall reflected in plant-life—waxing in the spring and waning in the fall. We see birds and other migratory animals move with similar periodicity, traveling synchronized with the seasons to amazingly exacting locations.

As we analyze these various pulses of nature, we notice a behavior of precise waves. We see a distinct and precise rhythm repeating and oscillating through the media of our environment. We see nature's oscillations pulsing through the oceans, causing waves and weather conditions. We see larger periods of ocean tidal rhythms bringing an exchange of ocean creatures and their food to and from the seashore. We see the rhythmic upwelling of cold waters from the ocean depths rotating and recycling the ocean's various biochemicals and marine life. Meanwhile, these surface waters are spun and rotated by the wind through recycling temperature gradients.

We also see a similar rhythmic pulsing throughout our atmosphere; recycling temperature, water vapor, and various gas mixtures with periodic precision. We see rhythmic oscillations pulsing through space, sending us the radio, light and other radiation waves from twinkling stars billions and trillions of light years away. We see our closest star, the sun, periodically radiating heat and light along with cyclic solar storms that in turn affect behavior.

The rhythms of living chemistry began to be translated into scientific knowledge some time ago. The rhythmic behavior of the universe gave rise to the use of mathematics. This was evidenced in the texts of Mesopotamia. The math within nature was apparent to the Greek philosophers of the sixth and seventh centuries B.C. Mathematics were used by the ancient Egyptians as early as 3000 B.C. Earlier we find mathematical formulation recorded in the texts of the Chinese monarchs of 3500 B.C. They set forth various measurements and calculations, on subjects ranging from architecture to the stars. Earlier than this, we find the ancient Sanskrit texts of the 4500 B.C. Indus valley civilization calculating the earth's rhythms. These early mathematical insights came to influence the scientific culture of later societies as we have investigated the precise nature of motion and movement. From the earliest of these recordings, we find a common acceptance that the physical world moves with a synchronized pacing or pulse. This pacing came to be measurable and repetitively precise. These ancient cultures also observed these relationships with a reverence toward a larger conscious mechanism—an elegant non-local effect with purpose.

The measurement of nature's rhythmic order descended onto western science through the capable doorway of the ancient Greeks. The famed Greek Pythagoras of the sixth century B.C. was considered by many in the West to be instrumental in developing a mathematical basis behind the rhythms of nature. Pythagoras and his students utilized reason, logic, and the observation of nature to find an affinity between the rhythms of the elements, the harmony of music and mathematical relationships of integers and their ratios. Though it is understood that Pythagoras guided many of those principles directly, credit for many insights presented as Pythagorean is due to a number of philosopher/scientists who learned and taught cooperatively within the Pythagorean community.

Through the works of Philolaus of Tarentum, we learned Pythagoras expressed the rhythms of song and instrumentation within a context of pitch, scale, octaves and harmony. All of these were brought into rationale through mathematical relationships. This same approach led the Pythagoreans to perceive various other relationships within nature. While Pythagoras may or may not be responsible for the famous *Pythagorean Theorem,* he is still considered the "father of numbers." He is also credited with the form of philosophical and logical reasoning that blossomed later through the teachings of Plato, Aristotle, Socrates, and Ptolemy.

Second century Greek Claudius Ptolemaeus was also known as Ptolemy. Ptolemy was a famed mathematician, astronomer, and natural scientist from Alexandria. He was responsible for a number of treatises that influenced natural scientists over the next 1500 years. His book *Harmonics* focused on the rhythmic qualities of music theory. His *Optics* treatise covered the realms of light rays and vision, and his book *Geography* established many of the principles utilized by geographers and cartographers in mapping and quantifying spatial relationships.

Ptolemy's *Harmonics* repositioned the Pythagoras' approach of relationships between harmony and music within a stricter definition of mathematical ratios. His work delivered music theory from the clutches of the fourth century B.C. Greek Aristoxenus of Tarentum, who proposed music harmony to be relative to what he termed the *"irrational exercise of perception."* While Ptolemy broadened music harmonies into various other relationships using the concords such as the fifth (3:2) and the fourth (4:3), his mathematical proofs—grounded in the scientific method—became fundamental in the process of relating the physical world to the precision of waveform mathematics.

The harmonic wave nature of the elements is illustrated by the early nineteenth century research of Oxford University physics professor Henry Moseley. Professor Moseley followed Mendeleev's periodic table construction with radiation emission measurements. Using x-ray diffraction, he determined that each element emitted a unique frequency of radiation. These frequency relationships, he found, also correlated with the orbital valence relationships. As atomic number count increased among the elements, the wavelengths decreased and the frequencies increased. Moving along the elements of the periodic table, frequency measurements increased in a stepped fashion and tapered with elements with complete valence shells.

Dr. Alexander Beddoe illustrated in 2002 that these frequencies can be correlated with sound frequency. Each row of elements corresponds with a stepping up of octaves. While the fourth row of the periodic table (potassium, calcium and so on) corresponds with the seventh octave, the third row (sodium, magnesium and so on) coincides with the sixth octave. Meanwhile, the second row correlates with the fifth octave and the first row corresponds with the fourth octave. The rows under the fourth row fall into the seventh through ninth octaves. Dr. Beddoe also charted these frequency-octave correlations, illustrating a helical shaped graph not unlike the Mayan periodic table presented earlier.

Precision and order at the atomic level is also evident when considering the accuracy of the atomic clockworks. In today's standard for timekeeping—the atomic cesium clock—radioactive cesium provides a steady stream of radiative waveforms that pass through a magnetic field to routinely oscillate a crystal. The emission from cesium is so rhythmically accurate that our society now quite literally sets its clocks to it.

The relationships between the elements and their atomic energy levels illustrate they have a common mathematical basis. When we look at these relationships using different models of measurement, we find the same common basis among the elements, indicating arrangement around a common integral multiple. When a molecule reaches a point of stability through combination, subatomic particles are being shared between atoms through resonation. In clear terms, this means a fulfillment of the waveform sequence within a *harmonic array*. This array is illustrated by the columns and rows of the periodic table. Consider how two columns of numbers can be converted to graphical form allowing us to see how each row and column relates to the other.

The periodic arrangement of the elements might be comparable to an instrument having sequentially arranged strings, with the first tuned to a basic note. Each sequential string can step-up the tuning from this first string to reach a full complement of musical keys. This enables the strings to be played together in harmony.

Waveform Structure

When most of us think about waves, we think of the ocean. We think of waves pounding onto the beach. Stirred up by the forces of wind and weather, large waves will march onto the reefs and beaches, standing up with ferocious crests. The beauty and power of a large wave lifting and crashing onto the rocks or beach is often the subject of popular photography and film. What we may not realize is that each single wave is communicating an event that took place thousands of miles away: A particular mix of wind, temperature, atmospheric pressure and moisture combining in just the right way to instigate a *weather system*.

This weather system converts its potential into waveforms in the surrounding ocean waters. Should we look at a storm's confluence of elements from space, we will see nature's characteristic spiral. Harmonically, we see this same spiral shape within a cross-sectional view of an ocean wave.

A wave is a repeating *oscillation of energy:* A translation of information through a particular medium. Waves can travel through solids, fluids, gases and space. Waves are not restricted to a particular medium, either. Most waves will move through one medium and continue on through the next medium where those mediums intersect. A sound, for example may vibrate a drum skin first. Where the drum skin meets the air, it oscillates the air molecules to translate the sound information throughout the medium. Where the air connects with the *tympanic membrane*, the information waveform is translated to the malleus, incus and stapes of the middle ear. After vibrating through to the round window, the oscillation is translated through the cochlea into nerve pulse oscillations. This means that the original wave of the drum beat transversed several mediums before being sensed by us.

A repeated oscillation or waveform through a medium against the backdrop of time is a *rhythm*. This tendency to move with a repetitive pace translates to a recurring *waveform*. As a recurring result is associated with a causal event, we can say that rhythm is the repetitive cycling of information waveforms through the mediums physical world.

Every movement in nature has a signature rhythm: The earth oscillates in specific types of seismic waves—some causing damage but most hardly noticeable. We each walk with a signature pace as our feet meet the ground. Our vocal cords oscillate to the reflection of our thoughts with a unique pace and timing. Our heart valves oscillate with the needs of circulation. Our lungs oscillate as we breathe in and out—unique to our lung size and cells' needs for oxygen. Even rugged, seemingly solid structures like rocks oscillate—depending upon their position, size, shape, and composition. A cliff by the seashore will oscillate with each pounding wave. A building in a windy city will uniquely oscillate with the movement of the wind through the streets. Each building will oscillate slightly differently, depending upon its architecture and location.

All of these movements—and all movements in nature for that matter—provide recurring oscillations that can be charted in waveform structure. Moreover, the various events within nature come complete with recurring cycles. While many cycles obviously repeat during our range of observation, many cycles have only recently become evident, indicating that many of nature's cycles are beyond our current observation range.

Natural oscillations balance between a particular pivot point and an *axis*. The axis is typically a frame of reference between two media or quanta. An axis showing quantification may illustrate time in reference to height, time versus temperature, time versus activity or time versus other quantifying points of reference. Waves will also transist between media. The ocean wave is the transisting of waveforms between the intersection of the atmosphere and the water: the storm system. The water's surface tension gives rise to the ocean wave as it refracts the pressure of the storm system. The storm system's waveform energy will be radiated through the ocean to the rocks and beach.

Nature's waves are relational to the rhythms of planets and galaxies. These rhythms translate to electromagnetic energy and kinetic energy, which translate to the elements of speed, distance, and mass. Momentum, inertia, gravity, and other natural phenomena are thus examples of the cyclical activities that directly relate with nature's wave rhythms. Every rhythm in nature is interconnected with other rhythms. As a house is built with interconnected beams of framing, the universe's waveforms are all interconnected with a design of pacing within the element of time.

The most prevalent waveform found in nature is the *sinusoidal wave* or sine wave. The sinusoidal wave is the manifestation of circular motion related to time. The sine wave thus repeats through nature's processes defined by time. For example, the rotating positions of the hands of a clock translate to a sinusoidal wave should the angles of the hand positions be charted on one axis with the time on the other axis.

Sinusoidal waveforms are thus the typical waveform structures of light, sound, electromagnetic waves and ocean waves. Late eighteenth and early nineteenth century French physicist Jean Fourier found that just about every motion could be broken down into sinusoidal components. This phenomenon has become known as the *Fourier series*.

The cycle of a sine wave, moving from midline to peak, then back to midline then to a trough and back to midline completes a full cycle. If we divide the wave into angles, the beginning is consistent with 0 degrees; the first peak is consistent with 45 degrees, the midline with 90 degrees and the trough with 270 degrees. The cycle repeats again, as we make another revolution around the sine wave circle.

Other wave types occurring in nature might not be strictly sine waves, yet they are often sinusoidal in essence. The cosine wave, for example, is sinusoidal because it has the same basic shape, but is simply *phase-shifted* from the sine. Other waves such as square waves or irregular sound waves can usually be connected to sinusoidal origin when their motion is broken down into composites.

We see so many circular activities within nature. We see the earth recycling molecular components. We see the recycling of water from earth to sea to clouds and back to earth. We see planetary bodies moving in cyclic fashion, repeating their positions in periodic rhythm. We see the seasons moving in cyclic repetition. We see organisms living cycles of repetitive physical activity.

While not every cycle in nature is precisely circular—the orbits of planets or electron energy shells for example—they are nonetheless linked within a grander cycle. Linked cycles often contain various alterations as they adapt to the other cyclic components. This modulation can be described as *adaptation*—a harmonic process between waveform matter and life.

This all should remind us of the notion of the *circle of life*, which has been repeatedly observed throughout nature in so many respects that it is generally assumed without fanfare. Circles recur in human and animal activity, social order, customs, and individual circumstances. The tribal circle is common among many ancient cultures—and for good reason. In modern society, we have circular conferences, round-table meetings, and cyclical ceremonies. The potter's wheel, the grinding wheel, and the circular clock are all examples of circular symbols in our attempt to synchronize with nature. Just about every form of communication and transportation is somehow connected to circular motion. For this reason, it is no accident that the wheel provides our primary and most efficient means for transportation. The motion of walking is also circular and sinusoidal, as the legs rise and fall forward, rotating the various joints.

In nature, we observe two basic types of waves: *mechanical* and *electromagnetic*. A mechanical wave moves through a particular medium: sound pressure waves as they move through air, for example. Mechanical waves can move over the surface of a medium. Ocean waves and certain earthquake (seismic) waves are examples of mechanical *surface waves*. Another type of mechanical wave is the *tortional wave:* This mechanical wave twists through a spiral or helix.

The electromagnetic wave is seemingly different because it theoretically does not move through a medium of any composition. Einstein assumed space is a vacuum and the ultimate electromagnetic wave, light, moved through this vacuum with constant speed. Dr. Einstein's theory supposed that time is collapsed within space: Instead of time and distance being separate, he supposed a singular element called *space-time*.

Yet in 2001, collaborative research led by Texas A&M University physics professor Dr. Dimitri Nanopoulos, Dr. Nikolaos Mavromatos of King's College in London, and Dr. John Ellis of the European Center for Particle Physics in Geneva confirmed that additional influences can alter the speed of light. Their calculations showed the speed of light varies to frequency. Furthermore, in 1999, University of Toronto professor Dr. John Moffat calculated that the speed of light has actually slowed down over time. Space may actually be a bona fide medium after all.

Nature displays two basic waveform structures: *transverse* and *longitudinal*. Visible spectrum, radio waves, microwaves, radar, infrared and x-rays are all transverse waveforms. As these waves move, there is a disruption moving at right angles to the vector of the wave. For example, should the wave move along a longitudinal x-axis, its disruption field would move along the perpendicular y-z axis. This might be compared to watching a duck floating in a lake strewn with tiny waves. The duck bobs up and down as the waves pass under the duck's body. In the case of the transverse electromagnetic wave, the disruption field is the magnetic field.

In the longitudinal wave, pressure gradients form regular alternating zones of *compression* and *rarefaction*. During the compression phase, the medium is pressed together, and during the rarefaction, the medium is expanded outward. This might be illustrated by the alternating expansion and compression of a spring. Instead of the wave disturbing the medium upward and downward as in the case of a transverse wave, the medium is disturbed in a back and forth fashion, in the direction of the wave. Examples of longitudinal waves are sound waves and most seismic waves. In the case of sound waves, air molecules compress and rarefy in the direction of the sound projection.

These two types of waves may also combine in nature. An ocean wave is a good example of a combination of transverse and longitudinal waveforms. Water may be disturbed up and down as it transmits an ocean wave, and it may convey alternating compressions and rarefaction as it progresses tidal currents.

Waves are typically referred to as radiation when the waveform can translate its energy information from one type of medium to another. In this respect, ocean waves can be considered radiating as they translate their energy onto the sand. In the case of seismic waves, they translate through land to buildings and people. The classic type of radiation comes from electromagnetic waves such as x-rays or ultraviolet rays, which can travel through skin or other molecular mediums after transversing space.

Waves are typically measured by their wave height from trough to crest (*amplitude*), rate of speed through time (*frequency*) and the distance from one repeating peak to another (*wavelength*). Waves are also characterized by their wave shape. Examples of wave shape include sinusoidal waves and, square waves, as we've mentioned.

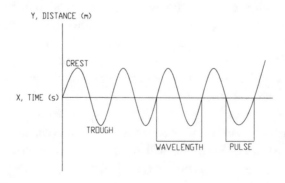

The frequency of a wave is typically measured by how many wave cycles (one complete revolution of the wave) pass a particular point within a period of time. Therefore, waves are often measured in CPS, or *cycles per second*. The *hertz*, named after nineteenth century German physicist Dr. Heinrich Hertz, who is said to have discovered radio frequency electromagnetic waves. Note that hertz and CPS are identical: Both the number of complete waves passing a given point every second. Other frequency measurements used include machinery's RPM *(revolutions per second)*, special radiation's RAD/S *(radians per second)*, and the heart's BPM *(beats per minute)*.

Wavelength is frequently measured in meters, centimeters, or nanometers to comply with international standards. Each radiation type is classified by its wavelength. A wave's wavelength has an inverse relationship to its frequency. This is because a shorter wave's length will travel faster through a particular point than a longer length will. Note also that speed is the rate measured from one point to another, while frequency is the rate of one full repetition to another past a particular point. Therefore, a wave's wavelength can be determined by dividing its speed by its frequency. Of course, a wave's speed can also be divided by its wavelength to obtain the frequency.

Despite popular science literature's penchant for naming only one aspect of a particular wave (often wavelength or frequency), we must consider the other specifications for clarity. When we describe a sinusoidal waveform, we can state either its frequency or wavelength, since the two will be inversely related. Otherwise, the wave's amplitude is an important consideration, as this relates to the height of the wave from peak to trough. Among sinusoidal waves, larger amplitude will accompany a larger wavelength. We also might consider the specific *phase* of a wave, its medium of travel, and again its wave shape. Together these help us arrive at a more precise set of specifications, which allows more accuracy in describing particular waveforms. While one or more of these specifications might be used to describe a particular wave in popular media, in reality all should be considered. Here we will refer to a unique combination of these specifications with the term *waveform*.

Waves travel with some form of repetition or periodicity. The very definition of a wave describes a repeating motion of some type. This repetition, occurring with a particular pace and particular time reference, together forms a rhythm. We see wave rhythms all around us. Can waves be chaotic? To the contrary, it is their very consistent, non-chaotic rhythm that allows us to interpret light, color, sound, or warmth with duplicating precision. All of these waveforms connect with the senses because they have consistent and congruent oscillations. In sensing the world around us, we do not perceive each wave individually. Rather, we perceive the information waves are carrying.

When an information-containing waveform collides or *interferes* with another information waveform, the result is often a more complex form of information. As waveforms collide throughout our universe, they comprehensively present a myriad of information via interference patterns. The information is only available to us to the extent we can sense and interpret those interference patterns, however.

We can thus conclude that nature is composed of combinations and interactions of longitudinal and transverse waveforms of different varieties. The classic waveforms vibrating through space and radiating through physical molecules are fairly easy to isolate, chart and measure. Within nature, however, waves collide and interfere with each other to create informational systems beyond our ability to measure. The complete picture of interference patterns created by nature's innumerable waveforms is quite simply outside our range of observation.

The more precise reason why not all waves are sinusoidal is that nature is complicated by these different types of interactions between different types of waveforms. When dissimilar waveforms collide, there is a resulting disturbance or *interference pattern*. Depending upon the characteristics of the two colliding waveforms, this interference could result in a larger, complex waveform—or *constructive interference pattern*. Alternatively, should the waveforms contrast each other; their meeting could cause a resultant reduction of waveforms—a *destructive interference pattern*.

The interactive quality of two waves as they collide lies within their similarity of wave *phase*. If one wave is cycling in positive territory while the other is cycling in negative territory, they will most likely destructively interfere in each other, resulting in a reduction of information. However, if the two waves move in the same phase—where both cycle with the same points on the curve—then they will most likely constructively interfere with each other, creating a greater complexity of information.

As a result, two waves are compared by being *in phase* or *out of phase*. In-phase waveforms will often meet with superposition to form larger, more complex waveforms. Out-of-phase waveforms will often conflict: reducing and canceling their effective rhythms in one or many ways. This canceling or reduction during interference is not necessarily bad, however. Destructive interference can also communicate various types of information.

The degree that two or more waves will interfere with each other—either constructively or destructively—relates to their *coherence*. If two waves are coherent, they are either completely in-phase or out-of-phase. They will thus create either greater complexity or significant cancelation. Waves that are different but not fully out-of-phase are considered *incoherent*.

Waveform coherency is not too different from speaking coherency. Coherent speaking refers to sounds that are better understood by the listener. Whether the communication is interpreted by the listener as positive or negative speech is beside the point. The clarity of the communication is indicative of its coherence. In the same way, coherent waves interfere significantly constructively or destructively as they interact.

Resonance occurs when individual waves are expanded to a balanced state—one where the amplitude and period is the largest for that waveform system. Thus, *resonating waves* typically occur when waves come together in constructive interference. This results in a maximization of their respective wave periods and amplitudes. This is illustrated when two tuned instruments play the same note or song together. Their strings will resonate together, creating a convergence with greater amplitude, which will typically (depending of course upon the surrounding environment) result in a louder, clearer sound. We also see (or hear) this when we create the familiar whistling sound accomplished by blowing into a bottle spout: To get the loudest sound, we must blow with a certain angle and airspeed—positioning our lips with the shape of the bottle. Once we find the right positioning, angle and speed, we have established a resonance.

As waves move from one media to the next, they will partially *reflect* or *refract*. *Reflected waves* will bounce off the new medium, while *refracted waves* will move through a new medium with a different vector and speed, depending upon the density and molecular makeup of the medium. The ability of a particular medium to provoke these changes is referred to as its *index of refraction*. Some mediums will reflect certain waveforms while refracting others. Most mediums will also absorb certain types of waveforms, as we will discuss further. The type of waveforms reflected and absorbed will usually determine the medium's perceived color and clarity.

As we have mentioned, *surface waves* are typically seen at the surface of a particular medium where that medium interfaces with another medium. Surface waves are seen on the surface of oceans and lakes, for example. Surface waves are mechanical in nature and thus tend to respond to surface pressures from the interfacing medium. In the case of surface seismic waves, the collision of the wave with a building may mute the waveform with one type of building material and exaggerate the waveform with another type of building material.

Surface waves are divided into two basic types—the first being a *capillary wave*. The capillary wave is a carrier wave that forms during the beginning of the build-up process. Therefore, it is considered a smaller wave—often seen as smaller ripples on the water as the wind freshens. The second type of surface wave is a *gravity wave*, typically having a larger wavelength and speed than the capillary wave has. It is the gravity-type *rogue waves* that seafarers respect for their shipwrecking abilities, for example.

In deeper water, a combination of transverse and longitudinal wave motions combines to form *monochromatic linear plane waves*. This forms a type of wave called an *inertial wave*. Inertial waves are typically moving within rotating fluid mediums. Inertial waves are common in not only the ocean and among lakes, but also within the atmosphere and presumably within the earth's core. The various currents and winds within the atmosphere all travel in inertial waves of varying lengths. Surface waves will interact with these inertial waves to move energy over the surface of their medium. This energy movement allows surfers to ride a wave from the outside to the inside of the tidal region, for example.

A *simple harmonic* is a recurring wave (usually sinusoidal) that repeats its own rhythmic frequency. When different waveforms converge and their frequencies are aligned—they are multiples or integers of each other—their waveform combination becomes *harmonized*: There is a mathematical multiple between them. In other words, harmony is based upon waveforms having a multiple of the same fundamental integer. For example, waveforms with frequencies at the same multiples will harmonize. Other waveform aspects of a wave can also create harmony. Waveforms having the same amplitudes or wave shapes—or multiples thereof—will be harmonic on different levels. Though their resulting interference pattern might not appear the same as a frequency-harmonic combination, we can still recognize their interaction as harmonic.

As forward-moving waves interact with returning waves, both waves will become compressed and dilated. This effect is known as the *Doppler Effect*—named after nineteenth century Austrian physicist Johann Christian Doppler. If the incoming waves have the same waveform, frequency, and amplitude, this will create a *standing wave*. If they do not, either the incoming or the outgoing wave will divert the waves it meets, and distort those waves in one respect or another. This distortion would be analogous to the oblong or parabolic orbitals of solar systems and electrons, which are distorted from sinusoidal by oncoming waveforms or magnetic fields.

Standing waveforms will typically have the same frequency, wavelength, amplitude, and shape as they oscillate. This creates a balance and resonance that gives the retinal cell perceiver the illusion that those standing waves are solid objects.

As suggested by Zhang *et al.* in 1996, and confirmed by multiple physicists over the last decade, multiple electrons within shared orbitals among multiple atoms situated within a close-range matrix are best described as *multiple standing waves:* These are standing waveforms within minute space. They create some of the strongest forces in nature, as they compile the illusion of physical reality. The convergence of these multiple waveforms standing together in a harmonic resonating pattern for a unique period of time is best described as *architecture*.

Harmonic synchronized and resonating waveforms also continually undergo *displacement*, thus transferring their energy through convergence or interference with other waveforms. This convergence or interference displacement conveys the rhythmic energy and information traveling through these waveforms on to others, mixing to create the resulting cyclic nature of our universe. These conveyances would also render the perception of *movement* within the universe.

As researchers have probed deeper into the nature of energy and matter, we have found that everything around us is oscillating at a particular rhythm. All information and movement moves within waveforms. Even nonmoving 'solid' matter has the slower, standing waveform movement as mentioned above, even while it undergoes larger life cycle waveform phases. For example, we might see a mountain as non-moving, but in reality it is not just rotating with the earth through the pacing of time: The mountain is also undergoing a hardly-noticed cycle of growth due to the earth's rotation of heat and lava. This growth inter-cycles with the earth's recycling of molecular components, creating gradual reformation due to water, winds and weather. Finally, this 'solid' mountain may undergo a dissolution phase during a volcanic event, with its molecular waveforms cycling into fluid and gas states.

When we see an object with a consistent color, we recognize this color consistency because the frequency of the reflective color waveform is oscillating repeatedly. It has a particular consistency or pace through time. If we were to look at a mirror with a mirror inside the reflection view, we will see a repeating pattern of whatever is inside that second mirror. This repetition forms a visual wave pattern. It may not appear oscillating to our vision, yet its repetitious nature creates a waveform. We will also note in this array, the mirrors become increasingly smaller as they repeat. The vision of the repeating mirrors is not simply repetitive: It is rhythmically reductive—starting from the larger to the smaller with a precise pattern of reduction. This reducing pattern is also rhythmic and harmonic—allowing us the opportunity to see many mirrors in array within the one mirror view.

In 2002, Gabriel LaFreniere introduced a series of wave models incorporating Doppler effects and interacting standing wave patterns. Through his models and supporting calculations, he was able to present a logical case for the increasingly accepted hypothesis that electrons making up matter are standing waves, oscillating within the magnetic fields of space. His proof was called the *La-Freniere's wave,* a single basis wave pattern of standing waves in accordance with Lorentz equations. His moving illustrations also provided solid support for the theory.

Spirals, Tubes and Whirlpools

As coherent waveforms of nature interact and interfere, spirals develop. For example, when we see the rhythmic spiraling growth of leaves or branches in Fibonacci sequence around the trunk of a tree we are presented with an interference of Fibonacci waveforms and the vectors of growth coming from the living plant. This interference creates a spiral or helix pattern of leaves growing upward and outward. Should we spread out the spiral orientation of a plant into two dimensions—x and y coordinates—we would find that the branching reflects a sinusoidal wave pattern. Should we look down at the plant from its apex, we would see this spiraling or helical effect, depending upon the size and nature of the plant. Looking at a younger plant—where we could see the top shoots with respect to the bottom trunk—we will likely perceive a spiral. Should we look at a larger tree with a large trunk at the bottom with its branches swirling and widening to the top, we will likely perceive a helix.

These helical and spiraling forms provide the basic structures for life within the physical world. We see these structures present from the smallest elements of life to the largest elements; from the double helixed DNA molecule to the spiraling galaxies of the universe. We see the spiral within all types of anatomical shapes. The nautilus shell is most famous, but just about every shell formation also reflects this spiral, including the swirling of tornadoes, hurricanes, and weather systems. Our senses are also tied to rotational spheres and spirals. Our cochlear anatomy utilizes a spiral to convert air pressure waves to neuron impulses. Our eyes are circular, spiraling through the pupils to the retina; bending light with filtration before they hit the retinal cells. When we consider the twisting and bending path of light through our visual senses, we ultimately arrive at the trigonometric sinusoidal and spiral. Other displays of nature's spiraling energies include the magnetic fields of the earth; and biological displays of spiraling structures such as claws, teeth, horns, irises, ear pinea, and fingerprints.

Just as the sinusoid wave is derived from the circle, the classic spiral may be derived from the sphere. Beginning at any one of a sphere's apexes or poles, a spiral is formed if we move around the curvature of the sphere towards the opposite poles. This most basic type of spiral is known as the *spherical spiral*. The spherical spiral is also known as the *arithmetic* or *Archimedean spiral*, named after the third century B.C. Greek mathematician Archimedes of Syracuse. In this spiral, the distance between each layer (and spiral arm) is held equidistant. This creates an angular moment that is consistent throughout.

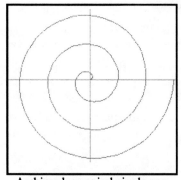

Archimedean spiral-single arm

There are various other types of spirals in nature. The Fibonacci sequence is often displayed within either helical or spiral forms. *Fibonacci spirals* are close relatives to the *logarithm spiral*. *Fermat's spiral*—named after sixteenth century Frenchman Pierre de Fermat—is related to the arithmetic spiral. In 1979, Helmut Vogel proposed a variant of Fermat's spiral as a better approximation of nature's Fibonacci spiral. This is the spiral observed within *Phyllotaxis*, which include sunflowers, daisies and certain spiraling universes. Around 1638, Rene Descartes revealed the *equiangular spiral*. This spiral reflects geometrical radii outward as polar angles increase. The relationship Descartes discussed (S=AR, which Evangelista Torricelli also developed independently during that era) has also been called the *geometrical spiral*. Edmond Halley's seventeenth and eighteenth century work revealed the *proportional spiral*. Jacob Bernoulli developed its logarithmic basis, revealing the *logarithmic spiral* shortly thereafter. Bernoulli gave it the namesake of *spira mirabilis,* meaning "wonderful spiral." It is said Bernoulli's fascination of the spiral led to his request it be engraved on his tombstone.

As pointed out by Giuseppe Bertin and C.C. Lin in their 1996 book, *Spiral Structure in the Galaxies*, the spiraling galaxies may well be generated through a combination of density waves that rotate in a slower rhythm than the rest of the galaxy's stars, planets and gases. This *density wave theory,* first proposed in 1964 by C.C. Lin and Frank Shu, explains that the harmonization of the angular paths and the mutual gravitational attraction of the galaxy's components form areas of greater density: This allows the spiral arm formation without a *winding problem*.

Much of nature is arranged in helix or spiral shape. What may not appear to be spiraling is likely requiring us to peer through its cross-section. For example, an ocean wave breaking over a reef may appear to be a half waveform as it is looked at straight on from the beach. However, a cross-sectional view of the same wave reveals its spiral motion: As we watch the water falling from one side of the crest—and crashing into the trough—the spiral effect comes into view.

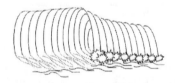

Ocean wave breaking (and spiraling) onto the beach

The combination of the forward movement of the wave to the beach and the sideways movement of water along the crest creates the surfer's classic spiraling *"tube"* or *"barrel."* To ride the tube or barrel requires the surfer to stay just ahead of the final eclipsing of the water with the trough. Should the surfer lapse into the center point of the spiral, the surfer will most likely be separated from the surfboard and experience the *"wipe out."*

The hurricane provides an additional example of this effect. Waves from two different pressure and temperature fronts interact to form the classic cyclone effect seen from satellite.

The hurricane's spiral is only visible from above. This means for thousands of years, humankind had no direct awareness of this spiraled form. Looking at a hurricane front from the land renders a view of the coming front 'wave' of rain and wind from the storm. While many speculated about weather systems as they experienced the 'eye of a hurricane,' and compared this with that other classic spiraling interaction of waveforms—the tornado—it was only as humans began to take to the air that these beautiful spiraling images unveiled themselves.

This is also the dynamic unveiled when we flush the toilet or watch water draining a basin. The water's swirling motion reflects the interference pattern of multiple waveform forces. These waveform forces are precisely mirrored by the classic electromagnetic structure: As the electronic vector pulses forward in one plane, the magnetic vector pulses outward into another plane. This is expressed in nature by the formation of the spiral. Because the earth is magnetically oriented with north and south poles, when we flush the toilet in the southern hemisphere, the direction of the spiral formed in the basin is clockwise. In the northern hemisphere, the same flush rotates counterclockwise. This is because of the earth's magnetic orientation, effectively "pulling" the water outward one way or other, as it is being pulled downward by gravity.

D'Arcy Wentworth Thompson's 1917 classic *On Growth and Form*, and Sir T.A. Cook's 1903 *Spirals in Nature and Art* both illustrated the many examples of nature's spirals. Mr. Thompson details how elements and organisms within nature have a tendency to coil. These include hair, skin cells, tails, elephant trunks, roots and cordiform leaves among others. Other interesting helix and spiral movements include the spiraled burrowing of rodents and the spiraled swimming of dolphins and whales.

In 1973, Dr. Michael Rossmann reported the finding of a protein structure where multiple coiling strands are linked together with two helical structures. The connection between the strands and the helices were found to be alternating, forming an available structure for nucleotide bonding. This structure proved to be one of many important helical molecules: Nicotinamide adenine dinucleo-tide (NAD), a critical coenzyme involved in cellular energy production and genetic transcription within every living cell.

Numerous other biomolecular structures are helical when we are able to observe their *tertiary* structure. Various polysaccharides, polypeptides, hormones, neurotransmitters and fatty acids produced by metabolism have helical-spiral molecular structures.

Then of course we can't forget the king of helical-spiral bio-molecules, DNA. DNA and its related RNA are protein molecules known for the storage and dissemination of the programming of the body's metabolism. Their helical-spiraling structure has mesmer-ized the scientific community for nearly six decades.

Furthermore, electron clouds have also proved to come in heli-cal-spiral dimensions. This spiraling micro-universe of atoms and molecules would have astounded the generations of thoughtful scientists over previous centuries.

At the same time, some physicists have been disturbed by the *paradox of the spiral*. This issue was noted by Dr. Einstein, who con-cluded this in discussion of the related *Faraday disc problem,* as apparently a radial conductance: *"It is known that Maxwell's electrody-namics—as usually understood at the present time—when applied to moving bodies, leads to asymmetries that do not appear to be inherent in the phenom-ena."* He went on to propose *"asymmetry"* arises when the currents are produced without a *"seat"* of forces. As we have previously dis-cussed, the magnetic field tends to exert a force vector moving perpendicular to that of electrical current. As this happens, angular momentum is inferred from the induction. When the torque of angular momentum arising from the conducting Faraday Disc is considered together with coherently interacting currents and fields, the dynamic of the spiral becomes evident (Serra-Valls 2007).

If we overlay nature's spiraling motion within the cyclical struc-ture of the molecular world, a tremendous symphony of alignment becomes apparent. As we observe this mysterious collection of movement and symmetry, we naturally seek to find the basis for the underlying tendency of nature to move into a twisting wave motion concluding in congruent spirals and helixes.

Dr. Einstein proposed we accept that the movements of nature are either moving relatively too fast or too slow for us to observe.

We can apply this to our understanding of the universe's wavelike, spiraling oscillations. For this reason, we find our research only gives us momentary glimpses of the complex waveform harmonic existing within the universe.

As we peer deeper into the electromagnetic interactivity between electronic current and its reciprocating magnetic fields, we unveil—through an analysis of induction—the potential disturbance they create. This implies a designed functionality between conduction and induction. All of nature's wave and spirals oscillate within a cooperative context. The fields of one electromagnetic rhythm will affect surrounding electromagnetic rhythms. The interrelationship between these rhythm motions indicates that their ability to continue their cyclical harmonic oscillation in each other's presence is ultimately organized on a grander level. A chaotic arrangement with this level of replicating depth of organization would simply be an oxymoron.

We can ponder more deeply the nature of water as we see the elements of multiple dimensions: The waveform and polar mechanics of water molecules, combined with the waveform nature of the motion of water.

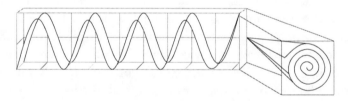

Wave in second and third planes

Again, we can compare these dualistic forces to the structure of electromagnetic motion. Electronic radiation is not that different from the motion of water. In both, we see a motion in three dimensions: Playing out the third dimension illustrates the magnetic field moving away perpendicular to the electronic vector of the electromagnetic wave. Because the electronic motion is radiating in an alternating fashion (sine wave), this magnetic vector moves with a helical, spiraling formation around and outward of the electronic vector. A representation of this effect is illustrated above. Here the electromagnetic sine is shown from side and cross sections.

Regarding the apparent differences between the spiral and the helix, we point out that when cross-referenced with the axes of time and space, a helix will convert to a spiraled helix. This may require a cross-sectional view to complete the image, however—just as we explained with a beach break wave. If we are looking at the wave breaking from the front view, we see a cylinder from the beach. It is the cross-sectional view of the wave (see illustration on page 68), looking down the length of the wave from the side that brings its spiral into view. In the same way, as time and space accumulates helical motion along one axis or another, we observe that one end of the helix will be more relevant than the other end. This progression may also be perceived as spiraling arms expanding outward as the helix approaches.

The three dimensional wave presents a helical spiral when the relativity of motion towards the perceiver is considered. We can illustrate the effect of time and space in motion by observing a train approaching us. The front of the train as it approaches us is closer and thus appears larger than the rest of the train. Though the train size is consistent through all cars, our perception at that point of time is of a large locomotive and small caboose. In the same way, traveling through time within the motion of a spiral would arrive at a helixed perspective: And vice versa for the inverse. Likewise, a person caught in the eye of a hurricane or tornado will not perceive the funneling shape of the storm. The helical or spiral view would only be perceivable from a distance or from above, respectively.

This visual relationship between time and helical-spiral motion also applies to polarity. As polarity bends the spiral motion in one direction or another, the motion assumes a helical orientation away from the bend. Because this is a waveform interaction, this bending creates the facility for information flow along the intersection region. This intersection of pulses and polarity is how molecules provide information.

Oscillating waveforms are information carriers. Spirals, then, are simply a conglomeration of waveform interference with the polar plane, providing a complexity of information. We might compare a waveform to a word and a spiral to a paragraph or even a book. We could pull a word out of a book, but its context would be lost without the rest of the arranged words of the book. While combined waveforms form interference patterns, spirals provide the platform for information flow within nature.

Simply said, information is conducted through spiraling waveforms. The medium or space-time may be disturbed by information waveforms, but the information does not move the medium. The information-wave *passes through*. The analogy that Dr. Einstein and Dr. Infeld used in *The Evolution of Physics* was to compare a wave to gossip that travels from one person to another over large distances, yet the people who communicated the gossip did not move. Only the gossip moved. In the same way, we can understand that the spiraling waveforms of nature are information carriers within standing mediums.

Does this relate to the electron clouds we discussed previously? The interactions of nature's waveforms to form resonating and sometimes standing waves are harmonic with those of atoms and molecules. Like spirals, electron clouds are created by wave interference and confluence. The shape and angle of the cloud depends upon the confluence of reciprocating electromagnetic waveforms. How do we know electron clouds maintain harmonic scale? The valence shells of twos and eights are specifically that: Harmonic frequencies of standing resonant waveforms. As these standing electron clouds are bombarded with radiation as demonstrated in mass accelerators, their resonation is disturbed, and radiation is precisely emitted.

Consider observing standing waves within a small pond of water caused by dropping a couple of small pebbles into the pond. While we see waves appearing to be standing in the same place as they meet each other, their motion is still reflecting the original pebble drops that disturbed the water. In other words, whatever motion is on the water reflects the original cause of the motion. If we were to drive a car over a cliff into the pond below, the resulting large waves within the pond will also reflect the weight and volume of the car. These waves would reflect onto the basin at the side of the pond to form standing wave patterns. These standing wave forms would 'memorize' the impact of the car upon the water.

The oscillating elements of nature are all spiraling waveforms; each having a particular rhythm, along with a unique combination of specifications like wavelength, frequency, amplitude, field, and phase—as well as spiral characteristics such as radius, loci and angular velocity. As spiraling waveforms interfere, complex interference patterns among molecular electron clouds and 'solids' take shape.

Most consider rhythms to be exclusively a characteristic of music. Certainly a gathering of interference patterns between harmonious rhythms creates a melodious song. However, is this not what is occurring all around us? All of the spiraling waveforms of color, temperature, wind, motion, sound, heat and light are radiating and interfering harmoniously to form the song of the physical world.

We might consider water a particularly melodious song within this orchestration. Water is an information carrier of particular interest to us, because it translates the beauty and wisdom of the universe: It is soft, yet it is resilient. It provides support for metabolism yet it will still tear away at the rocks next to the seashore. Within water, we find part of the mystery of the universe.

Earth Waves
The earth moves with cycling atmospheres, circulating waters, and vibrating terrestrial layers. These move synchronically with the forces involved in solar orbiting and galactic spiraling, and the various radiation of thermal and electromagnetic origin. All the while, the earth gracefully adapts to interference through a cycling of elements.

While covered by three-quarters water and most of the remaining topmost layers channeled with the vascular flows of aquifers, springs, streams and rivers, the earth's circulatory system is of the same quality the human physiology: Liquid-dissolved nutrients are pumped throughout the system—supplying minerals, proteins, lipids and phyto-nutrients throughout the ecosystem. This circulatory system gives sustenance to every living organism traversing within or on top of the earth's surface.

Just as our bodies have an epidural layer of skin enclosing and crossing the various layers of liquid, gas, heat, air and space, the earth has a similar enveloping system. This outer envelope or membrane is commonly referred to as its *crust*. As we probe deeper within the earth's crust, we find tremendous energy, motion, and composition among the various biological chemistries of the earth. Using observations gained through seismology and drilling, researchers theorize the earth is composed of several layers: the *crust*, the *upper mantle, the lower mantle* and the *outer* and *inner cores*. Within the crust layer—estimated at 1% of the earth's volume, about 30 kilometers deep including the oceans—researchers have observed a composition of various minerals and metals: We have observed calcium, magnesium, potassium, sodium, silicate, iron, aluminum, gold, silver, as primary, with numerous other secondary elements within the crust. These metals and minerals are typically found as oxides—structurally bound to oxygen. The most prevalent elements in the earth's crust are silica oxide (about 60%), aluminum oxide (about 15%), calcium oxide (about 5%), and magnesium oxide (about 4.5%). We also find about 1.5% of the earth's crust is water, circulating through the veins and arteries of aquifers and underground rivers, and a series of veins under the ocean's floor.

While the earth is far from precisely round, its approximate radius has been measured at around 6,400 kilometers. The earth's mantle is estimated to be nearly 3,000 kilometers thick and is estimated to cover 70% of the earth's volume. There are believed to be at least three strata of the mantle, the first thought to be a few hundred kilometers deep, the second being thought a few hundred more (guessed at between 500 and 700) and the lower mantle theoretically ranging from about 700 to almost 3000 kilometers. It is also believed there is a thinner crust of mantle layer—curiously referred to as *D*—between the mantle and the theoretical core. It is thought that this D layer is a layer of great movement and circulation.

The mantle is primarily differentiated from the crust in temperature, movement, and composition. The mantle composition appears to have more magnesium levels for example, and less silicon than does the crust. It appears the mantle is also subject to higher temperatures and liquefaction, which is thought to be responsible for the movement and tectonics of the crust. While the mantle tends to be in motion from heat, the crust appears to transfer that heat into more structured movement. Assuming this, the upper mantle is often divided into velocity zones—lower and higher. These are related to volcanic movement, convection and seismic movement. It is thought the middle mantle layers contain complex mineral compounds not found at the surface. Researchers propose this is the result of extremely hot mantle temperatures, which are thought to be well above 1000 degrees Fahrenheit and possibly trend over five thousand degrees in the regions nearer to the core. Of course, these are fantastic temperatures, well outside human experience. Notably, it is also thought the mantle has a circulatory system, which rotates minerals and nutrients between the outer crust, the inner core, and mantle.

Much of this information, including the following theoretical information about the core, has been deduced from the timing and movement of seismic waves and their echoes through the earth—much as sonar might be used to measure depth and fish count under water. Seismic waves are a type of wave that travels through the solid plane. Typical examples of seismic waves are earthquakes, volcanic eruptions, and reverberations from explosions.

Seismic waves are extremely long, typically about a kilometer in length. It is precisely because of this length that earthquakes and volcanoes can move so quickly through earth. While seismic waves are felt by most organisms through contact with the earth's crust, they are more precisely measured by an instrument invented in 1880 called the *seismograph*. There are a number of types of seismic waves. Two types of seismic waves have been the subject of more study, and these are used to deduce what may lie within the earth's surface: These are the *P-wave* and the *S-wave*.

P-waves are primary compression-oriented waves. They are explicitly formed because of a dynamic movement or jolt. S-waves are secondary shear waves. They typically result from the effects of P-waves. After measuring seismic waves around the world, Dr. Inge Lehmann postulated in the 1930s that the earth's core was actually not solid, but was made up of a layer of liquid surrounding a solid inner core. By measuring the effect of an earthquake felt in one location around the world, Dr. Lehmann found that the remote S-waves of the earthquake were apparently penetrating a first layer with some sort of refraction, followed by a bouncing off some sort of inner core. Dr. Lehmann proposed in her 1936 paper that this type of bending and bouncing back (refraction and reflection) were consistent with a solid layer covered by a liquid layer. Between those two layers, Lehmann suggested, was a thin envelope: This came to be known as the *Lehmann Discontinuity*. This hypothesis was apparently confirmed in 1970 when more advanced seismographic equipment was available. Dr. Lehmann received the William Bowie medal from the American Geophysical Union in 1971 for her pioneering research.

The earth produces more than simply seismic wave motion. The earth is also a gigantic thermal waveform producer. Its core produces intense heat, as we will discuss further. The earth has liquid and solid layers and several layers of atmosphere over its surface. The earth produces sound waves along with various electromagnetic waves. The earth's electromagnetic field vibrates at about 7-12 hertz. It was Nikola Tesla's work on global electromagnetic resonances in the early twentieth century that first established the earth's broad network of waveforms.

Then in 1952, Winfried Otto Schumann, after measuring the relationships between lightning and the earth's electromagnetic field, proposed the existence of a *waveguide governance factor* of the earth's network of waves. Dr. Schumann proposed this wave-guidance system was connected to the ionosphere: This effect was named the *Schumann resonance*. The theory was confirmed through seismic calculations a decade later. Interestingly, the frequency range of the Schumann resonance is very close to the range of human alpha brain waves. We might thus conclude that while we are in the alpha brainwave state—a state of relaxation but not quite sleep or meditation—we are resonating with the earth's waveforms.

The Earth's Inner Currents

While still being debated, the prevailing hypothesis holds that the inner core is made of some combination of nickel and iron. As for the outer core, some have suggested this layer is intermixed with a number of lighter compounds or even liquefied compounds. Seismographic equipment has since become more sensitive and computerized models are increasingly utilized. Additionally, drilling projects have been able to pull deeper and deeper samples from the crust. These additional observations have indicated the crust, mantle, and core layers are likely to be much more complex than has been proposed. This became evident for Texas A&M University's Jay Miller, head of a 2005 hole-drilling expedition. Dr. Miller stated that conventional theories of the earth's crust and composition *were "oversimplifying many of the features of the ocean's crust.... Each time we drill a hole, we learn that earth's structure is more complex. Our understanding of how the earth evolved is changing accordingly."* In addition, the project's co-chief researcher was quoted saying *"Our major result is that we have recovered the lower crust for the first time and have confirmed that the earth's crust at this locality is more complicated than we thought."*

Seismic data has been the main tool used to assemble most of these theories regarding the earth's layers and core. And recent drilling has given reason to believe that seismic data could have oversimplified the top mantle layers. It would be logical to assume that theories of the mantle and the core have also been oversimplified. Most geologists admit that we really do not know what is beneath the earth's crust. As our knowledge of wave movement and dynamics has expanded over the last few years, there is even some question about whether the seismic data indicating a layered mantle and single solid core might be deceiving.

For example, the Physical Acoustics Laboratory in Colorado's School of Mines Department of Geophysics (van Wijk *et al.* 2004) determined that an acoustic wave traveling through a solid piece of aluminum bounced off tiny holes or notches in the aluminum. This rendered a resulting wave with the same data as if that aluminum was layered—which it was not. It was concluded the bouncing effect picked up by Dr. Lehmann and others using seismic data could was likely caused by caverns or regions of different densities within the earth's mantle. This region or cavern seismic effect was termed the *pinball effect.* The theory of a round, solid core may thus be an oversimplification.

A 2008 study done at Sweden's Uppsala University indicates that the seismic data reveal an elasticity within the trajectories of wave conductance. This implies an irregular-shaped core. Focused upon the paradigm of a single-body core, the researchers contend that such a core would have to have an irregular cubic structure in order to account for the elasticity and fluidity of the seismic readings.

This data could also lead to another possibility. Consider first the pinball effect. Then consider the elastic seismic readings. To this, add observations of tectonic movement throughout the earth's crust, and the evolving thermal and lava flows arising from the crust and upper mantle. These observations render the likelihood of at a fluid interior and a variegated core system within the interior. The picture is not unlike the inside of our body: A series of organs immersed between a fluid medium.

This is not a new concept: Athanash Kircher's *Mundus Subterraneus* published a number of charts in 1664, including one depicting earth with a molten core and various interconnected sacs quite similar to a cell's organelles, interconnected with a circulatory system.

Most geophysicists agree that observations of magnetic fields, lava flows and drilling observations combined with data indicating a tremendous amount of heat is being generated within the surface of the earth. What is the source of this heat? We can logically assume this heat is generated from a durable generating source—which might assume a nuclear active core. We can also conclude the earth also has some sort of electromagnetic generative properties because of the strong presence of enduring magnetic pulses observed at the surface and arising with magma flows.

The amount of the earth's magnetic field ranges from 45,000 to 60,000 nT (nanoTesla) over the U.S. This huge variance is thought to be created by the existence of "buried magnetic bodies" under the earth's surface. This reality has been confirmed by the fact that magnetic field variances have been found in areas where there is an underground tank or other fixture buried. This is especially apparent for steel underground tanks, which have resulted in variances of thousands of nanoTeslas of magnetic fields.

We also find vein networks of nutritionally relevant fluids such as mineralized waters, petroleum, natural gas and liquid magma circulating through the upper layers. Among these circulating vessels we also find various veins of static strata with rich metals such as gold, silver, copper, crystals and so on. Petroleum creation involves a processing cycle that converts dying matter digested at the crust into pools of petroleum—a digestive process creating a cache of ignitable liquid gold from organic matter.

The slow process of petroleum creation starts with the decomposition of ocean biomass. This first yields an intermediate substance known as *kerogen*. Through an additional process called *catagenesis,* kerogen is converted into hydrocarbons—the chemical basis for petroleum. The resulting hydrocarbons accumulate and migrate through the porous rock of the crust, accumulating into reservoirs up to six kilometers deep.

Natural gas is considered a derivative of this process—the result of a further conversion process called *thermal cracking.* Thermal cracking is thought to take place among some of the hotter temperatures of the earth.

Coal accumulates as a result of a similar process of biomass conversion. However, the coal decomposition cycle utilizes land-based plant matter, as opposed to ocean biomass.

Are these not, as famously purported by Dr. James Lovelock (1979), symptoms of a biological organism?

Environmental research indicates the earth is now straining under the stress of its crust being poked, punctured, polluted, and robbed of vital fluids. While there are a number of precious nutrients—such as coal, gold, silver and diamonds—the one element not only precious, but critical to the functional nature of the earth's body is petroleum.

Earthquakes and Tsunamis

The oscillating rhythms of the earth and our physical bodies resonate with the same seismic waveforms. These seismic waves vibrate through the earth's crust as earthquakes, and through the ocean's waters as tsunamis. Over the past decade, some devastating tsunamis and earthquakes have killed hundreds of thousands of people. What causes these to happen?

The seismic wave has a very long wavelength. The long wavelength allows it to be felt by touch. Seismic rhythms are felt through the nerve sensors in the same way that physical movement is felt. Although we might sometimes be able to see the earth move during an earthquake, or even hear the cracking of the earth during one, this is only a result of the movement creating further waveforms, which the eyes and ears can sense. Otherwise, seismic waves and other grounded waves are only felt but not seen, heard, tasted or smelled. This is because seismic waves occur at the gross physical solid layer of matter.

Researchers are puzzled about the source of seismic waves. While geologists define the earthquake as a release of stored energy, there is not a known source of that energy. We are thus left with the experience of an incredible source of shaking and trembling without a known source. Here the solution to this mystery is provided by an understanding of the earth as a living organism. This is because living organisms produce biological mechanisms resulting in heat, movement, circulation, digestion, and so on. Earthquakes account for only a fraction—some say about 10%—of the total energy expended by the earth. If the earth is not a living organism, where does all this energy come from?

By watching our news media, one might think earthquakes are random and chaotic. This is far from the truth. In reality, earthquakes occur in a rhythmic fashion, occurring with periodicity and often in clusters. There are generally considered two types of earthquakes. One is called a *tectonic earthquake,* while the other is called a *deep focus earthquake.* While the tectonic earthquake theoretically originates at the upper crust within a hundred kilometers of the surface, a deep focus earthquake apparently originates through a process called *subinduction*—theoretically forming up to seven hundred kilometers deep, within areas of volcanic activity. These zones were developed in the 1920s and 1930s through the independent research of two professors—Dr. Hugo Benioff of California and Kiyoo Wadati of Japan; and are thus named Wadati-Benioff zones.

Earthquakes are related to a combination of rhythmic movements of the crust's tectonic plates and the circulation of lava. Their interaction creates a harmonic of confluence. Seismologists and geologists have studied both of these effects in detail, and have extensively charted out the earth's various tectonic plates. They have also attempted to map the movement of volcanic lava. Clustering earthquakes have been tracked and recorded over the last two hundred years with increasing detail. Distinct and periodic plate movement has been isolated in many parts of the world, with increased stress at the plate connections in California, Japan, New Zealand, Alaska, Portugal, British Columbia, and other loci around the world. Nearly ninety percent of all earthquakes and about eighty percent of the largest earthquakes occur in the Pacific belt called the *Pacific Ring of Fire.* This ring surrounds the pacific plate, which is for some reason the most active plate in the world. As researchers have looked at a map of directional earthquakes, they have noticed plate movement tends to move toward the Ring of Fire from most plates outside the Pacific plate, while the Pacific plate tends to expand outward from the middle during its activity. Many devastating tsunamis have occurred as a result of the interaction between this plate and its surrounding plates.

Some half a million earthquakes occur each year. Of these, 100,000 might be felt by humans and only 100 might cause damage. Since 1900 there has been an average of one 8.0+ earthquake per year and eighteen 7.0-7.9 earthquakes per annum. This rate is fairly stable.

As the tectonic plates have been cross-referenced with volcanic activity, a periodic pulsing appears to be evident.

Certainly, the mountains and mountain ranges are obvious exhibits of the earth's pulse. These huge growths of thermal energy appear around the earth with a synchronicity of their own. As we observe the mountains and crevasses of mother earth, we notice they present—if viewed within a cross-section—an undulating wave motion of mountains, valleys, and deep-water ravines. As we investigate the formation of mountains more deeply, we notice underneath these dramatic rock growths are veins of thermal and lava flows, pulsing through the earth's crust with a paced synchronicity resembling the pumping of blood or lymph through our circulatory system.

While still somewhat controversial, there is building evidence linking the rhythmic lunar cycle with the earth's tectonic movement. Correlations between the moon's cycles and earthquakes have revealed more specifically a link between eclipses and large earthquake activity.

In order for a solar eclipse to take place, the new moon and the sun have to be within one degree of the same declination. Due to the massive difference in the two bodies, this also means the moon must be positioned within the earth's orbit in such a way that blocks the sun completely. A lunar eclipse, in contrast, takes place during a full moon, which moves into the earth's shadow. This requires both the sun and moon to be exactly opposite each other with the earth in the middle.

The solar eclipse tends to affect the side of the earth where it shows itself more fully, simply because the two bodies are lined up with that side opposing the sun. This theoretically pulls the waters of the earth towards the moon. This affect appears evident in the tidal rhythms. However, along with tidal changes come other rhythmic changes. These take place because of the combined effect of blocking the sun's various waveform energies complicated by with the moon's own rhythmic force fields.

For thousands of years, the period around the eclipse of the new moon has been associated with earthquakes. The Greeks documented this cycle. Early Greek writers Thucydides and Phlegon recorded this link between earthquakes and new moon eclipses. Prior to that, Egyptian and Vedic cultures noted this trend. Over the past two decades, a number of seismology researchers have also proposed this link. A rash of recent quakes has also followed this trend. The San Francisco quake of 1989, the 1999 Turkish quake, the Sumatra earthquake and the tsunami of 2004 all occurred shortly before or after a solar eclipse. The Italian Physical Society published a study (Palumbo 1989) linking various other earthquakes to lunar cycles as well.

While this theory remains unproven, earthquakes appear to be related to the lunar cycles somehow. In 2004, researchers from UCLA's Department of Earth and Space Sciences published a report in *Science* (Cochran *et al.*), which correlated earthquake prevalence with high tides—both water tides and solid land tides. Others have confirmed this correlation: Notably Columbia University's Maya Tolstoy, who in 2002 revealed a tidal pressure correlation with deep ocean continental plate earthquakes (Handwerk 2004).

Undoubtedly, earthquakes and magnetic fields are related. While researchers initially thought of the earth's magnetic fields as rotating outside the earth's crust, anisotropic scaling has modeled and measured magnetic fields flowing both vertically and horizontally, even subsurface to the outside crust. These oscillating magnetic fields predispose the movement of magma together with tectonic movement. Magnetic fields and tidal changes work similarly, because they directly affect the pressure between the earth's plates (Moshe 1996).

A mysterious association between earthquakes and animals has also been seen. There have been many stories of animals acting disturbed well in advance of an earthquake. Well before the earthquake can be felt or heard physically—at least to our senses and equipment—animals have evacuated nests, begun running wildly and in general acted erratically. There have been many anecdotal observations of dogs, cats and other animals acting wildly days before an earthquake. In 1975, the Chinese government evacuated Haicheng based upon the observation of erratic activity of animals. Much of the city was evacuated, and as a result, only minor human loss and injury occurred from the 7.3-magnitude quake that followed days later.

In 2003, The Quantum Geophysics Laboratory at Osaka University (Yokoi *et al.*) reported that mouse circadian diagrams showed unusual circadian rhythmic activity just prior to the 1995 Kobe earthquake. The researchers reported drastic increases in locomotive activity, changes in sleep, and other effects in mice before the quake.

As we have mentioned, most animals have an incredible sense of direction and destination. This is witnessed during the incredible migrations of tens of thousands of kilometers by caribou, lobsters, whales, turtles, birds, and so many other organisms. As researchers have looked for clues as to where this sense of direction comes from, it was found that most of these animals have a sort of magnetic compass within certain cells of the brain and nervous system. Just as a compass needle points north, these animals are able to sense the magnetic fields of the earth using them to create geomagnetic maps of sorts. Birds are apparently able to organize a grid-like mapping of the earth, enabling them to steer back on course around obstacles or weather fronts. Cruel studies of turtles, lobsters, and mole rats have altered magnetic fields around the subject, resulting in their reorientation towards the appropriate direction dictated by the position of the magnetic forces.

Mole rats for example, burrow tunnels—sometimes 200 meters long or more—towards the south and place their nests at the end of those burrows. If the magnetic field changes, their burrows will redirect to the southern-most direction of the magnetic field. Loggerhead turtle hatchlings immediately have this sense of direction upon birth. Their 'magnetic compasses' give them an instant sense of where to migrate (Trivedi 2001; Handwerk 2003).

Furthermore, the research of Heyers *et al.* (2007) has unveiled recently the likelihood that birds actually see the geomagnetic field. Cruel neuronal tracing within the eye and forebrain of migratory birds indicate highly active rhythmic impulses consistent with visual signal pathways during magnetic compass bearing. *Crypotochromes* contained in the neurons in the eye and in the forebrain appear to confirm this hypothesis.

While many insist the universe and planet works through chaos, there is little evidence of this as we observe biological processes with living organisms traveling the planet. We used to assume living creatures accidentally wandered from place to place each year. It was only when we could follow their migrations that we were able to understand the precision of their navigation.

Humans were not overlooked when it comes to an innate ability to navigate. Certainly, there is reason to believe that ancient humans were at least partially migratory. This migratory sense is what is thought to have predicated humans finding their way to distant islands and other remote regions of the planet. Humans also have magnetic neurons, although they are rarely used. Our scientific attraction to magnets and our use of them as compasses casts a bit of irony when we consider that migratory animals use internal versions for their direction finding.

Over the past few decades, scientists have noticed that earth's main magnetic field seems to be weakening. This weakening of the geomagnetic fields may be a signal that the field may be reversing. Rock analysis reveals that magnetic field reverses have taken place periodically during earth's history, somewhere in the neighborhood of every 300,000 to 500,000 years on average, with quite a variance. The last one occurred about 750,000 years ago. Undoubtedly, a reversal of the north and south poles would have a dramatic impact upon life on the planet. Whether this is a cataclysmic event or not is to be determined. The bottom line is that the earth's magnetic fields oscillate in very long periods just as so many other elements oscillate with waveform frequency. In other words, these geomagnetic fields may be part of a macro-period waveform: The cycling of a larger biological system.

The Waves of the Water Cycle

Water's cycles are just part of this larger biological system. We can now understand the most obvious types of wave structures acting within water: Surface and tortional mechanical waves. Water radiates in these structures as it translates information and action. We've also discussed the waveform mechanisms that exist within water at the molecular level: The quantum waves that transverse electromagnetic and polar-oriented electron clouds and weak hydrogen bonds.

There is yet another waveform that transverses water: This is a macro-waveform wherein water is transposing from one elemental form to another: between the atmosphere, the earth, the groundwater aquifers and springs, the oceans, lakes and rivers, and the living organisms of the planet:

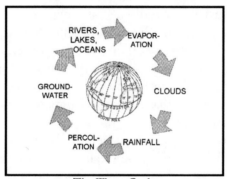

The Water Cycle

This water cycle has no beginning because water is at all stages of the cycle at any particular time. If we were going to choose a beginning, say when water is vaporized within the clouds, then the first part of the cycle begins when water falls to the earth during rainfall, snow or ice. As it falls, it forms snow and ice on the ground, it flows as rivers or streams, or it percolates into the ground and becomes absorbed into aquifers within rock formations below the surface. If these aquifers are under pressure and/or heat, their waters are pushed up to the surface in the form of springs. They may also be manually pumped to the surface using well pumps. Any of these means eventually accumulate within rivers or lakes, from which water becomes evaporated back into vapor cloud form. This water may also flow down to the ocean, where it is also subject to evaporation and the informational wave action of the oceans. During this passage, water is utilized by living organisms, whose bodies provide a means for vaporization.

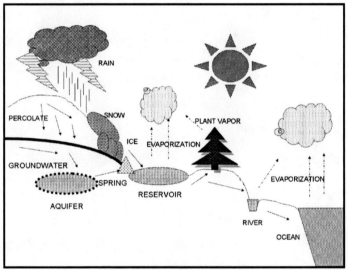

Nature's Recycling of Water

All living organisms utilize water. Those living within the atmosphere, (plants, mammals, etc.) will vaporize water. As we exchange oxygen and carbon dioxide, we utilize and expend water, sending it into the atmosphere. When we breathe, for example, we send out water vapor. Plants also produce water vapor from the water they take in from the ground. While our atmospheric exchanges are opposite, both humans and plants utilize groundwater or surface water for water consumption.

Once this evaporation or vaporization process recycles water back into vapor form, it is now ready to become liquefied again, as it falls back to earth to continue this macrocosmic waveform we call the water cycle.

~ Three ~

Toxic Waters

Water's beautiful and natural rhythms are being undermined by humans. As we've burned fossil fuels and monkeyed around with chemicals, we have opened a Pandora's Box of synthetics, unleashing toxicity upon our waters. Nature's pure waters are quickly becoming cesspools of toxic soup.

The Synthetic Age

Over the past century, humankind has unleashed a firestorm of chemical manipulation upon the planet. The industrial age and the greed of corporate giants have launched upon nature the cruelest form of disaster: The dumping of toxic chemicals into our precious waters. Supposedly, chemicals were going to increase our quality of life and make life easier. This prospect has completely backfired.

As this grand synthetic experiment has unfolded, we have discovered that most synthetic chemicals are not only toxic: they now risk humankind's future existence. After only a few decades of synthetic chemical manufacturing, we are beginning to suffer the horrific price synthetic chemicals come with. We are faced with increasing epidemics of allergies, asthma, cancers, COPD, and many autoimmune disorders. The water we drink has become toxic. Much of our drinking supplies are laced with DDT, PCB, nitrates, and hundreds of other dangerous toxins. Much of the commercial food we eat is now to full of various synthetic residues. We are gradually discovering that agribusiness' use of chemical fertilizers and pesticides is poisoning our foods and bodies. The toxins are building up in our cells—mutating DNA and suffocating our immune systems.

Most of the furnishings we purchase now are filled with formaldehydes, synthetic materials and other synthetic preservatives. Most office buildings and many houses still contain hazards like asbestos and other components that cause toxicity. Our entire environment is laced with synthetic chemistry. If the human race stopped chemical production today, it would still take centuries for our planet to degrade and neutralize these toxic chemicals.

The core issue with synthetic chemicals is that they interrupt the fragile balance existing among nature's biochemical recycling systems. As a result, they clog the arteries of our ecosystem. Today there are mountains of synthetic chemistry loading up our dumps, landfills, lakes, rivers, and oceans. These mountains are decomposing very slowly—outgassing and breaking down into potent toxins. These toxins are percolating through our soils into our ground-waters. Americans generated 1,643 pounds of mostly toxic trash per person in 2005. A mere 32% of that was recycled.

Plastic and Plasticizers

Much of this waste is plastic. The problem with plastic is also its perceived benefit: It lasts far longer than do natural materials. While a plastic bag might not tear and rip as fast as a paper bag as we walk from the grocery store, a plastic bag will have as much as a 500-year half-life. That is a long time. What happens to plastic while nature works biodegrade it? Tiny plastic pieces and particles clog our soils and waters. For this reason, our lands, waters, and bodies are becoming increasingly laced with hydrocarbons and plasticizers.

Plastics are made through reactions between monomers (small molecules) and plasticizers (polymer binders) to create longer-chain molecules. Monomers are typically hydrocarbons such as petroleum. Combining ethane monomers with plasticizers forms polyethylene. Combining styrene monomers with plasticizers renders polystyrene. Combining vinyl chloride monomers with plasticizers results in polyvinyl chloride, or PVC. Combining propylene monomers with plasticizers gives us polypropylene.

Nature produces its own types of natural polymers such as rubber. In an attempt to improve upon nature, the lab of Alexander Parkes in 1855 mixed pyroxylin from cellulose with alcohol and camphor to form what is thought to be the first type of plastic. This clear, hard plastic was 'improved' by Dr. Leo Baekeland decades later with a polymer process using phenol and formaldehyde in the first decade of the twentieth century. The resulting "Bakelite" became a wildly successful product, as it effectively replaced shellac and rubber as a general sheathing material. Because it was heat-resistant and moisture-proof, it quickly became the insulator of choice for engines, appliances, and electronics. Dr. Baekeland eventually sold his General Bakelite Company to Union Carbide in 1939 and retired a very wealthy man to Florida. Yes, his life was certainly made easier through the 'miracle' of chemistry.

Nylon was an invention of DuPont researchers in the late 1930s. It was made initially with benzene from coal. The introduction of polypropylene as a synthetic rubber followed shortly thereafter. Polypropylene was an accidental discovery made by a couple of researchers who were trying to convert natural gas for Phillips Petroleum. The American industrial complex gearing up for World War II focused its attention on this synthetic version due to a shortage of natural rubber. Thanks to synthetic rubber, each military person was estimated to have 32 pounds of rubber in clothing and equipment. A tank needed about a ton. We might consider that America's military might is at least partially due to its synthetic rubber making. Again, chemistry has seemingly made our lives easier.

The synthetic polymer revolution surged after the Second World War. The plastic revolution raged, as both consumers and manufacturers worked together to replace naturally derived goods with synthetic polymers.

One might argue that that combining earth-borne commodities like hydrocarbons cannot be so toxic. After all, hydrocarbons are produced within the earth as part of a recycling process. However, the process of converting these hydrocarbon monomers into polymers requires various catalysts and polymer plasticizers to complete. Plasticizers are used in plastic production to give the long polymer chain its flexibility. Without plasticizers inserted between the chains of monomers, there could be no flexibility among the substance. Without plasticizers, polymers are clear, hard substances: rock-like. The various gradations of flex added to polymer chains give the resulting plastic its particular usefulness and characteristic. A plasticizer will provide strength along with this flexibility, making the material difficult to tear or break.

Most plasticizers are *phthalates*. Phthalates are derived from phthalic acid, an aromatic ringed carbon molecule also referred to as dicarboxylic acid. Originally synthesized in 1836 through the oxidation of naphthalene tetrachloride, phthalic acid can also be synthesized from hydrocarbons and sulfuric acid with a mercury catalyst. Most aromatic carbon rings like the phenyl ring or the benzyl ring made using this process have proven to be hazardous to both our environment and health. Note there are a number of aromatic carbon rings that are produced in nature as well. These do not come with the same hazards for some reason.

Benzene, for example, is the typical source of the phenyl plasticizer. Benzene has been classified as a volatile organic compound and a carcinogen by the Natural Institutes of Health's *National Toxicology Program*. Benzene is among the top twenty most used industrial chemicals. It is used to make adhesives, paint, pharmaceuticals, printed materials, photographic chemicals, synthetic rubber, dyes, detergents, paint and shockingly, even food processing equipment to name a few. Today benzene is found throughout our environment—in our air and water—and has been implicated in numerous cancers.

Benzene is but one of hundreds of different plasticizers now in use in the production of different grades of plastics. Most are either aromatic carbons or otherwise toxic compounds. Bound within hydrocarbon polymer chains, plasticizers may appear innocuous. However, as plastic polymers break down in the environment, these plasticizers are released. Our backyards, landfills and oceans—our entire environment for that matter—are silently being inundated by the release of these plasticizers.

We will discuss many of the types of common plastics and their toxicity issues in the next chapter. Here we will simply point out that researchers are becoming increasingly aware of the risk plasticizers present to our environment and health once they are released. Even with tremendous resistance from plastics manufacturers, the word is slowly getting out.

The Costs of Synthetics

The costs of synthetic chemicals are extensive. Estimates suggest some 80,000 chemicals have been approved for commercialization over the past fifty years. The 1976 *Toxic Substances Control Act of 1976* was set up to evaluate chemicals being introduced. Only about 65,000 have been reviewed. Furthermore, only a small percentage of these chemicals have been carefully analyzed and reviewed as to their environmental and health effects. Several hundred thousand die in the U.S. from cancer each year. Millions die worldwide from this disease suspected to be caused primarily by cellular mutation resulting from chemical toxicity.

The Environmental Working Group's *Human Toxome Project* has revealed some frightening statistics regarding the poisoning of our bodies by chemicals. In one study of nine adult participants, blood and urine contained 171 of the 214 toxic chemicals for which they were analyzed. These included industrial compounds and pollutants like alkylphenols, inorganic arsenic, organophosphates, phthalates, polychlorinated biphenyls (PCBs), volatile organic compounds, chlorinated dioxins, and furans. In another study, the EWG found 287 of the 413 tested chemicals in the umbilical cord blood of ten mothers after giving birth. These included the chemical types mentioned above and more, including fifty different polychlorinated naphthalene compounds (EWC 2007).

A polychlorinated biphenyl is a grouping of chlorine atoms bonded together with biphenyl. Biphenyl is a molecule composed of two phenyl rings. It is an aromatic hydrocarbon occurring naturally in coal and petroleum. When synthetically combined with chlorine—another naturally-occurring element—the result is PCB, a highly toxic mixture of 209 chemicals. PCBs were banned in the early 1970s when biologists studied a population of dead seabirds and found they died of a toxic dose of PCBs. For more than forty years, PCBs have been used in paints, pesticides, paper, adhesives, flame-retardants, surgical implants, lubricating oil and electrical equipment.

Referred to innocently as "phenols" for many years, the PCB ban followed many protests for a number of years. Massive PCB contamination in the Hudson River was found caused by local electrical manufacturing plants. Some two hundred miles of the Hudson was eventually designated a toxic *superfund site*. This woke us up to PCB toxicity.

PCBs break down slowly and bio-accumulate in living organisms. When PCBs get into our waterways they build up in the smallest organisms and work their way up the food chain, eventually reaching humans. Today the ban on PCBs does not include many applications considered "closed," such as capacitors and vacuum pump fluids. This means there are still considerable PCBs in our buildings and electrical equipment. PCB poisoning can cause immediate liver damage. Symptoms can include fever, rashes, nausea, and more.

While PCB production has declined, primarily in the U.S. and other first world countries, PCBs are now found throughout our environment, and within our water systems. Recently a research team found PCB traces in snow samples from high atop Mount Aconcagua in Argentina. Mount Aconcagua is the largest mountain in the Andes, towering at nearly 23,000 feet. As this snow melts, PCBs will flow with once-considered pure glacial waters.

Biphenyl A is another sort of biphenyl, used in many types of containers, including baby bottles. BPA can easily leach into food or formula when the bottle is exposed to heat or sunlight. A 2000 Centers of Disease Control study found 75% of those tested had phthalates in their urine, and subsequent studies have found some 95% of the U.S. population has detectable levels of biphenyl A within body fluids. Biphenyls are considered *xenoestrogens,* or endocrine system disruptors. Long-term effects as their residues build up in our cells, organs and tissue systems are largely unknown.

By some accounts there are nearly nine hundred different pesticides being used in the United States. Of those, at least thirty-seven contain organophosphates—one of our more toxic chemical combinations. Organophosphates kill insects through nervous system disruption. These neurotoxins are also toxic to humans' nervous systems. The nerve gases Serin and VX are organophosphates, for example. Organophosphates block cholinesterase—a key neuro-enzyme—from working properly within the body. With cholinesterase blocked, acetylcholine is not regulated. Unregulated acetylcholine causes an over-stimulation of nerve activity, resulting in nerve damage, paralysis, and muscle weakness.

Organophosphates are spreading through ground water, air and dermal contact. Many water systems are now quite polluted with a variety of organophosphates. Initial symptoms can include nausea, vomiting, shortness of breath, confusion, and muscle spasms. Some of the more common organophosphates include Malathion, Parathion, Diazinon, Phosmet, Clorpyrifos, Dursban and others. The EPA actually banned Diazinon and Dursban in a phase-out beginning in March of 2001, to last through December 2003. Curiously, both Diazinon and Dursban are still in use today. Phased bans like this theoretically take several years to allow companies to run out their inventories. Also since these bans were aimed at consumer products, organophosphates are still used profusely in commercial agriculture—our food production.

In a 2003 study done by the *Centers for Disease Control and Prevention,* thousands of people were tested for 116 chemicals. Thirty-four of these were pesticides such as organophosphates, organochlorines, and carbamates. Nineteen of the thirty-four pesticides were found in either the blood or urine of this test group.

Chlorinated dioxins are also pervasive in today's environment. Significant sources include cigarettes, pesticides, coal-burning factories and diesel exhaust. They are now found among greywater systems and are becoming more pervasive in drinking water systems. Dioxins are also byproducts of the manufacturing of a number of products, including many resins, glues, plastics, and chlorine-treated products. Dioxins also bio-accumulate in fatty tissues and can take years to fully degrade. Dioxins are known endocrine disruptors. They have also been linked to liver toxicity and birth defects.

Thanks to the human industrial complex, there are now thousands of *volatile organic compounds* in our environment. A VOC is classified as such if it has a relatively high vapor pressure, allowing it to vaporize quickly and enter the atmosphere. Gasoline, paint thinners, cleaning solvents, ketones, and aldehydes are a few of the chemicals considered sources of VOCs. Methane-forming VOCs like benzene and toluene are considered carcinogens. VOCs are often used as preservatives for pressed wood and other building materials. As a result, many buildings contain VOCs locked within its building materials. They are soaked in or built into the fabrication of these materials. VOCs will not all stay trapped in these materials, however. They will slowly outgas over time, maintaining the 'sick building' status for years to come. This outgassing process is speeded up when the building is demolished or taken apart. As the building materials are broken up, VOCs can be released at toxic exposure levels into the surrounding environment. This kind of exposure becomes relevant following floods, hurricanes or other natural disasters, where buildings are broken apart and their chemicals merge into the surrounding waterways.

VOCs will form ozone as they interact with sunlight and heat. VOC poisoning symptoms include nausea, headaches, eye irritation, inflammation of the nose and throat, liver damage, brain fog, and neurotoxic brain damage. Using cleaning or painting solvents indoors is a common cause of VOC poisoning.

In a study by Janssen *et al.* (2004) in conjunction with *The Collaborative on Health and the Environment,* some two hundred diseases were found to be attributable to exposure to industrial chemicals. The diseases listed are some of the most prevalent diseases of our society: cancers, cardiovascular disease, autoimmune diseases and so on. The researchers found that over 120 diseases were strongly and *specifically* linked by research to exposure to specific industrial chemicals. For another 33 diseases, the evidence linking the disease to specific chemicals was considered "good." For the rest of the diseases, research indicated a definite link but the evidence was considered "limited" (Lean 2004).

Asbestos is becoming less used since the Environmental Protection Agency passed the *Asbestos Ban and Phase Out Rule* as part of the *Toxic Substances Control Act* in 1989—which was for the most part overturned in 1991 by the U.S. Fifth Circuit Court of Appeals. What have remained are various specific bans such as those from the *Clean Air Act* and remnants of the TSCA, including some continued restrictions supported by Congressional rulings. The CAA has stimulated various bans since 1973. Although paper- and cardboard-based asbestos has been banned along with certain spray-on substances, many new materials still contain asbestos. Beyond the banned goods, there is nothing preventing manufacturers from using asbestos. Current goods with asbestos include cement sheets, clothing, pipe wrap, roofing felt, floor tiles, shingles, millboard, cement pipe, and various automotive parts. The important thing to remember is that the EPA does not monitor manufacturers for their ingredients. In general, asbestos inclusion into today's building materials should be considered a given. Once the building is broken apart by disaster, those materials become part of our waterways.

Formaldehyde falls into the same category. Today so many building materials and furniture are built using formaldehyde. These include pressed wood, draperies, glues, resins, shelving, flooring, and so many other materials. The greatest source of formaldehyde appears to be those materials made using *urea-formaldehyde* resins. These include particleboard, plywood paneling, and medium density fiberboard. Among these, the medium density fiberboard—used to make drawers, cabinets and furniture tops—appears to contain the highest resin-to-wood ratio. Another resin called *phenol-formaldehyde* or PF resin apparently emits substantially less formaldehyde than the UF resins. The PF resin is easily differentiated from UF resin by its darker, red or black color. Incidental *off gassing* of formaldehyde into the indoor environment from fabrics or pressed woods can result in a variety of ailments. The merging of formaldehydes into our water systems creates another risk, especially following exposure to sun, heat, sanding or demolition. It should be noted that cigarettes are also sources of formaldehyde.

There are many other chemical toxins—including many yet to be discovered—in our building materials. Knowing some of this information, it is probably safe to say that any kind of building or decomposition of a modern building will likely impart various hazardous chemicals, most likely including asbestos and formaldehyde, into our air, soils and waters. This means that any kind of sanding, crushing, fire or demolition project should be dealt with extreme caution. Particle masks are advised to avoid breathing in VOCs and asbestos during such a project. Keeping the building waste out of waterways and groundwaters is a more difficult challenge.

Medical Waste Dumping

Our industrial manufacturing-based society has been dumping massive amounts of synthetic chemistry into our waters, our air and our soils. This is only partially driven by the need for strong or fire-retardant buildings. Some of it is simply driven by our need to look good and feel no pain.

Pharmaceutical medicines are increasingly clogging our waterways with chemicals. In 2007, researchers from Finland's Abo Akademi University (Vieno *et al.*) released a study showing that pharmaceutical beta-blockers, antiepileptic drugs, lipid regulators, anti-inflammatory drugs and fluoroquinolone drugs were all found in river waters. The concentrations of these were well above drinking water limits. The researchers also found that water treatment only eliminated an average of 13% of the concentration of these pharmaceuticals. This means that 87% of these pharmaceutical medicines remained in the drinking water, ready to dose each and every person drinking that water with prescription medication.

Many of the creams and cosmetics women apply to their skin today are also toxic. Their toxins are absorbed into the skin and into our waters via excretion and showering, and during their manufacture. Research has indicated women who use cosmetics daily are absorbing nearly five pounds of chemicals. In a 2004 study of more than ten thousand personal care products used by 2,300 people, the Environmental Working Group determined the average adult uses nine personal care products containing 126 different chemicals. Of the 28 products tested by the study, one-third contained at least one chemical classified as carcinogenic. Nearly 70% of the products had ingredients potentially tainted with chemicals linked in one respect or another to various complications such as hormone imbalances, fatigue, skin irritation, or cancer.

Some of the more typical chemicals or chemical types contained in cosmetics include parabens such as ethyl paraben, propyl paraben, butyl paraben, and isobutyl paraben. Parabens have been considered carcinogens since their components were found in breast tumor tissues (Soni *et al.* 2005).

Polyvinlpyrrolidone is derived from petroleum and is also called povidone-iodine. Research has suggested it interacts with the thyroid gland, the kidneys, and creates cellular systemic toxicity (Zamora 1986). It is also toxic to synovial cells and articular cartilage cells (Kataoka *et al.* 2006).

Diazolidinyl urea's prevalence in cosmetics is widespread and second only to parabens. This chemical is a preservative, releasing formaldehyde when in contact with the skin. For this reason, it is known to cause contact dermatitis (Hectorne and Fransway 1994). Other effects such as headaches, fatigue and depression are also suspected from formaldehyde absorption.

Stearalkonium chloride has been in use for many years by the fabric and paper industries. Its softener and anti-static properties are well known. However, this chemical is also a known skin irritant and allergen.

Propylene glycol is used for many cosmetics and personal care products. It also runs through manufacturing plants into our waterways. This is the chemical that killed hundreds of people recently in

South America as an ingredient in toothpaste. Propylene glycol is a solvent: a primary ingredient in antifreeze and brake fluid. OSHA requirements for working around propylene glycol require protective gear be used to prevent skin contact. Exposure has been known to cause headaches, nausea, eye irritation, and skin irritation (LaKind *et al.* 1999).

Diethanoloamine and Triethanolamine or DEA and TEA respectively, are lubricants and surfactants, which help to wet the skin and spread ingredients. Both can form carcinogenic nitrosamines when combined with other ingredients. Cruel dermal application on mice damaged liver cells and altered fetal brain development (Niculescu *et al.* 2007). Cell death in the hippocampus was also shown in cruel mice studies (Craciunescu *et al.* 2006).

These are just a few of the hundreds of potentially debilitating chemicals used in our medicines, cosmetics and personal care items. Many of these are also made with a host of synthetic colors, synthetic fragrances, and petroleum derivatives. Many are hormone disruptors, and have been implicated in cancer, allergies, contact dermatitis, liver disease and many other ailments. Some of these ingredients can take hundreds of years to biodegrade, and in the meantime will build up in our drinking water and bio-accumulate up the food chain of marine creatures.

Worse, as manufacturers produce these chemicals, unintended chemical combinations horrifically flow from their plants into nearby rivers, streams, lakes and oceans.

Fertilizers and Pesticides

The massive dumping of pesticides and herbicides by agribusinesses, park and golf course managers and homeowners threatens to demolish whatever semblance of pure water is left in our ecosystems.

Cotton, for example, is also one of the most chemically treated and most polluting crops. Five of the top nine pesticides—naled, propargite, triflualin, cyanide and dicofol—are either Category I or II (Environmental Protection-rated) chemicals, which are the most toxic classifications. There are estimates that about one-third of a pound of chemicals goes into each cotton T-shirt. Just in the San Joaquin Valley California alone, it is estimated that 18 million pounds of these chemicals are dumped annually onto a million acres of cotton fields. Furthermore, it has been estimated that no more than a quarter of crop duster-sprayed pesticides actually reach the crop. The rest drifts for miles, onto neighboring lands and waters, including residential areas and drinking water supplies. In 1995, endosulfan (a common cotton pesticide) leached into an Alabama creek from nearby cotton fields. An estimated 245,000 fish were killed over a range of sixteen miles from this typical cotton pesticide.

Nature maintains a delicate but critical nitrogen cycle. There is a precise balance of nitrogen in the atmosphere, the soils, and within each organism: Just enough to serve a biological purpose for all involved. Every species is involved in the cycle: exchanging and converting nitrogen to useable forms of nourishment as needed.

Enter agribusiness and chemical fertilizers. It is not enough to add natural forms of nitrogen to the soil such as compost. The beneficial addition of nitrogen chemical fertilizers into the soil has dramatically increased crop production for agribusiness farms. While adding something already available seems innocent enough, the dumping of pure nitrogen without the nutrients necessary to engage the bacterial decomposition process ruins the entire cycle.

Without the complex nutrients produced by the nitrogen-fixing process, the soil begins to erode and thin. The heavy load of unused nitrogen leaches through the soil, settling into the ground water. This nitrogen leaching creates a build-up of dangerous nitrates within groundwaters.

Ammonia-based fertilizer, our genius invention to fertilize nitrogen-fixing plants, has backfired on us. Most nitrogen fertilizers utilize ammonia. Ammonia is a harsh toxin. It will typically break down into nitrates. Nitrates now slowly seep through commercially farmed soils down to the once pure deep-water aquifers that supply much of our drinking water. At higher levels, nitrates have been shown to disrupt hemoglobin's ability to bind with oxygen. This can cause brain damage and various other metabolic disorders.

Nitrate build up has been poisoning ground water in agricultural areas throughout the world. In areas of heavy fertilizer use, undrinkable ground water is reaching increasingly deeper wells. Nitrate levels above about 50 parts per million can make a person sick.

Higher levels have been known to be fatal. Nitrate levels in public drinking water are therefore tightly regulated. Levels over 50 parts per million are typically not allowed in municipal water supplies and shared wells.

Though toxic levels of nitrate are monitored, lower nitrate levels also have inherent risks. In one study done at the Riley Hospital for Children in Indianapolis (Mattix *et al.* 2007), regions with higher nitrate levels in drinking water experienced significantly higher rates of congenital abdominal wall abnormalities.

In addition, nitrogen-rich fertilizers choke rivers and oceans with extra nitrogen, causing abnormal blooms of algae. These massive algal blooms cut off oxygen supplies and lead to the die-offs of many species of marine life. *Dead zones* have been reportedly growing in many of the world's waterways, as we will discuss shortly. The cause is the massive use of nitrogen-based synthetic fertilizers.

The use of pesticides on agricultural land, playgrounds, parks, home lawns, and gardens throughout the United States is staggering, and it is growing. In 1964, approximately 233 million pounds of pesticides were applied in the U.S. By 1982, this amount tripled to 612 million pounds. In 1999, the U.S. Environmental Protection Agency reported that some five *billion* pounds of these chemicals were applied per year throughout America's crops, forests, parks, and lawns.

One of the more increasingly popular pesticides is imidacloprid, a neonicotinoid. Introduced by Bayer in 1994, imidacloprid is used against aphids and similar insects on over 140 different crops. Touted as a chemical with a fairly short half-life of thirty days in water and twenty-seven days in anaerobic soil, imidacloprid's half-life is about 997 days in aerobic soil. While it has a lower immediate toxicity compared with hazards like DDT, imidacloprid's use is now widespread. It is rated by the EPA and WHO as *"moderately toxic"* in small doses. Larger doses can disrupt liver and thyroid function. While this pesticide does well at killing off increasingly resistant pests, it has also been shown to decimate bee populations.

A world without bees, as described in Rachel Carson's classic *Silent Spring,* would insure a destiny of hunger and destitution in human society. In France for example, some 500,000 registered hives were lost in the mid-1990s. Imidacloprid was implicated, and was subsequently banned for many crops in that country. Massive bee destruction has occurred in other regions of Europe also appear connected to imidacloprid use, but of course the pesticide manufacturers dispute this. A 2006-2007 loss of hives throughout Europe and the U.S.—referred to as *colony collapse disorder*—is now being connected to the increasing use of imidacloprid and other pesticides. These chemicals are thought to weaken the bees' immunity to viruses and other infectious diseases. Imidacloprid and other pesticides were designed to kill insects. What are bees then?

In addition to this nightmare, all of these pesticides are leaching into our groundwaters, our rivers, lakes and oceans. Residues are in our drinking water. When will we get the hint that these pesticides are actually *humanicides*?

Cleaning Chemicals

Cleaning agents are typically used with water and thus immediately enter our greywater systems. According to the U.S. Poison Control Centers, about ten percent of all toxic exposure is caused by cleaning products, with almost two-thirds involving children under six years old. While we might be shocked to find a child toying with a bottle of drain cleaner containing sulfuric acid, hydrochloric acid and lye, we do not think twice about feeding this same product into our waterways. While we wear gloves to protect our skin from the harmful affects of ammonia and bleach while we do our cleaning, we assume we won't have to touch these chemicals once they are poured down the sink.

In a 2002 U.S. Geological Survey report on stream water contaminants, 69% of stream samples revealed non-biodegradable detergents, and 66% of the samples contained disinfectant chemicals. Phosphates—central ingredients in many commercial laundry soaps—have been banned for dumping in over eleven states in the U.S. because of their dangerous effects upon the environment. Yet many people still use these soaps without any consideration of their effects upon our waters.

We might consider that one small individual disconnect (our own) with the planet does little harm. However, when we consider there are about 300 million of these "small" individuals in the U.S. alone, the toxic burden becomes cumulative.

Toxic Oceans

Illustrating this, among the beaches of California, long known for their pristine blue ocean waters, there were a record 25,000 beach closings in 2006. These closings were the result of polluted ocean waters—so polluted swimming was considered toxic.

As we look to the ocean increasingly for nutrition, we face concerns not only of profitability and population size, but also of sustainability and stewardship. Over the past few years two important studies have been released—the *Pew Oceans Commission Final Report* and the United States Congress *Oceans Commissions Report*. These two reports sent an urgent message to our marine and coastal industries, summed up by Dr. Wallace, Research Associate at the California Academy of Sciences: *"Too much is being dumped into the oceans, too much is being taken out, and the ocean's coastline habitats are quickly being destroyed."*

These combined factors are increasingly problematic to a human population seeking to sustain life on the planet. Research by Slovenian researchers Tatjana Tisler and Jana Zagorc-Koncan (2003) has shown that we are drastically underestimating the effects of toxic industrial waste. Our typical method for toxicity research has been to study each individual chemical and its possible toxicity. What we are missing with this type of research is the combined effects of the thousands of chemicals we are putting into our waters. As these chemicals mix, they create a toxic soup of new chemical combinations. Some of these are combinations are exponentially more toxic than the individual chemicals.

The issue of soup toxicity is tantamount for the health of our oceans. Marine life studies are showing higher levels of mercury, lead, arsenic, cadmium, and other heavy metals. These are showing up in combination within fish, bottom dwellers, and marine mammals alike. Polychlorinated biphenyls (PCBs), petroleum, *E. coli*, and other bacteria from waste run-off are also bio-accumulating up the food chain with these heavy metals and other toxins.

Our oceans are also filling up with plastic particles. As plastics break down into smaller particles, they are absorbed by filtering marine plants and aquatics and passed up the food chain. Research led by Captain Charles Moore of the *Algalita Marine Research Founda-*

tion (2001; 2002; 2008) found an astounding six-to-one ratio of plastic particles-to-plankton in some areas. This means that for every pound of algae—the key nutrient for nearly all marine life—there are six pounds of plastic in the oceans. This also means that our marine life is eating plastic particles with their meals: and so are humans who eat fish.

Captain Moore was first alerted to the plastic problem in 1997 when he sailed through a region of the Pacific Ocean between Hawaii and California called the *North Pacific Gyre*. He came upon a large area of floating garbage, consisting primarily of plastic debris. The *Great Pacific Garbage Patch* is now documented from a number of studies, the earliest from a 1988 National Oceanic and Atmospheric Administration paper.

Requiring some 500 years to breakdown, plastics are known to disrupt hormones and accumulate hydrocarbons as mentioned earlier. It is estimated that about twenty percent of the plastic polluting the oceans comes from discarded plastic pellets used to make plastic by manufacturers. These pellets are being swept or blown into the water from careless manufacturers and transport companies. The other eighty percent of the ocean's plastics is estimated to come from daily consumer use and the careless littering of oceans and runoffs.

Dead Zones

Our oceans, lakes and seaways are dying. This is due to a combination of toxic chemical industrial waste, toxic personal waste from households, and the widespread use of chemical fertilizers.

Nitrogen-rich fertilizers seem through our soils, choking rivers and oceans with extra nitrogen, causing abnormal blooms of algae. These algae blooms cut off the supply of oxygen for other fish, suffocating fish and other marine species. The massive marine life die-offs and overwhelming algae blooms together are gradually transforming the entire marine environment into lifeless regions now referred to *dead ocean zones* or *hypoxia regions*. These dead ocean zones are increasing throughout the planet. They have been growing dramatically, especially in regions known for heavy chemical fertilizer use and commercial farming. A huge dead zone is now growing in the Gulf of Mexico, for example. In 2007, the size of this one dead zone was estimated at 6,000 square miles and growing.

These dead zones are reversible. Dead zones in the Black Sea and the North Sea have been reversed through decreases in fertilizer use and industrial chemical dumping in those regions (Mee 2006).

All we have to do is vote with our checkbooks: Simply refuse to buy or use any product that contains chemicals that will destroy our waterways. How do we know if a product will hurt our waters' ecosystem? Stay informed. If in doubt: if we cannot eat it, we should not be dumping it into our waters.

~ Four ~

The Fluid Human

The makeup of our cells is primarily water: intercellular fluid makes up about 60% of our body's total water. Each cell is also bathed in water. Outside the cells, we find about 40% of the body's water, including the blood and the interstitial fluid. This water is not simply water, however. It is rich in ionic minerals and nutrients.

The cell membrane regulates the ionic and nutrient content between the cells' inner and outer environments. Cell membranes contain phospholipids 'stacked' into molecular arrays bound with precise molecular polarity. This polarity permits the formation of microscopic pores or channels through which the movement of nutrients and ions between the cell membrane is regulated.

Phospholipids are critical to these pores, and to the health of the cell. Phospholipid misalignments will flag T-cells that the cell is in a diseased state. Phospholipid misalignment also leads to a loss of brain and nerve cell conductivity. One of the key conductivity phospholipids is phosphatidylserine (PS). PS is interspersed among cell membranes, especially among brain and nerve cells. We also know that PS content tends to decline with age.

The Ionic Anatomy

The cytoplasm inside the cell membrane is typically abundant with positively charged potassium ions, while the water outside the cell is teeming with positively charged sodium ions. Their polar affinity allows their transport between the cell membrane through pore system called the *sodium-potassium pump*. This pump system is one of many different types of pump and pore systems that exist within the cell membrane, balancing the flow of water and nutrients into the cell with the flow of waste out of the cell.

The polarity of ions such as sodium and potassium ions creates an electromagnetic affinity within tiny receptors inside these pores. This affinity provides a gateway system between the inside and outside surfaces of the cell membrane. This also helps give the membrane a stable partition. Water provides the foundation and solvent for the ionic currents that flow through this partition.

These tiny pores within the cell membrane, created by spaces between stacked phospholipid molecules, are also called *ion channels*.

Ion channels have tiny gates that open to allow particular nutrients into the cell, and particular waste materials out. The ions typically stimulate the switching mechanism of the channel, and often escort the nutrients through the channel.

There are many types of ion channels within the cell membrane, even among sodium and potassium ions. In addition to the sodium-potassium pump there are single sodium channels and potassium channels that help move nutrients between the cell membrane.

This entire process is called *cellular diffusion* and *active transport*. These terms describe the activity of how cells bring in nutrition and pass out toxins through the cell membrane, utilizing these ion channels. Throughout the body, different types of ion channels transport specific types of nutrients in and out of cells, depending upon the function and requirement of each cell and organ system.

For example, calcium channels provide information in the form of completing an ion voltage circuit for neurons. Calcium ion channels are found primarily among brain, organ, and nerve cells. Calcium gateways conduct information through depolarization, by turning on and off the release of neurotransmitters and hormones.

Chloride channels regulate cellular nutrition. More than thirteen types of chloride channels have been discovered. Each type regulates different nutrients and functions.

Among most cells, cyclic nucleotide channels regulate the entry of certain nucleotides, driving the production of proteins (including DNA and RNA), along with energy production and cellular clock function. The heart's pacemaker neurons function extensively with cyclic nucleotide channels, for example.

Research has unveiled many many other types of ion channels, including cAMP and IP3 channels, and many many others.

There are also many different types of pore structures among ion channels. For example, some potassium ion channels have a double-pore system, as opposed to the single pore system of many other potassium and other ion channels. Cation-selective double pore channels provide an exchange of voltage potentials. The double-pore potassium channels regulate tone and flexibility among blood vessels, for example.

The body's pore system is driven by mineral ions. There are about 80 known macro and trace minerals in the body. As nutritional research into macrominerals has continued, we have gradually come to understand that every mineral—macro and trace—plays an important metabolic role. Should the human body be lacking in any of these elements, imbalances in the body's metabolism begin to occur. Some of the more prevalent macrominerals include, among others, calcium, potassium, magnesium, sodium and phosphorus. These are called macro because they exist in larger quantities in the body. These minerals contribute to the metabolic activities of the vast legions of catalysts, proteins, enzymes, cells, organs and so many other elements of the body's physiology.

The balance between macro and trace elements is one of the key governing factors in maintaining physiological balance. Zinc, for example, was long considered not that critical to health. Some clinicians thought that zinc was poisonous. Recent research has found that this trace element is a key factor for at least one hundred enzyme and immune system processes. Zinc is a participant in immune function, growth, wound repair, DNA production and enzyme reaction. Without zinc, the body will function in a depressed immune state.

Another trace element is copper. Copper, for example, is critical to the production and function of superoxide dismutase, one of the body's most critical detoxification enzymes.

It might be surprising that other important trace elements—including fluorine, cadmium, bromine, chlorine and even uranium—are also needed by the body, albeit in minute quantities. In larger quantities, these elements can be toxic. In minute quantities, they are essential for metabolic functions, including innumerable enzyme reactions, protein sequencing, immune cell composition and many others. Without a consistent source of trace elements, our body's metabolic operations quickly become handicapped.

Ions can form acids or bases. In traditional chemistry, acids and bases are defined by hydrogen atoms—or proton proportions. An acid is typically described as a substance with an excess of hydrogen atoms ($H+$), which acts as a net proton donor. A base, on the other hand, is considered either a hydroxide ($OH-$) donor or a proton acceptor—a substance often described as having excessive electrons. Net charge is also used to describe acids or bases. An acid solution is one with a net positive charge, while a base solution has a net negative charge. An acid is often referred to as cationic (with cations) because it has a positive net charge, while a base will have a negative charge and thus is referred to as an anion.

A measurement of the level of acidity or alkalinity using a logarithmic scale is called pH. The term pH is derived from the French word for "hydrogen power," *pouvoir hydrogene*, which has been abbreviated as simply pH. pH is measured in an inverse log base-10 scale, measuring the proton-donor level by comparing it to a theoretical quantity of hydrogen ions (H+) in a solution. Thus, a pH of 5 would be equivalent to 10^5 H+ moles worth of cations in the solution. (A mole is a quantity of substance compared to 12 grams of the six-neutron carbon isotope.) Put another way, a pCl (chlorine) concentration would be the negative log of chlorine-ion concentration in a solution, and pK would be the negative log of potassium-ions in a solution.

The pH scale is calculated between 0 to 14, for 10^{-1} (.1) to 10^{-14} (.00000000000001) range. The scale has been set up around the fact that pure water's pH is log-7 or simply pH7 (.0000001). Because pure water forms the basis for so many of life's activities, and because water neutralizes and dilutes so many reactions, water has became the standard reference and neutral point between an acid and a base. In other words, a substance having greater hydrogen ion concentration characteristics than "pure" water will be considered a base, while a substance containing less H+ concentration characteristics than water is considered an acid.

Of course, a solution concentration may well be lower than log-14 or higher than log-1, but this is the scale set up based upon the typical ranges observed in nature. Using this scale, any substance measuring a pH of 7 would be considered a neutral substance, though it still has a significant number of H+ ions.

In humans, a pH level in the neighborhood of between 6.5 and 7.5 is considered a healthy ionic state depending upon which body fluid is being measured. This range is either slightly more acidic than water or slightly more alkaline than water, either of which allow ionic current flow through the body. If the body's fluids are substantially higher or lower than these levels, there is likely an im-balance of mineral ions in the body.

To test the body's pH, a test paper such as pHydrion is sprin-kled with saliva or urine. Saliva is typically more acidic than urine, depending upon our recent consumption of food and beverages. Assuming no fluids or foods within the last hour, an optimal saliva pH should range from 6.8 to 7.4. Urine, on the other hand, will optimally range from 6.5 to 7.0 in a healthy person.

Better put, a 6.5-7.5 pH range offers the appropriate currency of energy flow between ions. The alkali metals, alkali earth metals and a few other elements provide the means for maintaining ionic stability. These include hydrogen sodium (Na+), potassium (K+), calcium (Ca+), magnesium (Mg+) and lithium (Li+) and others. These are specifically oriented for the exchange of ion polarity within the body's cell membranes.

The balance of ions within and around cells, including the neu-rotransmitter fluid between nerve cells, is critical to our body's equilibrium. A state of disequilibrium, for example, takes place when a person has become intoxicated from alcohol or psychotro-pic drugs. Here the ionic balance within the neurotransmitter fluid is altered, affecting the ion channel flow of information between nerve cells. This in turn affects coordination, physical response, perception, mood, and other neuron-dependent functions. Alcohol also suppresses vasopressin secretion, which promotes a state of dehydration within the body.

Balanced ion states are critical for nutrient flow into the cell. For example, ion-channel receptors stimulate sodium-glucose chan-nels to establish glucose equilibrium. These are called *glucose receptors*. These receptors are connected to the specialized channel gates that sit on the surface of the cell membrane, and are switched on by stimulation from the hormone *insulin*.

In addition to providing channels for the exchange of nutrients and toxins, nerve cell sodium/potassium pumps provide a mecha-nism of the exchange of ionic information. As electromagnetic pulses traverse the length of the nerve cell, sodium ions are pulled into the nerve cell, while potassium ions are pushed out. Each ion pulse produces a specific piece of information. This functions somewhat similar to the 1s and 0s of computer machine language code. As most of us know, this rather simple computer machine system of 1s and 0s (or on or off states) allows for complex instructional messaging. In the case of the potassium/sodium pumps, the on or off state is provided by the differing polarity between the potassium and sodium ions.

The ion channel can provide more than a simple on-off state in the form of an open or closed gateway. Most ion channels allow three possible gateway states. These include *deactivation, activation* and *inactivation.* (A simple on-off switch would be either activation or deactivation.) Both the deactivated state and inactivated states close the gateway, and the activated state opens the gateway. The difference between the two closed gateway states is that a deactivated gate is blocked by an opposing open gate, while the inactive gate is simply closed with no opposition.

Most of the body's biochemical processes are *hydrolytic.* In other words, most metabolic reactions are water-dependent, requiring hydrolysis. Water is required to complete the metabolic step, and water molecules are often part of the reaction. The hydroelectric ion transport currents through the ion channels of the cell membrane stimulate many of these metabolic reactions—such as the ATP energy manufacturing cycle. Many metabolic reactions that don't utilize water molecules still require water as the essential foundation to buffer and transport ions. Water is the main substrate and the central solvent for a vast network of metabolic biochemical processes occurring simultaneously within the body.

The Pathology of Dehydration

When the body becomes dehydrated, a number of physiological responses occur. Initially, when the cells among the body's least vital regions become exhausted of water, various ionic channels will close to preserve fluid for vital tissues. As this happens, the movement of ions, nutrition, and fluids in and out of those cells will dramatically slow down or even shut down.

The system of drought management within the body is driven by histamine, vasopressin and renin-angiotensin. These hormone/neurotransmitters stimulate physiological responses that preserve the body's water and attempt to maintain homeostasis within the body in the face of dehydration. Once histamine release is stimulated during the dehydrated state, renin is produced, which stimulates the production of angiotensin. These together increase the pressure on the blood vessel walls, which increases blood pressure, causing a state of hypertension.

These in turn stimulate vasopressin (antidiuretic hormone) and force the kidneys to tighten urine filtration. Tightened filtration makes the kidneys concentrate urine so the body can reuse more of its water. This urine concentration is not good for the kidneys, however. Kidney damage can also result from chronic urine concentration. Uric acid crystallization, also a byproduct of eating too much protein, can accumulate to cause kidney stones.

During the dehydrated state, the body prioritizes and rations its reduced availability of water very pragmatically and intelligently. The areas where hydration is reduced first will be the less vital regions of mucous membranes, joints, tendons and other non-life-threatening areas—as opposed to the vital circulatory-rich organs such as the brain, heart and liver.

As dehydration continues, prostaglandins and kinins stimulate inflammatory processes that have dramatic affects upon these vital organs. Brain and nerve damage, cardiovascular damage, and liver and kidney failure can result from a chronic dehydrated state. These inflammatory factors also produce pain responses. Chronic fatigue and pain syndromes, along with allergic and autoimmune responses, have been linked to dehydration.

One of the first regions of the body affected by thirst is our mucosal membranes. Our mouth, nose, ears, throat, lungs, intestinal tract, urinary tract, and genitalia openings are all lined with epithelium covered with mucous membranes. These membranes protect the epithelial cell linings from damage associated with microorganisms, particles, toxins, acidity and foreign substances.

Our mucosal membranes consist primarily of water and mucopolysaccharides. They contain various immune cells. Most also contain probiotics that help defend our body against invasion.

Reduced or inadequate water intake almost immediately thins out these mucosal membranes. As they thin, the cells lying within the membrane become exposed to toxins and microorganisms. This in turn seriously dampens the body's ability to counteract infection. This 'front-line' mucosal membrane is a critical part of our immune system. The wearing down of these mucosal membranes can open up the possibility of infections of the lung, throat, sinuses, urinary tract, stomach, ears and intestines.

Other internal tissues are also dramatically affected by dehydration, as cells reduce their water holdings and intercellular waters are reduced. As a result, there is a domino affect of various disorders associated with chronic dehydration. Many arthritic and joint issues appear be directly related to dehydration. In the case of joint issues, water is an important part of the slippery cartilage that lies between bone ends in a joint. Dehydration causes the cartilage to begin to break down (Batmanghelidj 1992).

Negative effects upon cognition and psychomotor performance have also been observed. Using neurophysiology testing, Grandjean and Grandean (2007) found that a mere 2% body water loss depressed the nervous system significantly.

Dehydration can also affect childhood learning. In a study from the University of East London (Edmonds and Burford 2009) with 58 children between seven and nine years old, those who drank more water performed better on cognitive and visual attention tests.

Other pathologies appear to be related to even mild dehydration as illustrated by Manz (2007). These include cystic fibrosis, renal toxicity, urinary tract infections, constipation, hypertension, various coronary and artery disorders, and glaucoma. Evidence from the CF/Pulmonary Research and Treatment Center of the University of North Carolina (Boucher 2007) has revealed a link between hydration and cystic fibrosis as "low airway surface liquid volume." This is another way of saying that the mucosal membranes lining the airways are dehydrated.

We also can link a lack of water consumption with various digestive disorders such as GERD (gastroesophageal reflux disease), ulcers, and irritable bowel syndrome (Batmanghelidj 1992). In a state of dehydration, the pH chemistry of the stomach radically changes. Again, the mucous membranes of the esophagus and stomach wall become thinner and less protective. This is because water is the central component of mucous and gastrin, which in turn buffers the HCL component of stomach secretions. Water is also a major element in the sloughing and division of the cells of the walls of the stomach and intestines. Intestinal cells are some of the shortest living cells of the body. Cells of a healthy digestive tract will divide and slough off within days, leaving the body with virtually a new stomach mucosal lining within days. Dehydration can create genetic mutation among these new generations. This mutation may allow the cell to function with less water, but often at a price. Once mutation occurs, the cell may assume foreign attributes. As the immune system senses these foreign attributes, *autoimmunity* may arise.

Ailments associated with chronic dehydration

allergies	arthritis	diabetes
asthma	chronic fatigue	kidney disease
colitis	Crohn's disease	irritable bowel
headaches	angina	claudication
candidiasis	hiatal hernia	gout
liver disease	neck pain	depression
stress	multiple sclerosis	PMS
hypertension	high cholesterol	atherosclerosis
COPD	peptic ulcer	obesity
heart disease	insomnia	cystic fibrosis
varicose veins	GERD	muscle cramps
stroke	Alzheimer's	Parkinson's
infertility	scleroderma	anxiety
panic attacks	indigestion	constipation
gastritis	cystitis	UTI
rheumatism	eczema	schizophrenia
cirrhosis	PAD	neuropathy
glaucoma	polyps	ear infections

These are only a few of the many symptoms of chronic dehydration. Because most of us have unique physiologies, we often have unique responses, depending upon our metabolic vulnerabilities. Disease etiologies are often complicated and interactive, and chronic dehydration may play a contributing role or a dominant role in these pathologies.

One of the important elements of this issue is that as the body ages, the thirst sensation decreases. The thirst sensation is sharp as the body is in development, and is especially noticeable when the blood volume is low. The maturation of the body's metabolism and proportion continues until about 18-21 years of age. During development, the body's need for water is critical, and this drives the thirst sensation. Thirst sensation begins to decline at about 21, and continues a steady decline into the elderly years. A number of studies have documented elderly dehydration and this decrease in thirst sensation (Vogt *et al.* 2009; Ferry 2005; Kenney and Chiu 2001).

Healthy Hydration

There are two central issues to consider as we determine appropriate water consumption. The first is water loss and the second is water absorption, which relate directly to quality and volume. Obviously, the two issues are related. As Dr. Jethro Kloss pointed out decades ago (1939), the average person loses about 550 cubic centimeters of water through the skin, 440 cc through the lungs, 1550 through the urine, and another 150 cc through the stool. This adds up to 2650 cc per day, equivalent to a little over two and a half quarts (about 85 fluid ounces).

Most health professionals suggest optimal water volume around eight 8-oz glasses per day. In 2004, the National Academy of Sciences released a study indicating that women typically meet their hydration needs with approximately 91 ounces of water per day, while men meet their needs with about 125 ounces per day. This study also indicated that approximately 80% of water intake comes from water/beverages and 20% comes from food. Therefore, we can assume a minimum of 73 ounces of fresh water for the average adult woman and 100 ounces of fresh water for the average adult man should cover our minimum needs. That is significantly more water than the standard eight glasses per day—especially for men.

It is not surprising that some health professionals suggest that 50-75% of Americans have chronic dehydration. Fereydoon Batmanghelidj, M.D., probably the world's foremost researcher on water, suggests one half ounce of water per pound of body weight. Drinking an additional 16-32 ounces for each 45 minutes to an hour of strenuous activity is also a good idea, with some before and some after exercising. Temperature and elevation extremes, and extra sweating or fevers all increase daily water requirements.

Most experts agree that as soon as we feel thirsty, our bodies are already experiencing dehydration. Becoming consciously thirsty is the point where tissue and cell damage is taking place. Water is critical for the smooth running of all of our cells. Areas likely to suffer during mild chronic dehydration include the stomach and digestive tract; the joints; the eyes and the liver. Some health experts have estimated as little as a 5% loss of body water will decrease physical performance by up to 30%.

We can watch our urine to make sure we are getting enough water. Our urine color should range from light yellow to clear. Darker urine indicates dehydration. A bright yellow urine color typically indicates the supplementation of riboflavin (B2)—present in many multivitamins.

Pregnant or nursing women may want to increase their intake by two to three glasses per day. Dr. Batmanghelidj proposes that morning sickness may well simply be a symptom of dehydration. Most beverages can be included in that total. The Academy study mentioned above includes caffeinated beverages at a one-to-one ratio. However, we should note that caffeine is a mild diuretic agent, so if caffeinated beverages are being consumed at above-average levels, more fluids are needed to accommodate for the increased fluid loss. An additional four ounces should be added for every eight ounces of coffee or caffeine soda included in water intake according to some experts.

Sodas with sugar and caffeine have a diuretic effect, reducing hydration. Many sodas also contain refined corn syrup and/or aspartame. Aspartame has been linked with a number of neurological side effects. Many sodas also contain sodium benzoate. According to 1999 research led by Dr. Peter Piper from the University College in London (Kren *et al* 2003), sodium benzoate harms mitochondria within cells. This effectively starves those cells of their energy production. Sodium benzoate is also a common ingredient in pickles, some Chinese sauces, jams and some fruit juices.

If a dominant portion of our water intake comes from sugary sodas or diet sodas with chemical additives, additional water is suggested to balance their diuretic and toxic effects.

Urination frequency depends largely upon the volume of water we are drinking and the size of our bladder. If we are not urinating at least four times a day we are probably not drinking enough water. At the same time, urination frequency can vary widely between people. Some people are able to accumulate urine in the bladder and kidneys for several hours, at varying degrees of concentration. Some concentrate better than others. Some simply have smaller bladders, and must urinate more frequently. While urination frequency may indicate enlarged prostate or urinary tract issues, it may also simply indicate habitual urgency response or a small bladder.

Our bodies utilize water during sleep. Therefore, it is important to hydrate immediately upon waking. A large glass of room temperature water first thing in the morning will speed absorption, replenishing water loss. Water taken prior to brushing will also deliver mucous from our mouth and esophagus to our stomach, aiding the stomach's mucosal gastric lining (an ancient Ayurvedic remedy).

Nature's Ions

Mineralized waters from springs or wells can have a pH of 7-8 because of their interaction with nature's nutrients. As water flows through rock and soils, minerals and trace elements are pulled away to merge into the water as ions or dissolved solids.

The most prevalent mineral gleaned during water's travel is calcium carbonate ($CaCO_3$) present in most rocks and limestone. Dolomite ($Ca(Mg)CO_3$) is also a Ca+ ion donor.

Magnesium is another major mineral present in rocks—prevalent in most spring or well water. Magnesium is known for producing muscle and cardiovascular efficiency.

Other common minerals natural water draws from the earth include selenium, silica, iron, copper, potassium, sodium, and many others. Mineral profiles of rock deposits show rocks can contain over 80 trace minerals. 'Trace' here means content in the parts per million or parts per billion. While passing waters may not pick up every mineral, the further a water has traveled through unpolluted rocks and soils of the planet, the more nutrients it will contain, and the purer it will likely be. This is because minerals draw toxins through chelation and covalent boding. In other words, mineral ions draw various contaminants, bacteria and pollutants out of water.

Research is still investigating the human need for many minerals and trace elements. Calcium is one of the more researched minerals.

Studies have shown that absorption of calcium from water rivals calcium absorbed from milk (Couzy 1995; Heaney 1994). These studies have also showed no significant resorption difference, illustrating that calcium from water is well utilized by the body.

Natural mineralized water or 'hard water' has been linked with increased cardiovascular health (Tubek 2006). What elements in hard water give it these benefits? Calcium, magnesium, cobalt, lithium, vanadium, silicon, manganese, and copper along with other trace minerals provide the link. These minerals have been shown to be beneficial to the body in one respect or another. Just about every enzymatic and metabolic process in the body utilizes minerals and trace elements. Like water, they are essential for health.

There is considerable evidence indicating that cancer risk is lowered and possibly prevented through the ingestion of a balance of trace minerals. Selenium has been linked with lower prostate and lung cancer risk. Zinc has been linked with lower breast cancer risk. Arsenic has been associated with lower lung and bladder cancer risk, and cadmium has been associated with lower lung cancer risk (Navarro *et al.* 2007).

Mineral research to date has primarily focused on deficiencies of individual macrominerals. As a whole, this research, together with epidemiological studies from the World Health Organization, indicates that it is the *combination* of macrominerals and trace elements that creates the greatest potential for health benefits.

Lawrence Wilson, M.D., a leading expert on mineral balancing, has documented many years of clinical experience in analyzing subjects' hair and blood minerals. Dr. Wilson (1992) has also prescribed numerous mineral supplement strategies to rebalance deficiencies in one mineral or other. Dr. Wilson also established various mineral balancing ratios between macrominerals such as calcium, sodium, potassium, zinc, lead, copper and others. For example, using hair analysis, Dr. Wilson established that an ideal sodium-potassium balance is around 2.5:1. Levels below this ratio indicate issues related to sodium pump mechanisms, such as adrenal stress and exhaustion. Dr. Wilson also calculated the optimal sodium-magnesium ratio at 4.17:1. Ratios below this (but above 1:1) were indicative of adrenal activity leading to high blood pressure, high blood sugar, and excess gastric acidity. Dr. Wilson's work also indicated an optimal calcium-potassium ratio of 4:1. Higher ratios indicate sluggish cellular thyroid activity, while lower ratios indicate overactive thyroid activity. Dr. Wilson also documented various other mineral relationships with various pathologies.

Dr. Wilson also found that certain minerals become *metabolic analogues*, or substitutes for deficient minerals. In a zinc deficiency, for example, copper and cadmium can substitute for zinc in enzymatic metabolic reactions. These can create anxiety and nervousness. In situations of calcium deficiency and lead overexposure, lead can substitute calcium. Dr. Wilson observed this substitution creating the propensity for seizures. Using precise mineral rebalancing therapies, Dr. Wilson has contributed to the recovery of thousands of patients for many years.

To date, research has yet to determine the minimum allowances for most of the macrominerals, let alone the trace elements. For example, various studies have confirmed that zinc, selenium, copper, arsenic, cadmium, and silica are all necessary for health (Bourre 2006). However, their precise deficiency levels have proved difficult to establish. Protocols for determining cellular mineral deficiencies and their effects have remained elusive.

While blood tests have been predominantly been used to gauge mineral levels, the blood is constantly shifting minerals from different tissue locations around the body as needed. Blood levels are thus difficult for determining deficiencies among tissues or cells. We might assume that high levels in the blood indicate high levels in the tissues. This assumption conflicts with other clinical research, however. For example, we know that blood calcium levels can be quite high (hypercalcemia) while bone calcium levels can be low and bone loss is occurring. The leaching (or resorption) of calcium from the bones to maintain blood levels of calcium has been well established. This has been elucidated over the past few decades by James McDougal, M.D.

Because blood levels of minerals can be deceiving, Dr. Wilson's clinical applications with mineral testing have relied more heavily on hair analysis. Others have criticized hair analysis, pointing to accuracy issues relating to sampling and analysis. Dr. Wilson has answered these concerns with protocols that minimize inaccuracies and increase analytical perspective.

Natural Mineral Balancing

The earth's mineral waters are often composed of more than 80 trace minerals, including several important macrominerals. The key macrominerals in water are calcium, magnesium, sodium, potassium and phosphorus. This mineral content is due to water's interaction with the rocks, sand, and soils of the planet.

The World Health Organization's research reports have suggested that water concentration levels of 10-30 mg/L magnesium and 10-50 mg/L calcium were enough to decrease cardiovascular disease rates. Questions have been raised regarding mineral waters' possibly contributing to kidney stones or gallstones. However, there are a myriad of other factors related to these stones, notably protein overeating and uric acid formation. Ramello *et al.* (2000) confirmed there was no link between water hardness and kidney stones.

There is no controversy that both calcium and magnesium—like many other minerals—are extremely important to the overall health and metabolism of the body. While calcium is involved in muscle contraction, nerve conductance, bone structure, heart contractibility, blood vessel wall and lung flexibility; magnesium is involved in at least 300 critical enzyme reactions. Both minerals increase flexibility among muscles and artery walls, while stimulating nerve response. Calcium and magnesium play many other important roles in the body. World Health Organization research has shown that water that is low in calcium and magnesium dramatically raises the risk of heart disease, osteoporosis and other diseases.

Research has also confirmed that naturally mineralized water increases water absorption. This occurs on an ionic level. The ionic structure of mineralized water resonates better with the sodium ion channels of cell membranes and intestinal junctions. This is due to the gateway acceptance of the ion content of mineralized water through these ion-regulated channels.

Mineral content orients water with ionic polarity. This influences the water molecules' spin and collective surface tension. This in turn relates to the ability of water to form structured clustering. While the argument has been made that ions within mineral water cleave and disassociate, we cannot logically separate water from its ionic content. Ionic content regulates surface tension and adhesion. These in turn directly affect absorption.

Water Softeners

Water softeners draw important minerals like magnesium and calcium out of water using a combination of sodium and zeolite minerals. Zeolites are ion-exchanging minerals that attract and cleave mineral ions. As these beads become saturated with minerals, the recharging system in the water softener passes the beads through salt crystals, replacing the mineral ions with sodium ions. This process leaves a significant amount of sodium in the water.

In one study (Yarows *et al.* 1997), softened well water varied from 46 to 1219 milligrams sodium per liter with an average of 278 mg/L. *This in addition to the sodium already contained in the water.* 17% of the households tested above 400 mg/L. The higher the sodium before the softener, the higher the resulting sodium content. This study also measured various municipal waters, which resulted in an average of 110 mg/L, with the highest registering at 253 mg/L. This means that if a person were on a restricted sodium diet of say 1500 milligrams a day, just three liters of household water with a 250 mg/L sodium content would take up half the day's maximum sodium intake.

We mentioned earlier a number of studies have suggested that hard waters with magnesium and calcium had a protective affect for cardiovascular disease and heart disease. More than eighty studies have documented research in this area and many of these were reviewed and summarized by the World Health Organization in a 2004 report called *Nutrient Minerals in Drinking Water and the Potential Health Consequences of Long-term Consumption of Demineralized, Remineralized, and Altered Mineral Content Drinking Waters.* This report documented a number of negative health consequences from drinking demineralized water, while remineralized mineral content waters faired better.

Furthermore, Kozisek reported in his 2004 report to the World Health Organization, *Health Risks from Drinking Demineralised Water,* that distilled or otherwise low mineral waters have decreased thirst-quenching abilities and potentially harmful effects upon the linings of the intestinal tract and digestive system. Apparently, intestinal epithelial cells undergo alteration without mineral ions present in drinking water.

The above report also underscored research showing that consuming low mineral content water also has negative effects upon the body's homeostasis mechanisms, thereby altering the body's enzyme and hormone mechanisms. Increased diuresis (urine output); increases excretion of cellular ions; decreases secretions of thyroid hormones and aldosterone (ADH); increases cortisol levels; alters kidney function; lowers red blood cell volumes; and reduces bone ossification—contributing to bone loss. This report also cited research showing that distilled and demineralized waters cause a repositioning of water around the body, decreasing intracellular fluid, increasing extracellular fluid and increasing plasma fluids. This in turn stimulates increased urination and further mineral loss.

Epidemiological studies over the past ten years have confirmed that drinking soft water increases the risk of mortality from cardiovascular disease. Sodium-enriched soft water has also been associated with higher risks of bone fracture; increased risk of certain cancers; heightened risk of motor nerve damage; increased risk of sudden death; and higher levels of pregnancy disorders (Monarca *et al.* 2003; Nardi *et al.* 2003; Sauvant and Pepin 2002).

Whether they work or not, new magnetic softeners that theoretically repolarize water coming into the house are far healthier.

Municipal Tap Waters

According to a recent U.S. Geological report (Barber 2009), approximately 410,000 million gallons were withdrawn per day from water sources by Americans in 2005, including industrial use. This means that most of our tap water originates from local reservoirs fed from runoff from a variety of sources. Many of these sources are theoretically pristine, such as mountain snowmelt. Some are not so pristine. Some are fed by rivers that flow through farmlands that carry fertilizers and pesticides, and/or carry waste streams from industrial operations.

One of the biggest problems occurring with creek water or river water is the runoff of toxic waste and agricultural chemicals. Studies in the San Francisco Bay, for example, revealed that chemical fertilizer and pesticide runoff from nearby farms was one of the greatest sources of the water pollution in the bay. Drinking water reservoirs are also often fed by streams that connect to commercial agriculture. Other sources of toxic chemicals in drinking reservoirs include industrial chemical byproducts from manufacturing facilities. These include thousands of chemical pollutants being dumped or chemicals seeping into groundwater. They also include chemically treated septic tanks; leaking underground gasoline tanks; fertilizers applied to lawns and farms; and the dumping into marine environments by commercial shipping discharge, marine oil leakage, antifouling paint application, and marine head chemicals.

A study released in 2005 by the Environmental Working Group found 260 contaminants in drinking water supplies around the country. Of these 260 chemicals, the U.S. Environmental Protection Agency regulates 114 to some extent; and another five have been assigned secondary standards—non-enforceable minimum contamination goals. That leaves an astonishing 141 chemicals with no standards in the drinking supplies of over 195 million people. Not all 141 chemicals are being served to all 195 million people at once, however. The report specified that at least 40 of these 141 chemical toxins were being fed to at least one million people, while another 19 were being supplied to at least 10,000 people. In some cases, single water supplies had up to twenty unregulated contaminants. In other words, some water supplies are much worse than others, depending upon their proximity to manufacturing facilities, commercial farms, golf courses, sewage treatment plants, and underground fuel storage tanks.

The report also broke down the unregulated contaminants into several categories; including methyl tertiary butyl ether or MTBE from gasoline, perchlorate from rocket fuel, fifteen water disinfection byproducts, four plasticizers, seventy-eight consumer and industrial production chemicals, and twenty gas, coal and other fuel combustion chemicals. Fifty-two of these unregulated chemicals have been linked to cancer. Seventy-seven have been linked to reproductive or growth problems. Sixteen more have been connected with compromising the immune system.

By far the biggest source of both regulated and unregulated chemicals in this study was industrial waste with 166 chemicals, followed by agricultural pollutants with eighty-three chemicals.

Household and urban pollution came in third with twenty-nine chemicals, and water treatment plants contributed a jaw-dropping forty-four pollutants to tap waters.

Agriculture spreads 110 billion pounds of chemical fertilizer over almost 250 million acres per year according to a 2002 USDA report. This is equivalent to about one-eighth of the entire United States. Meanwhile about one-tenth of the U.S. is being drenched with herbicides and pesticides.

Meat production is another dramatic contributor of pollutants. There are about 248,000 feedlots in the U.S., primarily housing cattle or pigs. These feedlots produce about 500 million tons of manure annually, laden with hormones and antibiotics. This means our thirst for commercially farmed meat is limiting our future ability to consume our body's most precious requirement: water. As Fawell and Nieuwenhuijsen (2003) document in their review of various water contaminants throughout the world, water contamination has been linked to a variety of disease pathologies, especially in areas with increased industrial and commercial agricultural economies.

We can therefore conclude that drinking municipal tap water can be a risky proposition. While the occasional sip of unfiltered tap water is probably not going to do much harm, the risk lies with the consistent drinking of tap water over a long period of time. This of course brings us to the topic of water treatment.

Chlorinated Water

Certainly, municipal tap water needs treatment. Chlorine and chloramines are standard treatment additives in most all U.S. municipal water treatment plants. Is this a good thing or a bad thing?

There is good reason for chlorine purification. Chlorine has been the standard for water treatment for over a century. Because of its use, public water-borne bacterial diseases have dramatically decreased. Chlorine itself is a natural element, known primarily to be the ionic element of sodium chloride—the salt of our oceans. It is also a necessary trace mineral, used for various enzymatic and metabolic functions in the body. In heavy doses, however, chlorine can burden the body's toxin load. Though the body can readily detoxify or utilize chlorine, chlorine breaks down into other harmful chemicals when added to water. While EPA guidelines only require about .2 parts per million for the municipality to purify water, levels are often increased to handle higher bacteria levels, which can occur during seasonal low water levels and sewage spills.

Chlorine readily breaks down in sunlight and during transport through pipes. The byproducts of this breakdown are trihalomethanes (TTHM) and haloacetic acids (TAA5). In the United States, the Environmental Protection Agency regulates these two byproducts in municipal drinking water. Over the past few years most municipalities have reduced total trihalomethane (TTHM) levels to 80 ug/L (equivalent to 80 parts per billion) and 60 ug/L (60 ppb) respectively. Meanwhile, many states have mandated tougher standards, some to the tune of 10 ug/L or 10 parts per billion for municipalities within their jurisdiction.

Meanwhile, the FDA's mandated level for TTHMs in bottled water is 100 ug/L. While we might assume bottled waters would not contain trihalomethanes, the NRDC's 1997-1999 tests concluded that many bottled waters had substantially higher TTHM levels than municipal water mandated levels. Many had levels ranging from 20 to 90 ppb TTHM. While levels below the EPA's and FDA's mandates have not been shown to pose a significant health risk, the bioaccumulation effect is uncertain. TTHM's are metabolized through the liver and kidneys, so they could certainly burden an unhealthy body.

As for the haloacetic acids, there are five that can result from chlorination of municipal waters. These are monochloroacetic acid, dichloroacetic acid, trichloroacetic acid, monobromoacetic acid, and dibromoacetic acid. Levels of these treatment byproducts are regulated by the EPA at 60 parts per billion.

As to whether TTHMs or TAA5s are more toxic than some of the deadly bacteria the chlorine removes; most of us would probably prefer chlorine treatment to microorganisms. Many water-borne microorganisms including *Giardia lamblia, Cyptosporidium* sp., *Salmonella* sp. and *Entamoeba histolytica* are highly and immediately toxic, causing dysentery and even death if untreated. At the end of the day, the residual risk chlorine byproducts from standard chlorinated municipal water treatments pose is significantly lower than the risk of bacterial infection. The pertinent questions include whether there are viable alternatives, and what kind of filtration system is appropriate for screening out chlorine and its byproducts.

Chloramine Treated Water

The municipal water additive to be more concerned about is the newest version of chlorine treatment: chloramine. Chloramines like monochloramine, dichloramine and trichloramine are produced by combining chlorine with ammonia. This creates a hardy molecule— one that does not break down as readily as chlorine does in water. For this reason, most EPA researchers believe that because chloramines last longer, less can be used. They also believe that since they do not break down as readily, there will be less TTHM content in the water supply. In addition, chloramines treatment doesn't affects water's odor and taste as much as standard chlorine treatment.

However, because chloramines do not break down as readily, they provide more potential accumulation risk and thus may be more toxic in the long run. They can also shift from one molecular form to another, from monochloramine to dichloramine to trichloramine. Trichloramine is the most toxic of the three, although the EPA questions its existence in treated waters.

Aquarium fish will typically die in chloramine water. Chloramine stresses the gills of fish, and chloramine content above .3 ppm will kill most fish. The Canadian Environmental Agency (CEPA) reported that water main breaks that released chloramine waters into nearby waterways produced major salmon dieoffs. Chloramines also react with certain rubber materials, damaging hoses and gaskets in dishwashers and washing machines. The State of New Jersey Material Data Sheet on chloramine characterizes it as an irritant that can cause pulmonary edema with higher exposure levels. This is especially true with regard to trichloramine.

There are a number of questionable byproducts as chloramine breaks down. These include the nitrosamine NDMA or dimethylnitrosamine. NDMA was first found in drinking waters in Northern California, and as the California Department of Public Health investigated, they found NDMA in other treated waters, notably those treated with chloramine. Shortly thereafter, the EPA published Method 521 to establish a laboratory means for determining nitrosamine levels in drinking water. The maximum contaminant level or MCL of NDMA has not been determined. The Office of Environmental Health Hazard Assessment set an advisory for NDMA, but no regulation has been established. NDMA is considered a potential carcinogen. Other byproducts suspected from chloramine-treated water include hydrazine and iodoacids. Hydrazine is also considered a possible carcinogen.

Meanwhile, the World Health Organization reports that chloramine is 2,000 times less effective for removing *E. Coli* and 100,000 times less effective for removing rotaviruses. At the same time, the WHO considers chloramine significantly more toxic than chlorination.

One might wonder why the push for chloramine treatment with these facts? The issue at hand is the TTHM levels, which the EPA has put strict limits on. While chloramine may produce reduced levels of these when compared to chlorine, the potential for these other toxins should be reviewed more closely by municipalities and regulatory bodies.

There are options for municipal water treatment. Total TTHMs from chlorine treatment can be reduced with additional filtration and ozone treatment. Anyone with chloramine-treated water should lobby their municipality to discontinue chloramine treatment.

Nature's Filtration Systems

The purity and nutritional abilities of water are tied to its ionic and electromagnetic properties. Water is naturally purified as it is cleansed by the earth's mineral content. The ionic and electromagnetic properties of water are formed as the water flows through the rocks and crevasses of the planet. During this journey, water picks up the ionic charges of a living earth. As a result, water flowing through natural rocks will be cleaner than water that runs through pipes. This is because through polarity, the ions and carbon elements within the rocks magnetically adhere to the toxins and pollutants within the water to draw them out. Rocky purification systems also remove bacteria as well, by providing a level of alkalinity that bacteria do not thrive within. For these reasons, most virgin well water is quite pure and bacteria-free, even if the well lies below a septic field that has toilet water dumped upon it.

While quantum and molecular analysis might tell us that waters with different pH, polarity, spin, and surface tension could be problematic for hydration purposes, the simple solution is to draw water from the natural springs and wells around the planet. This assures us that the water has been cycled through the earth's purification and filtering structures, and given the appropriate mineral content. The process natural water cycles through includes evaporation, pressurization, rainfall and/or snowfall, and then a filtering through the earth's rocks and sediment of the earth. This cycle orients the water to the electromagnetic rhythms of the earth, lending to a specific molecular structure, polarity, pH, spin, and surface tension—the precise specifications our bodies happen to require. Natural rock minerals draw toxins and microorganisms from the water through a process called *adsorption*. Adsorption utilizes Weak Van der Waals forces to attach and adhere to contaminants in water like tiny magnets.

By nurturing and protecting the elements of nature that provide these filtration mechanisms, we assure ourselves the consistency of supply and nutrient content.

The better water's ionic quality, the healthier the water will be. The more effective it will be in hydrating our body. In other words, water that resonates with our body's fluids will be better absorbed and utilized. It will also create less of a burden on our liver, kidneys and other vital organs.

In short, water naturally flowing through the contours of the living planet will have the magnetic polarity and electromagnetic characteristics that closely align with those of the living human body. This statement is supported not simply by a study of one hundred clinical subjects, or even one million subjects. It is supported by billions of subjects over a span of millions of years of drinking the earth's waters. This scientific conclusion comes from the most available and extensive scientific testing imaginable—one where every living organism has taken a part. This million-year epidemiological study has been pervasive, with significant controls and placebos in the form of unseen nutrients, pollutants and infective microorganisms.

On the other hand, those who have more recently died or become sickened by drinking contaminated water provide us with circumstantial evidence that the industrial age has introduced poisons into our water cycle. Basically, humankind has combined nature's chemistry in unnatural ways: ways that encumber the very structural elements that provide purification systems for water. Our pumping one of the earth's natural fluids—petroleum—and then burning and releasing this throughout our environment could be likened to a person forcing his feces into his mouth. Feces might be fine within the colon and decomposing within the soil, but it is not healthy to eat. In the same way, the burning of the earth's petroleum into the atmosphere creates a toxic atmosphere, and the planet is choking on it.

As for dysentery and other diseases caused by waterborne microorganisms, the issue again is related to humankind's lack of respect for nature's cycles. Dysentery and parasites are not necessarily caused by natural water. They are caused by drinking water that has been sitting for too long. Any water that has been sitting without movement for very long will attract microorganisms, especially if there is any kind of organic matter to nourish the microorganisms. Most of nature's fresh water supplies carry organic matter.

This can be proven quite easily: We can take some some clean, fresh spring water (not chlorinated) with little or no microorganism content, and put it in a bowl, and mix some fresh fruit into the water. After about two or three hours, we can put the mixture under a microscope to find it teeming with microorganisms. This is because the water provided a culture medium for microorganism growth. In the very same way, virtually any unchlorinated water pool, pond or lake is likely to carry a number of pathogens.

How did humans survive before chlorination? Humans survived drinking water that flowed through the rocks of streams and outcroppings. Water from clean sources flowing through enough mineralized rocks will provide wholesome and clean drinking water. This is not to say that tainted upstream sources will become clean downstream. The filtration process should involve soil percolation and sufficient mineral rock exposure to remove impurities. This means the water must come into intimate contact with clean soils and mineralized rocks for a considerable amount of time.

Evidence for this is that human populations have thrived from regions where there was plenty of clean water that filtered through mountainous regions. For this reason, we find that many great cultures arose from valleys flowing with waters that filtered down through mountain streams and springs.

We should thus consider not only the source of our water, but its movement. Water sitting for long periods without movement will become a medium for microorganisms unhealthy to the body. On the other hand, water moving over rocks, streams, and aquifers that channel water over naturally electrostatic mineral rocks of various compositions are more suitable to drink both from a nutritional and sanitary perspective. This is reflected by the stronger, healthier organisms that have thrived around clear mountain and valley springs.

Water from a virgin stream flowing gently through the rocks fed from an underground spring in a pristine environment would likely have extraordinary mineral content along with a minimal level of microorganisms. This type of water has the suitable polarity, oxygen content and nutrient levels for healthy consumption.

This type of water is also, as most of us have evidenced by drinking fresh mountain spring water, most refreshing. Fresh spring water simply tastes great. Why? Because our bodies were designed to drink spring water. Our bodies absorb and utilize spring water most efficiently, and spring water is the healthiest type of water for our bodies. Regardless of whether our bodies adapted to the water or whether the water was designed for our bodies, the bottom line is there is a match between the two: Like hand and glove.

Today's rivers and streams are not so virgin. They are likely to host various types of *E. coli* and other bacteria, organophosphates from fertilizers and pesticides, and various other toxins from our industrialized environment. Today, unless the water source is a deep underground aquifer in excess of 500 feet, our water will likely require filtration and/or treatment.

Reverse Osmosis Water Filtration

In other words, unless we live next to a deep well spring or draw from a deep, clean well, we will need to add additional filtration into our drinking water supplies. Certainly, filtration is strongly suggested for any municipal or urban water source. Reverse-osmosis systems are among the most popular water filtration systems. While RO-filtered water has its downsides, RO filters may be appropriate when there is a chemical toxicity not removable through other means of filtration. These can include nitrates and high levels of arsenic.

Reverse osmosis works by pressurizing water through a partially permeable membrane. This membrane will typically have a very small micron size: typically around .001 to .0005 microns in size. Meanwhile toxins and microorganisms typically have micron sizes that range from 1-2 microns down to .005 microns. This means that most microorganisms and toxins will be screened and filtered through a reverse osmosis system.

Prior to the thin membrane, some reverse osmosis filters also have two to three other filtration chambers. Carbon is often used. This means that water will filter through carbon prior to going into the membrane. This will provide two benefits: First, it will remove more impurities. Second, it will speed the flow somewhat by removing as much as possible prior to the thinnest membrane.

One of the downsides to all this filtration is that it can leave the water lacking in mineral and ionic content. Mineral content, as we've discussed, is critical to the hydration factor of water. Minerals are also required for health. While some mineral ions will make it through the sieve, this does not apply to all minerals. Therefore, the resulting water from reverse osmosis may be lacking in a variety of minerals. This may not be a problem if we are getting enough minerals elsewhere in our diet. This would include, of course the many trace minerals that our cells require.

One way to solve this, as we'll discuss in detail later, is natural mined mineral salt. Salts that have been harvested from mines are typically complete with a host of minerals. The two most popular mining regions include the Utah salt mines and the mines of the lower Himalayan Mountains. These salts contain upwards of 60 or 70 trace minerals in natural form. If our water were running through these mines as they had in the past, our water would have these minerals in it.

Using these salts in our cooking or simply stirring a bit into the water be a good way to insure we are getting mineral nutrition. Care must be taken to make sure we have adequate iodine in our diet, however. Iodine is added to processed salts for good reason.

Iodized salts are readily available in most processed foods and can easily be alternated with mineral salts for a guarantee.

Some have accused reverse osmosis systems of removing oxygen from water. This may partially be true when considering a multi-stage pressurized system. Home reverse osmosis systems are typically not very oxygen-poor, however. At any rate, adding oxygen back to water is quite simple. We can simply half-fill a glass bottle, put the lid on and then shake the water before drinking. This will add plenty of oxygen to the water if it is oxygen-poor. Simply stirring water with a utensil can also add oxygen.

While not the best choice for filtration, reverse osmosis may be one of few choices for some households.

Activated Carbon Filtration

Carbon filtration is probably the most used forms of water filtration today. This is because the element of filtration is derived from coal, so it is readily available.

Activated carbon is coal pulverized into a micro-thin powder. The "activation" is because the powder provides more surface area for toxins and bacteria to become attached to. This again is called adsorption. It is the action of toxins becoming attached electro-magnetically and drawn out of the water. Carbon is one of the main elements that nature also uses to filter, as mentioned earlier. By pulverizing the carbon, the journey water has to take is dramatically shortened. Water doesn't have to travel through miles of underground rocks or streams to become purified. It can just run through a matted wall of carbon with a sieve. An ounce of activated carbon powder has roughly an acre of surface area.

This powdered carbon filtration provides a significant reduction in toxicity, typically in the 99% range, depending upon the content of the water. Carbon will not adsorb certain elements however, such as arsenic and nitrates. It will also gradually lose its filtration ability as more and more of the carbon powder is neutralized by the toxins, and thus "deactivated." The carbon powder can also become degraded over time through oxidation.

Carbon filtration systems also utilize granular forms of carbon. This creates a carbon piece that is larger than a grain of powder, and thus able to adsorb a greater quantity of toxins. Granular systems are often used by municipalities.

Carbon filtration systems can effectively remove many microorganisms, chlorine, chlorine byproducts, lead and various other heavy metals, without exhausting the water of many of its mineral qualities. For this reason, carbon filters provide a safe and practical means for protection from contaminants.

Large municipal treatment plants utilize *staged filtration,* using various filter mediums, including sand, lava and other materials. The filter material's mineral content, particulate size and consistency will differentiate its ability to draw out specific contaminants.

Ceramic Filtration

Ceramic filtration more closely approaches what nature does. Ceramic filters are composed of low rock sediment pulverized to increase its surface area. Like carbon, this natural rock surface adsorbs toxins and microorganisms. Some of the same levels of filtration and sometimes even higher can be achieved with ceramic filtration, depending upon the materials used and the pulverization process. Some ceramic filters may also contain small particles of silver. Silver particles help to provide an antibiotic effect upon the water being filtered. Silver is highly toxic to microorganisms, yet healthy for humans.

Ceramic filtration will also provide a healthy dose of mineralization to the water, with little loss of oxygenation. Water filtered through a good ceramic filter would probably come closer to natural spring water than many of the other filtration options.

Ceramic filters are a good choice for several reasons: Ceramic filters use ionic polarity forces of attraction and adsorption similar to the earth's processes of purification through rocks. Ceramic filters are made from rock, clay and other natural materials, so they are environmentally sustainable and more durable.

Ceramic filters also last longer—they treat more gallons and thus 'deactivate' much more slowly. A good ceramic filter can last two or three years in normal household conditions. A consideration to make regarding a ceramic filter unit, however, is that algae may grow on them, requiring periodic scrubbings.

Ultraviolet Filtration

UV-filtration is one of the newest and most intriguing forms of water filtration. This is because UV will break apart many toxins including chlorine, and eliminate most microorganisms without affecting the ionic or mineral properties of the water. In fact, UV-filtration may well add to the ionic nature of the water by helping to free minerals and oxygen for drinking.

UV systems typically contain a UV chamber that introduces a 254-nanometer radiation waveform into the water. This precise waveform damages the genetic material of most microorganisms, destroying their ability to reproduce. It also breaks down key toxins, very similar to the process the sun uses in breaking down chemicals.

Many food manufacturers and pharmaceutical companies utilize UV-filtration systems because of their reliability and efficiency. Because other filtration methods require a constant recharge or change of filters, they are less desirable in the long run. A carbon or ceramic filter can gradually lose its effectiveness throughout the filtration period, leaving the filtered water with some inconsistency. This has minor consequence in a small system as long as filters are changed on time. For larger volume flows, this becomes a bigger issue. In other words, UV-filtration provides a consistent and measurable level of constant filtration.

In a UV-filtration system, however, the bulb will need replacing at some point. Most UV bulbs have particularly long lives. Some bulbs are rated at 9000 hours. This means if a person used their filter two hours per day, the bulb should last about twelve years.

Probably the biggest downside is that UV-filtration systems are typically more expensive than the other forms of water filtration. Costs have been coming down as the technology becomes more available to homeowners.

Ozone Filtration

Ozone filtration systems are also very durable and do not require the filter replacement that carbon and ceramic require. Ozone is made of three oxygen atoms, as opposed to oxygen, which consists of two oxygen atoms. As ozone is shot into the water, the third oxygen atom breaks off and oxidizes contaminates and microorganisms. This oxidation process is not unlike the process that chlorine uses, but the oxidation process of ozone is 150% times more active than chlorine's oxidation. Ozone is usually shot into a water tank through a machine that converts oxygen to ozone. This is a fairly low-energy operation, but it does require electrical energy. The result, however, is highly desirable, as it leaves the water full of oxygen.

Complete ozonation of a water source can be a more expensive proposition than many other filtering choices. The advantages over other filtering and disinfectants are that it leaves oxygen in the water and can remove practically every contaminant, assuming adequate ozone is added. This can be an expensive proposition, however. This is why many municipal ozone treatment plants also supplement their treatment with chlorine.

Survival Purification

The United Nations has suggested that some 25,000 people die every *day* from water-borne illnesses. Most of this is from microorganisms that cause gastroenteritis, dysentery, cholera, giardiasis, malaria and others. By contrast, the CDC reported in its 2008 report on water morbidity and mortality that five people died in 2005-2006 in the U.S. as a result of water-borne illness. Those of us in the modern world have the blessing of water treatment. Many countries do not have this luxury.

The challenge any of us may someday face is being away from any reliable filtering system and being left with questionable water. Water that has been sitting for too long will likely have microorganism content that could make us very ill. This will usually be apparent immediately upon smelling the water. If the water "smells" at all, it is likely contaminated.

There are hundreds of microorganisms that can infect our water. The most common are *Cryptosporidium* spp., *E. coli*, *Giardia lamblia*, *Leptospira* spp., *Salmonella* sp., *Entamoeba histolytica*, *Vibrio cholerae*, and various parasites. These thrive from a combination of standing water and animal feces, as well as from the increased growth of nutrients created by extra nitrogen. These factors point to chemical fertilizers and industrial animal farming.

If we can get the water into a bottle, we can leave the bottle in the sun for several hours. This will kill most of the microorganisms, depending upon the heat of the sun. The sun can be intensified by putting foil or a mirror behind the bottle. The combination of heat and UV rays should kill most of the microorganisms.

A more reliable way to disinfect the water is to boil it. Most microorganisms will die after about five minutes of boiling. Ten minutes is preferable to be on the safe side.

A solar still can also be used to evaporate the water into a basin. Makeshift solar stills have kept many a mariner stranded at sea alive. The basic premise here is that as water is vaporized by the sun, it can be trapped by an overhead plate and dripped down into a lower chamber or pan out of the sun's heat. Here the distilled water will gather, able to quench ones thirst.

If available, iodine may be used, but it will not kill every microorganism. *Cryptosporidium*, for example, is not removed by iodine. Iodine tablets or crystals are usually available from hiking stores. A vitamin C tablet is typically used after the iodine to remove the iodine taste and content from the water.

Certainly chlorine is the easiest solution if it is available. Only a small amount is necessary. Two drops of 5% chlorine bleach to a liter will remove just about every microorganism known to cause illness. The water should then be put aside in the sun for thirty minutes or so. This will help remove some of the chlorine taste and metabolites. Stowing away a small bottle of chlorine bleach into the backpack for a hiking trip is quite an easy proposition.

Distilled Water

While it probably results in some of the highest water purity, distillation is not very efficient, nor does it result in the best quality of water. The evaporation method of distillation naturally leaves out much of the mineral and ionic elements that give the water its nutritional benefit. Water to be distilled must undergo an intense heating process for efficient evaporation. This process effectively leaves behind most of the water's dissolved solids. Minerals and trace elements make up the bulk of dissolved solids.

Indeed, there are many benefits of distilled water for certain purposes. Irons and radiators work better with distilled water because some minerals can corrode certain metals. There are also a few circumstances where distilled water can be used to promote health. These have to do with drawing out certain minerals and toxins from the tissues. This practice, however, should be supervised by a health professional, and distilled water should never be used during fasting.

The concern with distilled water is that its purity attracts and dissolves substances it comes into contact with. This also goes for air. Distilled water draws carbon dioxide from the air, increasing the acidity of the water and giving it free radical properties. Within the body, distilled water will draw minerals from the tissues, and as the water is excreted from the kidneys, there will be a net loss of minerals. Not such a good scenario.

At the same time, if the water is full of salt, nitrates or other difficult toxins to filter, distillation may be one of the few options.

There are many environments where distillation is necessary. In situations where a water source has been intruded with saltwater, or there are poisonous particles in the water, distilled water may be one of the few ways to drink the water. Should we have little or no water and we are surrounded by the salty waters of the ocean, we may need to distill the water to desalinate it. For a thirsty population, this may be a matter of life and death.

The obvious solution for a large desalination treatment process would be to allow the desalinated water to flow through an area with natural rocks to allow it to interact with the planet's mineral content before it is consumed. While desalination is not necessarily an unnatural process (as planet earth also does this), it is unnatural for us to drink it before it comes into contact with the minerals of the earth. Just as the earth circulates minerals as part of its circulatory process, our bodies also require these same minerals for healthy circulation.

Spring Water

We should take a moment to clarify what "spring water" is, because quite frankly, some of the marketing on waters has not been very straight forward with regard to labeling. A spring is a naturally occurring upwelling of water. It comes from a pressurized underground aquifer that pushes the water up to the surface. This is a real spring. Because some loosely use the word 'spring' to describe a stream of mountain water, the word has become somewhat of a misnomer. The likely origin for this misuse of the word is that some mountain streams actually originate from a spring. Some bottled water companies have misused the term 'spring water' on their labeling. They have identified well water as spring water. If the company utilized a pump to extract the water, the water is not spring water.

There are those who propose there is little difference between spring water and well water, but they forget that the earth is exerting a special force upon the water to push it to the surface. This force typically comes from a deep volcanic tube that is alive and generating heat and pressure. Volcanic rock is produced deep within the crust, and is typically made up of an extraordinary assortment of minerals and other nutrients. For this reason, volcanic soils are extremely productive for farming and gardening. Humans thrive from the nutrients in volcanic soils just as these plants do. For this reason, volcanic spring water is to be highly prized.

Spring water is naturally rich in a number of minerals and trace nutrients. Some springs are even naturally carbonated. In these cases, the pressure and heat from the aquifer has forced carbon into the water.

Most health experts agree that real spring water is the most nutritious form of water. Why? Because spring water is naturally filtered, and contains minerals in nature's combinations. This doesn't necessarily mean that today all spring water is clean...

Artesian Water

Artesian water also rises, but it only has to rise up above the level of the aquifer before it can be pumped in order for it to be called artesian. This means there must be some pressure being exerted onto the aquifer, which should also impart an abundance of minerals into the water.

Like spring water, the labeling of artesian waters has at times been loosely regulated. Some court cases have occurred between producers over this issue of definition. These have helped clarify the standard of identity for artesian water. From the illustration on the next page, we can see that the water must flow up to the top of the aquifer. The entire rock region, including the impermeable area is considered the aquifer, not just the water itself as many might assume. While artesian water may be pumped up, it must naturally rise to at least the top of the lowest portion of the aquifer before it can be pumped. If the water is pumped from below this point, it would have to be identified as well water.

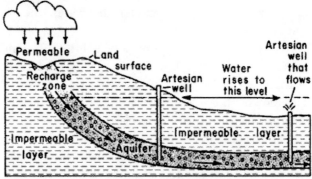

Well recharging and artesian withdrawal (USGS Image)

Well Water

Most well waters are also full of minerals, but likely not to the extent of most spring waters. This is highly dependent upon where the well is, and how deep the aquifer. A deep aquifer in the region of a natural spring may contain similar nutrients in its well water.

Well-drilling enterprises are typically equipped with special drills that will put a hole in the ground up to a thousand feet or more. Most home wells today in the United States draw water from 400-800 feet below the surface. Three or four decades ago, 200-300 feet was typical. This has been the result of finding increased levels of nitrates and other pollutants that have seeped down to these levels. Nitrates come from fertilizers that are put into farmlands, golf courses, parks and yards. These fertilizers have nitrogen-ammonia content that converts to nitrates as it percolates through the soils, as we've discussed.

Drilling deeper usually solves the nitrate problem. That is, until those deeper levels are penetrated with nitrates. The clock is ticking in rural areas surrounded by commercial farms. As long as chemical fertilizers continue to be used, within a few decades most well aquifers within a few miles of farmland will likely be contaminated with nitrates.

Most underground aquifers are recharged annually with rains and/or snowmelt. These wells can remain useful for many decades, and even hundreds of years. If too many people draw from the same aquifer or the aquifer is drawn down too quickly before it can be recharged, there may be trouble, however.

Wells are running dry in some parts of the world, and even some parts of the U.S. For farmers in India, Yemen and other arid parts of the world, wells have run dry, and farmers are scrambling to dig deeper wells or find alternate means of irrigation. This has not been as much of a problem in most regions of the United States. Most of the U.S. gets sufficient rainfall over its mountain ranges. Even an aquifer located hundreds of miles away from a mountain range may be recharged from the rainfall and snowmelt from that mountain range. This is the case for many of the plains areas of the U.S.

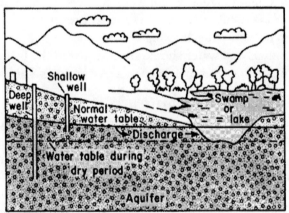

Shallow and deep wells (USGS Image)

This subject brings up the notion of dowsing. While dowsers have been lauded and memorialized as a traditional custom for finding water in many cultures, dowsing techniques remain thus far unproven by modern science. This author has reviewed a number of studies that raise serious doubts about dowsing.

In 1995, the U.S. Department of the Interior reviewed over 500 publications and studies on dowsing. Their conclusion was: *"It is doubtful whether so much investigation and discussion have been bestowed on any other subject with such absolute lack of positive results. It is difficult to see how for practical purposes the entire matter could be more thoroughly discredited, and it should be obvious to everyone that further tests by the United States Geological Survey on this so-called "witching" for water, oil or other minerals would be a misuse of public funds."* (Enright 1995)

We leave this topic with the notion that this does not mean that certain individuals have not had the ability to sense the motion or existence of water many meters below the surface of the earth. Certainly this is may be feasible by especially talented individuals who can sense changes in magnetism. Where are these individuals now, however? Will their results stand up to scientific scrutiny? Unfortunately, scientific review of just about every reputable study has shown no dowser success beyond the possibility of chance.

Depending upon the well's depth, well water may still require filtration. Filtration may be needed to remove nitrates, iron, MTBE and other contaminants. Some wells can also host microorganisms. These wells certainly require filtration to prevent these microorganisms from entering our drinking water.

In general, well water should be considered the healthiest source of drinking water with the exception of spring and artesian water.

Purified Water

Purified water is also somewhat of a misnomer. Purified water sounds pretty nice on a label, especially next to a picture of a beautiful waterfall. However, purified water is often simply municipal tap water run through a filtration system. This filtration system may be carbon filtration, reverse osmosis, UV, distillation or a combination thereof. Purified water is certainly a good choice in the absence of spring water or mineral water. It must, however, be clear that there is no standard on the content of purified water, other than minimum contaminant levels determined by the FDA.

However, if a purified water is produced through distillation, it is not desirable as drinking water. The other methods of filtration are acceptable. Most ultra-filtered 'purified' water producers will also add back minerals to improve the taste. Without these minerals (usually calcium and magnesium), the water would likely be quite unpalatable.

Mineral Water

Most mineral waters come from natural springs or wells that have an abundance of natural minerals. Mineral water is typically defined as requiring 250 parts per million of dissolved solids. These do not have to be particular minerals, but typically, calcium and magnesium make up the bulk of the dissolved solid content. Theoretically, the dissolved solids could also be iron or other less desirable solids, so the consumer should become aware of the water and/or read the label carefully to be sure of its mineral content.

The question is whether some water producers are adding in the minerals to achieve the required levels. This may well be the case, but most producers will not advertise this. We know that some 'natural' sparkling mineral water producers are adding carbon dioxide to the water to increase its carbonation. Theoretically, they are not supposed to add more carbon dioxide than what was originally in the water when it was harvested. But how close are they being watched? Most water producers are only inspected by local health authorities more interested in microorganism contamination.

Still, naturally sparkling mineral waters are typically a joy to drink. They provide great mineral content and their taste makes drinking adequate water much easier.

Hexagonal Water

Over the past few years, the concept of *hexagonal water* and *alkaline-ionized water* has been gaining attention. The research is compelling. As noted earlier, the evidence of water clustering is grounded in science. Through x-ray diffusion, observations of water molecules coming together into group formation bound with weak hydrogen bonds has been clearly documented. At the same time, many prominent scientists have described the health benefits of these waters as pseudoscience.

The debate appears to revolve around the importance of clustering, and whether water clusters provide any specific benefit to the body. Many also argue that even if there is a benefit of water clusters, they are unlikely to remain intact though water's assimilation into the body and cells.

This is because all the empirical data suggest that water clusters are transitory and elusive. They appear momentarily and then disappear just as quickly. More clusters form in the presence of certain dissolved solids, however. Indeed, Dr. Mu Shik Jhon's research has confirmed a link between calcium content and the number of hexagonal clusters observed in the water. Now whether additional hexagonal water encourages additional calcium availability or vice versa, we do not know. Dr. Jhon's position is that hexagonal water allows for better calcium solubility. *In vitro*, it appears from Dr. Jhon's research that water with increased hexagonal structures interferes with cancer cell growth rates. Curiously, it seems that this effect is also associated with calcium availability as well.

In an attempt to sort this out, Jhon measured 3T331 tumor cell growth in three types of solutions: One with unprocessed water; one with calcium chloride ions deposited into the water ($CaCl_2$); and one with calcium chloride ions plus mechanically ionized hexagonal water. By far the fastest tumor growth occurred with the unprocessed water. The two $CaCl_2$ waters had decreased tumor growth. The $CaCl_2$ water alone had a faster immediate reduction of tumor cell growth. However the hexagonal- $CaCl_2$ water began slower but after two days its reduced rate of growth moderately exceeded the $CaCl_2$ alone (Jhon 2004).

This increased effect may have also come from the hexagonal water's extra purity resulting from its treatment. While hexagonal water is portrayed as significantly better water, it also seems credible that that the calcium in the water may provide the alkalinity to have reverse the tumor growth. This would be consistent with the other research involving mineralized water and calcium. In fact, by Dr. Jhon's own admission, calcium provides the core electromagnetic potency for hexagonal water formation. Therefore, the absence of calcium would deter the water's ability to form hexagonal structures.

It should also be noted that this experiment was conducted outside of an environment of a living organism. There is currently little information about the cluster environment within a living organism, because fluids have to be removed in order to be tested.

In the presence of enzymes and nutrients, including calcium and magnesium, a healthy living organism will likely create a significant amount of clustering among its body fluids when compared with a laboratory environment. The logic for this? The body utilizes water for metabolism, which involves ionic exchange. The body's use of water might be compared to electrolytes inside of a battery. There is a constant current running through the water. The body produces concurrent electrolysis and oxidizing reactions—not unlike the machines that produce ionized hexagonal water.

At the end of the day, the earth's natural rocks and soils provide both the minerals and the electromagnetic orientation to allow the body to produce hexagonal structured water. The question, however, is whether the water that we are currently drinking from our faucets or water bottles provides these elements.

Ionized Water

It should be noted that many, though not all, of the hexagonal water advocates also sell expensive ionizing machines. Thus they may be biased by the promise of financial reward. This is not to say that ionizing machines do not produce healthy water: They can. They can enhance a water's pH using electrolysis—comparable to a car battery but without the sulfuric acid. The point of electrolysis is to separate ions by passing the substance through a series of polarized plates. These plates attract certain ions and leave others in the water depending upon the plate polarity and the ionizing machine's electronics.

This separation creates a movement of electrons (anions) to positive poles and positive ions (cations) to negatively charged poles. The questions are; does electrolysis significantly change the nature of water, and does that change survive the body's absorption process?

Pure water at 7.0 pH will contain a balance of mineral ions. Ionized water, depending upon the machine and upon the setting of the machine, can produce water with a pH of as high as 10. This higher pH results from a higher content of mineral ions in that water, and thus those ions will be available for absorption by the body.

It is for this reason that many people have claimed they feel better and their health has improved after drinking ionized water for a period of time. Because electrolysis effectively separates ions by charge, the machine can be adjusted to different settings, producing different pH levels. The ionizer can thus create a high level of alkalinity, and thus higher mineral availability.

As we've reviewed some of the research on mineralized water, we can see that mineral ion availability has many positive health benefits. Do these carry over to ionized water? Little peer-reviewed human research has been done specifically on ionized water, but research on mineral water and mineral ions, especially calcium and magnesium have shown water with healthy mineral ions produce bone, cardiovascular and liver health benefits (Scopacasa *et al.* 1998; Scott *et al.* 1996; Tubek 2006).

There are many other benefits of mineralized waters. Is ionized water simply mineral water, then? We might say that ionized water is like super-mineral water, because the mineral ions have been separated to produce the high alkalinity.

We have to be clear that we cannot actually make water alkaline or acidic. Water has a pH of 7.0 by definition. pH is based upon the balance of ions normally existing in nature's waters. Therefore, alkaline or acidic water does not really exist. There must be some dissolved solid or ion element added making the water more acidic or alkaline. Should we drink water with minerals in it, we will be drinking water with added minerals. The minerals are rendering the alkalinity. We can also drink water with lemon juice added, which will give us an acidic lemon water.

Lemon water brings up a significant point. While lemon water will have a low pH and register as an acid, the body will be influenced towards alkalinity once we drink it. This is because of the nutrient components of the lemon juice. The intestinal tract and its sodium ion channels correct the acidic issues of the solution upon absorption. However, the nutritional elements of lemon juice are particularly healthy for us, especially the citric acid and bioflavonoid. It is these residual nutrients in lemon juice (along with the water) that are ultimately nourishing to the body. This also applies to mineral ions within healthy water.

If our incoming water is tainted with toxic chemicals, ionizers will typically do a good job of separating contaminants from mineral ions, creating a filtered water with plenty of ions and a higher pH. This should be quite healthy to drink, and if we drink enough of this water, we should surely have health benefits because of its retained ion content.

Certain electrolysis ionizers claim to decrease cluster size. Whether these smaller clusters indeed increase water absorption and utilization is not proven, however. Surely electrolysis that produces higher mineral ion content should change the clustering of the water, and research has indicated this is true. Again, however, observations of cluster sizes and hydrogen ion superstructures have made outside of living organisms.

Most of our water is absorbed through either the stomach or the small intestine. This immediately affects the body's hydration levels within the blood and the liver. Water is absorbed through sodium ion channel diffusion within the intestinal membrane and gastric cells. Following this absorption, the body's liver interacts with the water, separating ions, solids and toxins. Thus, we might call the liver a tiny water ionizer.

The evidence for ionic water health benefits may not be convincing to everyone, but there is significant anecdotal discussion of its validity. Could this be a placebo effect? Truly, any chemist will accept that while water travels through volcanic rock, there is an ionic exchange taking place, leaving the water mineralized and thus "harder." To ignore the possibility that this mineralization takes place within water ionizers may also prove to be shortsighted. Certainly, evidence and experience clearly points to the reality that the earth's circulatory system is suited to render the best form of water for human consumption. If we cannot find any more of this water due to our destruction of our natural waters is there any harm in trying to duplicate nature's ionization process?

Typically, a water molecule has a tetrahedral angle. The oxygen ionic element is flanked by two hydrogen ions. Between each water molecule flank is a weak ionic bridge. This weak bridge allows water to cluster somewhat, giving water its surface tension. Through the work of Nobel Laureate Dr. Carlo Rubbia, it has been determined that these weak bonds are stimulated through an interaction with light, aligning each water molecule in a slightly different way. This results in each molecule of water having a unique electromagnetic frequency, depending upon its unique orientation with natural light. These are subtle bonding effects, synchronized by nature through resonation.

What the human body needs is natural living water. Living water is pure water that has been circulating through the living planet earth. As it has been circulating, it becomes ionized and alkalinized. These waters directly balance the acidic nature of our body's waste and toxin metabolism. Our body's metabolic process produces various waste products, most of which are acidic. If these are not neutralized by a fresh supply of mineral ions, they can damage our blood vessels, livers, kidneys and urinary tract.

The minerals like magnesium and calcium gathered from natural rock are merely residuals of the water's natural movements. This is the observable portion. Behind these minerals are the water's waveforms—some might also call these weak bonds—generated partially by the movement of the water through the rocks and partially by the various magnetic influences of nature's other elements. The dissolved ions existing in living water are simply one result of the water's interaction with nature. Water's subtle electromagnetic properties make water the universal solvent and foundation for metabolism.

Just as the physical body was designed to digest natural foods and produce vitamin D from natural sunlight, the body was designed to drink natural waters of rhythm.

Now if we live in an urban area where our only available municipal water sources are particularly toxic and questionable, and we have some extra disposable income, then we might consider purchasing an ionizer. Drinking this ionized water should be a great improvement over the water that is probably coming out of our tap.

On the other hand, for those of us without this kind of cash-flow, a ceramic or carbon filter should be sufficient.

Rainwater

While rainwater sounds like a great means for pure water hydration, it is actually not. Rainwater typically has a pH in the region of about 5.6 to 5.8 due to airborne carbonic acid. Levels below this (less than 5.6 pH) are considered *acid rain*. When carbon dioxide dissolves in the presence of water, it forms carbonic acid: The more carbon dioxide presence in the air, the greater the carbonic acid formation. Thus, most of our rain is primarily acidic in nature, and is not exactly the best source of hydration.

Certainly we can assume that rainwater was an excellent source of hydration before humankind began dumping toxins into the atmosphere. Because carbon dioxide has been present in our atmosphere for millions of years, we know (also from ice cores) that rainwater has always had some acidity. However, only extreme atmospheric situations such as an intense volcanic eruption could approach the acidity created by the massive carbon monoxide levels created by humankind's endeavors over the past century.

Many catchment systems utilize rainwater as a primary water source. While this is certainly better than no water, a better strategy would be to collect that rainwater within a *cistern* holding tank met with a ceramic or gravel filtration process inserted between the cistern and the faucet. Ceramic filtration might also help, to expose the water to some of the earth's natural minerals.

Water Absorption

The simple reason our bodies continue to survive in a chronically dehydrated state is due to the resiliency of water combined with the body's ability to conserve water when dehydrated.

When it is hit with polluted, toxic water, a healthy body will work to purify and molecularly orient the water for cellular use. The body will strip water of many chemicals through its passage through the digestive tract and liver. Before water is assimilated through the walls of the stomach and intestines, the stomach's secretions provide acidity to help rid it of microorganisms.

Ironically, these excretions are also primarily composed of water. Stomach acids produced by gastric cells from a healthy stomach wall lining will destroy most microbial content. After this sterilization phase, the sodium ion channels within the intestinal and gastric walls diffuse the water through to the bloodstream, which channels it through the liver for further purification.

A healthy liver will process about 1500 ml (about 50 ounces) of blood per minute. The water-blended blood is commingled within well cavities called sinusoids, where it is staged through stacked sheets of the liver's primary cells—called hepatocytes. Here blood is also met by interspersed macrophage immune cells called kupffer cells. These kupffer cells attack and break apart bacteria and toxins. Hepatocytes further filter and purify the blood before it is dumped back into the bloodstream. The hydrated blood travels out through the hepatic veins and into the inferior vena cava, where it is then pumped through the heart, oxygenated by the lungs, and then pumped into circulation.

The kidneys also provide a filtering function, as the glomerulus cells filter and recycle water back into the bloodstream.

If the gastric pit cells are not producing large enough quantities of hydrochloric acid and peptic acid; and the colonies of probiotics in our mouth and intestines are not strong enough, the intestines may allow entry of microorganisms with our water. The healthier the stomach lining and the better its secretions; the less likely bacteria will pass through the stomach to the intestines. Should enough bacteria pass through, dehydration becomes a new concern, as watery diarrhea caused by microorganisms and can cause a huge loss of fluid. Dehydration due to diarrhea is one of the main causes of death in dysentery and choleric situations.

In general, our bodies can handle and use surprisingly large quantities of contaminated water and remain alive. However, the collateral damage must be considered. Our concern with contaminated water becomes the burden on the liver and the body's various detoxification systems. When we consider the many toxins the body must deal with coming in from our air, food and water, in addition to the other thousands of metabolic tasks the liver must accomplish, burdening the liver is of critical importance to the long-term survival of the body. The liver itself performs many critical tasks: from secreting bile and digestive enzymes to filtering and recycling blood and assembling nutrients for the body's use. To overburden the liver with toxicity will eventually overload it, reducing its life expectancy and performance.

Bottled Water

We might assume bottled water is cleaner than municipal tap water. Bottled water is regulated in the United States by the Food and Drug Administration, while municipal tap water is regulated by the Environmental Protection Agency. The FDA rarely if ever tests bottled waters—unless there is a mass complaint or scare. Meanwhile, the EPA requires multiple daily tests on municipal supplies. Municipalities are also mandated to publish all test results. The

FDA mandates weekly testing are done by commercial bottled water companies, but those records are rarely if ever inspected, and are not available to the public or any public agency. In addition, bottled water brands are not required to reveal the source of their water. Does this mean that municipal water is cleaner than bottled water? Maybe, or maybe not. The point is that we don't know.

Plastic can leach a number of chemicals into the water in the presence of light and heat. The extent of leaching can vary, depending upon the grade of the plastic, the extent of exposure and the length of exposure. There are a number of grades and types of plastic now being used to store and ship water and other drinks. The grade and type of plastic bottle is stamped onto the bottom of most plastic bottles. This number is called a resin ID code. Often it will appear within a small three-arrow recycling triangle symbol. The number code indicates the grade and type of plastic.

There are seven basic codes in current use. There is polyethylene terephthalate (PET) usually marked with the number 1; polyvinyl chloride (PVC) (#3); polypropylene (PP) (#5); polystyrene (PS) (#6); polycarbonate (PC) (#7); and two types of polyethylene—high density (HDPE) (#2) and low-density (HDPE) (#4). #7 may also be nylon, acrylic, acrylonitrile butadiene styrene or a number of similar composite types.

Polyethylene terephthalate or PET is now probably one of the most distributed water container types, especially for smaller sizes. Most sodas and soft drinks, along with various waters, are now bottled in these containers. PET is a thermoplastic polymer resin, part of the polyester family. PET bottles may be clear or opaque. Most PET is made with a trans-esterification reaction between ethylene glycol (yes that green stuff put into radiators) and dimethyl terephthalate. The ethylene glycol is the typical byproduct of polymerization of PET. While resonated PET is very strong, unmodified PET's melting point is below the boiling point. Modified PET, used for most food applications, is more stable: it can be heated to 180 degrees Celsius for 30 minutes without melting. Most PET will have a *glass temperature* (the level where its molecules have more mobility) of about 75 Celsius, which is about 167 degrees Fahrenheit. In other words, this is the point where molecules of the plastic may leach indiscriminately into the liquid or food present.

However, this is a sliding scale and minute leaching begins at much lower temperatures. Research has confirmed that heat leaching is higher when PET is exposed to direct sunlight. At temperatures above room temperature or even at room temperature for extended periods, significant leaching of toxins from PET has been observed. Up to 19 different migrating chemicals have been observed from commercial amber PET bottles. Various fatty acids, plasticizers, and acetaldehyde have been discovered in PET research. Furthermore, foods microwaved in PET have revealed significant levels of cyclic oligomers. It is also thought that cyclic oligomers from PET bottles may also leach due to sun exposure.

That said, PET has undergone extensive toxicology and risk assessment research. *In vivo* and epidemiological studies—many of which were extensively documented by a 2000 report by the International Life Sciences Institute—have indicated that toxicity due to PET leaching is below levels thought to pose an immediate threat to our health. Certainly, the body has tremendous abilities of detoxification and adaptation. However, we must also consider their toxicity upon those whose immune systems are burdened. Whether PET-leaching toxins are significant toxins or merely additional toxins adding to the total stress burden on the body—they are still a concern. While small amounts might not pose a concern for the body's detoxification systems, continuous exposure is likely to cause a host of possible disorders over time. In other words, we have yet to realize the long term risks of PET.

Polyvinyl chloride or PVC plastic will typically be coated with a plasticizing resin called di-2-ethylhexyl-phthalate, usually referred to as DEHP. Along with several types of plastic bottles, DEHP is a popular coating on rubber hoses. Many hiking and camping bottles are made with PVC coated with DEHP. Many of us have probably drunk out of a PVC bottle on a bike or hike. After a few hours in the sun, the water will have a strong plastic odor and taste. The Environmental Protection Agency has determined that the MCLG or *Maximum Contaminant Level Goal* for DEHP is set at zero, while the regulated MCL requirement is set at six parts per billion in public drinking water. This means the aim is zero, but the reality is much higher. According to the EPA, nausea, vertigo and gastrointestinal pains are associated with short-term exposure (drinking);

while liver damage, genital and reproductive damage, and cancer are noted as potential effects of long-term use of DEHP. PVC is also a popular material used in various toys. These toys should be eliminated from kids' rooms, as they will release DEHP when they are played with. Medical grade silicone nipples and teethers are probably better choices than PVC toys. Even better are natural materials.

Polycarbonate bottles should be avoided especially if exposed to heat. Baby bottles and various types of water bottles are often made of PC. PC is also used in medical devices, dentistry, lenses, and clear storage containers. PCs are made using Bisphenol-A (or BPA). As a result, PCs are known to leach BPA into bottle contents as heat is applied. BPA is a monomer and considered an endocrine disruptor. Ironically, BPA was first synthesized in the 1930's for estrogen replacement. Research indicates that BPA appears to have negative effects upon physiological development, growth, memory, behavior, skeletal formation, prostate size, sperm count, and may be implicated in the Alzheimer epidemic. As mentioned earlier, BPA is xenoestrogenic. This means it mimics estrogens, and more than one study has linked it with dramatically increasing estrogen levels because of its affect upon estrogen receptors. This makes PC a potential contributing factor in the dramatic rise in breast cancer. Breast cancer does seem to occur more prominently in cultures with prevalent plastics exposure.

Plastic bottles with both low-density and high-density polyethylenes (LDPE and HDPE) have been known to leach polyalkylated phenols such as BHT and Irganox 1640 into their contents. Interestingly, both of these chemicals are also commonly used as chemical preservatives in food production. Their toxicity is not well established. The stabilizers used in polypropylene production have been observed as bioactive, indicating they may also be leaching into contents. Some of these are suspected to inhibit nerve conductance. Heat and light cause the most leaching of LDPE and HDPE, although the higher density polypropylenes appear to leach less.

While the cumulative effect of these compounds entering our bodies for many years has yet to be determined, there is some evidence that most plasticizers are estrogenic, which means that they can attach to estrogen receptors, and thus confuse the body's stimulation of different mechanisms such as growth and inflammation.

Estrogen ligand and receptor balance is also critical to our flow of various other hormones and neurotransmitters such as serotonin, dopamine, progesterone and many others. We should also note that rates of menopause, chronic fatigue disorders and breast cancers, all directly related to the balance of hormones, have been rising dramatically over the past 20 years.

Municipal tap water with a good filtration system provides a viable alternative to the plasticizers from plastic bottles.

The Environmental Costs of Bottled Water

In 2007, Americans drank nearly 9 billion gallons of bottled water, up nearly 7% from 2006, and more than double a decade earlier. The Pacific Institute estimated that 20 million barrels of oil are used per year to produce plastic water bottles. Ironically, about 1.85 gallons of water are also required to manufacture an average-sized plastic water bottle. About 72 billion gallons of fresh water are used per year to make empty plastic bottles.

Only about 20% of these plastic bottles are recycled. Roughly 60 million plastic water bottles are thrown away in the U.S. *each day*.

Furthermore, much of the plastic used for our water bottles is manufactured in China. China provides some of the lowest-cost plastic among the world's suppliers, and huge tanker ships navigate the oceans filled with container loads of plastic. Then (unless the water bottling plant has the injection molding equipment) the bottles are molded from plastic pellets at a bottle production plant. The empty molded bottles are then shipped to a water-bottler for filling. Once filled, the bottled water is then shipped to distributors, and the distributors ship the bottled water to the retailers. Consumers go to the retailer stores and carry the bottled water back home in their vehicles. So how many transportation miles do bottled waters travel to get to the consumer's home? Certainly a lot more than water coming out of the faucet travels.

Bottled water can undergo significant environmental exposure during all this transportation and storage. Once the water is extracted from its well, aquifer, or municipal reservoir—and many bottled waters are simply filtered municipal tap waters—it is usually filtered by distillation, reverse osmosis, or a combination of the two. Some might refer to reverse osmosis as triple filtration because it travels through three filtration membranes. Sometimes selected minerals are added back for taste—because our bodies naturally prefer mineralized water. Once filled into plastic or glass bottles, the water is then shipped around the world.

During this distillation and shipping process, different environmental exposures may affect the purity and stability of the water. Certainly we can agree that this water is far removed from the natural ionic waters nature produces. Shipping via modern transportation will expose the water to temperature fluctuations. This will cause the leaching of plasticizers and organochlorines from the plastic into the water.

Overseas water may be loaded onto a container ship from a hot, tropical environment, from where it undergoes a lengthy ocean voyage in the hold or on deck. Either location opens the possibility of extremes in temperature. Once arriving at the port, the water may undergo irradiation, which can cause further leaching. From the dock, the water will undergo other temperature changes and light exposure on its way to distributors and stores. By the time this water ends up in our mouth it may have undergone months of transportation and warehousing—most of it within a plastic container. Each of these environments induce different levels of heat, light and pressure variance. The unfortunate result may be a water full of leached plasticizers and other chemicals as mentioned.

In a 1997-1999 multi-year study of bottled waters by the Natural Resources Defense Council, over 1,000 bottles of water from 103 brands were tested for contaminants after reaching the shelves. Over one-third of the bottled water samples turned out to have contaminant levels greater or equal to levels typical of municipal tap water supplies. A third of 103 different bottled waters tested violated state limits or guidelines, with 22% violating enforceable limits, and 17% violating government water guidelines for municipal water treatment.

In addition to the purity issues, and the potential damage transportation and leaching effects, we should consider the environmental impact of all this carbon-intensive transportation. For a commodity most Americans can access from local reservoirs and aquifers, it appears financially and economically idiotic to waste our resources on shipping water around the world. Yet according to the

International Bottled Water Association, bottled water sales have grown from almost nil in the 1980s to over twenty-seven gallons per person in 2006. In just under twenty years, total gallons of bottled water sold burgeoned from less than 300,000 gallons in 1976 to more than 3,000,000 gallons per year in 1997. Imagine the waste in resources over this twenty-year growth period. These shipments could have just as well been grain shipped to the hungry. Today as we peruse our shelves at the store, we can see the distance some of our commercial waters travel: Fiji, Italy, Switzerland, and Hawaii. Often a single water shipment will take up an entire cargo hold of a ship.

While the water itself in a bottle of water might cost only a few cents, more than 90% of its total value comes from the activities of forming and packing the plastic bottle, shipping it, and paying the margins of distributors and shippers. Some have estimated that the cost of a bottle of water is 240 to 10,000 times the cost of filtering and purifying the same amount of tap water.

As far as containers go, glass containers are by far the most natural and resilient—made primarily of sand. Glass is extremely stable when exposed to light, pressure, and reasonable heat because of its elemental stability. Clay and ceramic containers, assuming they are made with natural clays or rocks tested for heavy metals and coated (if at all) with natural finishes, should also be considered. Porcelain cups are typically made from ceramic material and/or clay, and soft-paste porcelain is made with a mix of clay and glass. These are acceptable, assuming again, they are coated with natural finishes. Lead-based finishes are sometimes applied to cup ware, which is not suggested for hot liquids.

By far the most environmentally feasible and safest water container is simply a glass from our kitchen filled with well-filtered tap or well water.

~ Five ~
Therapeutic Water

Water is not just a hydration element. Water has been used in medicine for thousands of years. In fact, it is one of the oldest healing agents documented. Early hydrotherapy practice has been documented in ancient Ayurvedic medicine and Chinese medicine; as well as the medicines of the Greeks, Polynesians, Aborigines, North American Indians, Incas, Mayans, Japanese, and Egyptians.

Hippocrates was a proponent of hydrotherapy, and hydrotherapy treatment centers were very popular in Europe and the United States in the eighteenth, nineteenth, and early twentieth centuries. Vincent Priessnitz from Austria popularized many types of water treatments, including water compresses, cold-water therapy, and warm baths in the early nineteenth century.

Dr. Wilhelm Winternitz, an Austrian neurologist, observed one of Priessnitz's treatment centers and became one of the most celebrated proponents of water treatment. Dr. Winternitz designed a number of different water treatments and influenced American physicians such as Dr. John Harvey Kellogg, Dr. Jethro Kloss and Dr. Simon Baruch. Dr. Kellogg operated the famous Michigan Battle Creek Sanitarium for many years until it burnt down in 1902. The center utilized hydrotherapy as a healing agent. Dr. Kloss ran his own clinic and worked closely with the Battle Creek Sanitarium.

Despite its history of success, opposition to hydrotherapy came from pharmaceutical medicine circles in the decades following. Water cures became a target for the new medical establishment, and many hydrotherapy treatment centers were shut down between 1920 and 1950. Hydrotherapy experienced a resurgence in the U.S. following the post-World War II popularity of swimming pools and whirlpools. Today hydrotherapy is widely used in various modalities, treatments, and centers. Many new hot springs and wellness centers are unmistakably similar to the "sanitarium" centers. Today, many draw millions of people seeking both therapy and relaxation.

Physical therapists use hydrotherapy to retrain and nurture injured or post-surgical limbs. Water aerobics has become the quintessential form of exercise for the elderly because of its low impact and low stress on joints. Colon hydrotherapy is now used throughout the world to cleanse the colon of putrefied waste. Hot baths are now regularly recommended by conventional doctors for relieving stress and muscle fatigue. Many Americans sport hot tubs in or around their homes. While the sophisticated use of hydrotherapy is still considered alternative, most conventional physicians agree that water therapy can stimulate circulation and healing. A recent Italian study (Municino *et al.* 2006) of eighteen advanced heart failure patients using hydrotherapy illustrates this effect. After three weeks of daily water training, cardiopulmonary tests and quality of life all increased substantially.

Research has also confirmed that living near or exercising in water significantly lowers the risk and incidence of asthma. A number of studies have confirmed swimming reduces asthma occurrence. In two studies investigating whether swimming itself reduced asthma or whether weather or greater humidity near the water reduced asthma incidence in children, it was determined that just the act of swimming (over other forms of exercise) reduced asthma incidence (Inbar *et al.* 1980).

Most of us have experienced the soothing nature of warm water, or the energetic nature of cool or cold water. Water carries electromagnetic, thermal and of course fluid rhythms that balance the nervous system and the cardiovascular system. While water is by no means a cure-all, when used conjunctively with other natural healing processes, water has many powerful effects upon the body.

Hot and Cold Water

Hot and warm water increase circulation, relaxation (thus decreasing stress), joint movement range, and detoxification efforts. Hot water calms the body and slows the heart rate, as the body's blood vessels relax and dilate in response to thermal radiation.

Cold water constricts the blood vessels and leads to involuntary muscle contraction. This type of muscle contraction increases the body's immune function by pumping the lymphatic system. Lymph flow is circulated by movement and muscle contraction. Lymph circulation distributes macrophages and B cells throughout the body, enabling them to break down invading bacteria, viruses, and chemical toxins. In a German study (Goedsche *et al.* 2007) on twenty patients with chronic obstructive pulmonary disease, cold-water hydrotherapy was tested for immunostimulation, maximal expiratory flow, quality of life, and level of respiratory infection. After ten weeks of three cold effusions and two cold washings on the upper body per day, IFN-gamma lymphocytes increased, quality of life increased, and the frequency of infection decreased throughout the study group.

The Contrast Bath

For tight joints or sprains, we can alternate hot water and iced water. This is also called a contrast bath. The sprained or injured area may be placed into a bucket or pan of iced water, holding until the area begins to feel numb. The injured area can then be put into a tub or pan of hot water (test to prevent scalding). This can be held for several minutes, until the skin feels hot. The process can be repeated a number of times. If the injury is not a muscle or tendon tear—slightly moving the joint a little while numb may help speed healing. This will increase the microcirculation at the capillary level.

As reported by Preisinger and Quittan (2006) from the University of Physical Medicine and Rehabilitation in Wein Germany, muscle spasms were reduced by the application of hot and cold waters. While cold was more effective for reducing spasticity in motor neuron lesions, joint stiffness was reduced with hot water application. They also reported that pain threshold—the ability to endure pain—was increased by combined hot and cold water therapy.

Cold Showers

Daily cold water showers or a quick cold water rinse off after a warm water shower is invigorating and stimulating to the immune system and nervous system. It also helps balance the body's thermoregulation systems, cooling the body in hot weather, and heating the body (through muscle contraction) in cold weather.

As the cold water hits the skin, internal muscles autonomically contract. This effectively "pumps" the lymphatic system. Increasing the circulation of the lymphatic system in turn stimulates the flow of T-cells, B-cells, probiotics and other immune system mechanisms. Increasing lymph flow also increases detoxification, as lymph also carries toxins out of the body.

A cold shower also causes the skin pores to close. This leaves the body prepared to step out of the shower or bath. This reduces the potential of a basal cell chilling, which can stress the body. A cold shower will better prepare the body for the temperature change. Blood vessel constriction from cold water also stimulates the contraction of blood vessel walls. This serves to increase blood vessel wall elasticity, especially when the cold shower follows a warm or hot shower.

Sauna and Cold Plunge

Another way to accomplish this is the Finnish sauna and plunge system. The Fins are famous for their wooden saunas, built outside, near a cold-water plunge. A vigorous sweat in the sauna is immediately followed by the cold plunge. This ritual has also been a part of other cultures, including many American Indian tribes, who used *sweat lodges* with great health benefits. These cultures have a tradition of living long lives with strengthened immunity. (Note that cold showers are not advised after infrared saunas—warm is better here.)

The Hot Bath

The hot bath is an incredibly healing proposition. Hippocrates, known to western medicine as the father of medicine, stated that the hot bath *"...promotes expectoration, improves the respiration, and allays lassitude; for it soothes the joints and the outer skin, and is diuretic, removes heaviness of the heat and moistens the nose."*

A hot bath will open skin pores, allowing a detoxification and exfoliation of skin cells and their contents. For sore or damaged muscle tissues, the dilation of capillaries and micro-capillaries speeds up the process of cleansing the muscle cells of lactic and carbonic acids—the byproducts of cellular energy production.

Recovery times from strenuous activity are typically reduced by the use of hot water therapy. It should be noted that too much hot water for too long of a period can lead to cardiovascular stress should one not be accustomed to it. Hot water can also lead to heat exhaustion.

For best results, hot water applications or saunas should be limited to about 10-15 minutes at the hotter levels. This can be increased for lower temperatures. In a 2006 review by French *et al.*

from the *Monash Institute of Health Services*, hot- and cold-water treatments were compared and analyzed for the treatment of low back pain. They reviewed nine different trials on 1117 patients. They concluded that heat therapy was successful at reducing acute and sub-acute low-back pain. Another review of studies (McCarty *et al.* 2009) showed that regular thermal therapy, including hot baths and saunas, could improve insulin sensitivity similar to physical exercise.

Hot water also slows internal organ activity. This provides a soothing effect upon the innervations of these organs. The result is a calming of nervous tension.

Hot water is also *hydrostatic*—it gently massages the dermal layers. This effect increases microcirculation while relaxing and soothing muscles and nerves. This effect is increased when hot water is in motion, for example in a hot tub or whirlpool.

Hot water can also relax key intestinal issues. In a study of 18 healthy volunteers and 28 patients with anorectal disease, 10-minute baths at 40, 45 and 50 degrees Celsius were tested for rectal neck pressure and internal sphincter stress. The hotter bath temperature produced significantly better test results and better pain scores (Shafik 1993). (Always test hot water to prevent scalding.)

Hot Mineral Springs

From the deep within the earth's surface come special waters of a thermal nature. Geothermal heat from volcanic magma creates a ripe environment for heating and charging aquifers with high temperatures and a variety of minerals. For thousands of years, humans have revered hot springs therapy. Hippocrates, for example, was a great fan of thermal springs for therapeutic use. In his *Use of Liquids* treatise, Hippocrates spoke highly of the use of both hot water and thermal mineral springs. He proposed their use produces healing effects for many different ailments.

Today, thermal hot springs, many boasting ancient origins and use over centuries, exist all over the world.

Due to the earth's sulfur conveyor system, many of these hot springs waters are rich in sulfur in the form of hydrogen sulfide or sulfate along with other minerals. A hot spring can contain a wholesome mixture of bicarbonate, iron, boron, silica, magnesium, copper, lithium, and many other minerals. Some contain exotic elements such as arsenic—believed to help heal skin issues and digestive issues. In other words, not all hot springs are alike.

For example, the mineral content at the *Avila Hot Springs* in Avila Beach, San Luis Obispo County, California has the following content:

Minerals-Avila Hot Springs	Content
Sodium	326 milligrams per liter
Silica	72 milligrams per liter
Iron	25 milligrams per liter
Calcium	68 milligrams per liter
Magnesium	42 milligrams per liter
Chloride	83 milligrams per liter
Bicarbonate	1049 milligrams per liter
Sulfate	46 milligrams per liter
Borate	17 milligrams per liter

Avila's hot spring pushes up from hundreds of feet beneath the surface at around 130-135 degrees F. The water is mixed with cooler waters at the surface, where the therapeutic pools are kept at about 104 degrees F year round. The flow of this spring has been constant for the over 100 years that the hot springs pools have been operated. Prior to this, several springs here and up to 50 miles north in Paso Robles, CA were highly regarded for centuries by the Salinan Indians, who therapeutically bathed in these waters for relief from injuries and ailments.

Research has supported the value of hot mineral springs therapy. Researchers from the Faculty of Health Sciences of Israel's Ben-Gurion University and Soroka University Medical Center conducted a randomized, controlled and single-blinded study to test whether sulfur baths offered any real benefit to osteoarthritis patients. Forty-four osteoarthritis of the knee patients were divided into two groups. The first took two baths per week for six weeks in a sulfur-treated pool heated to 35-36 degrees Celsius (about 96-97 degrees Fahrenheit). The other group took two baths per week for six weeks in a pool at the same temperature but filled with tap water. The group treated with sulfur baths had significantly less pain that lasted six months following the treatment period.

Sulfur has been known for its ability to speed the healing of joints and connective tissues. Sulfur in the form of MSM (methylsulfonylmethane) has been demonstrated to relieve joint inflammation and pain. In one study (Kim *et al.* 2006), 50 patients with knee osteoarthritis took MSM for 12 weeks. The MSM group had significantly less pain and significantly more mobility than the placebo group.

Another form of sulfur is DMSO, or dimethyl sulfoxide. DMSO is a byproduct of the wood pulp industry. Its use dates back to 1953, when it was used as a solvent. In 1961, Stanley Jacob, M.D. noticed that DMSO readily penetrated the skin and seemed to relieve pain. Since then, thousands of medical papers and even some clinical studies and veterinary use have confirmed DMSO's ability to reduce pain and inflammation. Reports have confirmed that DMSO blocks nerve transmission (Evans et al. 1993). It relieves pain and inflammation in chronic musculoskeletal injuries such as rotator cuff tendonitis and tennis elbow injury (Lockie and Norcross 1967; Percy and Carson 1981). It reduces urinary tract inflammation (Shirley et al. 1978) and rheumatoid arthritis (Matsumoto 1967).

Sulfur is the third most prevalent mineral in the body by weight (Parcell 2002). It is utilized as a component in many enzymes, and is a central component of many cellular structures, including those of the skin, bones and cartilage. Sulfur is also utilized in an enzyme used by chondrocytes to produce cartilage. The dramatic effects gained by MSM and DMSO are unlikely in a sulfur mineral springs. However, because the active ingredient in both is sulfur, and because DMSO in particular can easily penetrate the skin, it is likely that the sulfur ions in mineral springs provide significant therapeutic effects if used on a regular basis.

Other mineral ions in hot springs have beneficial effects. Magnesium has been shown in many studies to relax muscles and ease tension. Magnesium also strengthens arteries and cardiac muscle. Calcium, of course, helps build bones and connective tissue. Calcium is also beneficial for the cardiovascular system.

Iron in hot springs has been associated with strengthening the immune system.

Bicarbonate in hot springs—also called "soda springs"—has been associated with easing tension and aiding digestion..

Mineral springs have also shown to have beneficial effects to the skin. A study at the thermal hot springs waters of Comano, Italy (Zumaini 1986) tested 39 patients with psoriasis. After 3-6 months of regular bathing in the hot springs, the average reduction in psoriasis lesions was about 50%. The authors also documented the compete regression of psoriasis in a number of the subjects.

Luckily, there are hot springs located in many regions around the world: A great way to relax and stimulate healing, and a healthy vacation idea at the very least.

The Epson Salt Bath

For those without a nearby hot springs, a simple bath can be easily turned into therapeutic waters. At home, we can duplicate a magnesium and sulfur mineral springs bath by adding natural mineral salts such as Epson salts to our bath water. Epson salts— originally named after the magnesium-rich waters of Epson, England—are primarily magnesium sulfate, which will ionize in the water into magnesium ions and sulfur ions. As mentioned, ionic magnesium is beneficial to body tissues, relaxing skin and muscle tension, and lowering stress. Sulfur was also discussed above.

The Epson salt bath can be supplemented with the addition of rock salt. Natural rock salt contains upwards of 80 minerals and trace elements, which can make the bath a nourishing soak for the entire body.

A drop or two of an essential oil such as lavender or rose oil into the bath will further support relaxation. Lavender oil in particular can significantly calm the nerves. In one study of seventy elderly patients with dementia, lavender aromatherapy significantly reduced agitation among the patients (Lin *et al.* 2007).

The skin is said to be the largest organ of the body and absorbs water quite readily. The skin is similar to a mucous membrane. The ancient seamen understood this fact well. When out to sea and the ship's water ran out, they would soak their garments in seawater to become at least partially hydrated.

For this same reason, our bath waters should not contain toxic chemical bubble baths, chemical-laden perfumed soaps, or heavily chlorinated water. The skin will readily absorb these toxins, putting an extra burden upon the liver and detoxification systems. Best to use filtered water and only natural additives.

The Sitz Bath

The sitz bath is sometimes thought of as a foot bath. This is actually a feet and hip bath. The sitz bath stimulates detoxification and relaxation for injuries, and cramping of the abdomen, hips, legs, and feet. The sitz is accomplished by sitting in a large washtub while putting the feet into another. The foot tub is heated about five degrees F hotter than the larger tub. The water level on the big tub can be about belly button high. A towel or blanket is laid over the exposed body to increase sweating. Best to cool the water for a few minutes before exiting the bath or get out when it naturally cools to room temperature. Epson salts and a drop or two of lavender can be used to provide additional therapy.

The Foot Bath

The foot bath is a great way to ease sore feet, increase circulation, ease chills, and ease abdominal cramping. The tub can be ankle to knee deep. Water is heated gradually from warm to very hot while feet are in. A blanket or loose clothing can cover the rest of the body up to the neck. A cold compress on the nape of the neck provides an extra therapeutic effect. 15 to 30 minutes is the recommended duration. Again, Epson salts may be added for additional therapy. Eucalyptus can be added along with a blanket wrap to ease congestion.

The Hose Bath

The hose bath is performed with one person spraying a hose from about ten to fifteen feet away from the subject, spraying up and down the spine, throughout the body. This can stimulate the immune system and decrease pain. It also can reach affected areas hard to get to with showers and baths. The water temperature can be contrasted or be at tap temperature, and shower hoses can help.

The Lavage

The nose bath or lavage is very good for sinus congestion, headaches and allergies. While specialized *neti pots* can be used, we can also simply pour warm saltwater-baking soda (pinch of each) in the palm of our clean hand, place the nose into the palm and lean back as we *snuff* the water up our nose. It can be pulled through to the mouth or held for a moment in the pharynx and pushed out through the nose. Neti pots are helpful because we can lean back and snuff through the sinus and pharynx when congested. The lavage can be done one nostril at a time or both at the same time. Alternating nostrils has the bonus of being soothing upon the psyche as well as decongesting.

The Steam Bath

The steam bath is especially helpful for lung infections, sinus congestion and headaches. The steam bath can be accomplished by the formal steam room, by the use of a humidifier, or simply with a hot bath in an enclosed room. A cool or coldwater rinse after is important for immune stimulation. Eucalyptus can be added to increase the expectoration effect. With this and all hot baths, water intake should be increased dramatically, depending upon duration.

The Medicated Bath

The medicated bath is a bath with specific botanicals or essential oils. A hot water bath may be medicated with any number of herbal or aromatherapeutic agents. An herbal or aromatherapeutic manual and health practitioner can be consulted for specific botanicals to use for particular issues, as there are many options. For a relaxing medicated bath, pour one to three drops of essential oil of lavender, sage, melissa or basil oil into the bath (or one drop of any three). For a headache, try a drop or two each of fennel, lemongrass, rosemary and/or chamomile. For muscle fatigue, try two drops each of wintergreen and rosemary essential oil. For joint pain, try a drop each of essential oils of lemon and pine (or juniper) together with four drops of rosemary oil. Alternatively, these herbs can be made into a tea on the stove and added to the bath water. Herbs can also be added directly to the water in fresh or dried form. Oatmeal, olive oil, Epson salts, rock salt and even a little clay can also be added for additional benefit. Prior to taking a bath with an additive, that additive should be skin tested by applying to a small part of the skin and letting it sit on the skin for 10-15 minutes.

The Mud Bath

Mud baths are often natural warm springs with clay mud zones, but they can also be made with warm water and natural clays. Mud baths are extremely detoxifying because clay draws toxins from the skin cells, while producing an alkalizing effect. Essential oils or botanicals can be added to the mud water to increase its medicinal benefit.

The Sponge Bath

Sponge baths, spray baths and hot water bottles are extremely beneficial for during times of injury or disability. A hot or cold sponge, rubber water bottle, or spray bottle can be used therapeutically to target specific areas of pain or injury. Relaxation and dilation occurs with heat, and stimulation and constriction occurs with cold. Contrasting can be done for a particular region or injury as well. The bottle, sponge, or spray can be applied directly onto the areas of pain, congestion, or inflammation. Open wounds or burns should be kept dry and clean, so they are not good candidates for this type of therapy.

The Water Wrap

Water wraps are best done with linen cloth or a cotton washcloth. The cloth is wetted with either cold water for immune stimulation, or warm water for respiratory or sinus congestion. The linen is then wrapped around the affected part of the body. The water also may be medicated. See the description for the medicated bath. A medicated wrap can be kept on the skin for thirty to forty-five minutes. A standard hot or cold wrap can stay on a bit longer, but not long enough to provoke shivering or a chill. Cool water wraps are very effective for cooling off on a hot summer day.

The Compress

Cold compresses or packs are clothes soaked in hot or cold water (depending on the circumstance) and applied directly onto the skin to reduce inflammation (cold) and stimulate the immune system (hot and cold). Ice water compresses can be produced with crushed ice in a bag or cloth or a bag of frozen vegetables. Compresses can also be medicated.

Skin Hydration

Water is the universal hydrator for dry skin. What's the rush to towel off so quickly? Rinsing our skin with clean water without toweling off will naturally increase skin's moisture. Alternating cold-hot-cold water with a washcloth cleanses the pores and hydrates the epithelial cells, while stimulating circulation to keep the facial skin vibrant. Salt water is particularly healthy for the skin. Natural rock salt is suggested for skin cleansing. Because salt is mildly antiseptic, salt water can also reduce blemishes.

Humidified Air

As mentioned previously, the air is full of water in the form of vapor. When water is vaporized within our atmosphere, it is called humidity. Humidity levels are typically measured as *relative humidity*. This is the level of moisture the air can contain at a particular temperature. This means that 100% relative humidity indicates that this is the highest amount of moisture the air can contain at that temperature. Warmer temperatures can hold more vapor than colder temperatures, which is why a hot humidity is especially uncomfortable.

Humidity levels can range from 100% percent at 100 degrees in the tropics, to 25% at the same temperatures in the desert. At zero degrees F, however, 100% relative humidity is equivalent to only 4% humidity at room temperature. So cold temperatures are typically very dry, even at higher relative humidity levels.

As most of us have experienced, higher humidity during warm weather is uncomfortable. Too low of a humidity level will also be uncomfortable, as it will dry our skin and irritate our lungs. Our lungs are full of moisture, and a more humid environment is typically good for the lungs.

What this all means is that typical winters are too dry and summers are too humid in most places. This can be exacerbated indoors if we are not careful, creating an unhealthy indoor environment.

The trick is to create healthy indoor humidity levels. This does not mean reducing outdoor air levels, however. It is important that we have a constant flow of oxygen from nature into our indoor environment. Not only does this give us good oxygen content: It also reduces the amount of radon that the house will contain. A closed up house attracts more radon than an open-air house because of the pressure gradient.

So how do we create a comfortable indoor humidity? Our bodies are most comfortable at 25% to 60% humidity at room temperature. Indoor humidity can be affected by a house's building materials, ventilation systems, whatever air conditioning or heating units are in place, and human activity. Simply being in the house will increase its humidity. When we breathe, we send out about a cup of water into our environment every four hours, effectively raising the humidity level by 6-8%. Most furnaces, fireplace fires and forced air heating units will also dry the atmosphere. Most refrigerant air conditioners also dry the air as their evaporator coils draw water vapor. Swamp coolers or evaporative coolers increase the indoor humidity (and use less electricity). Also how we cook, take showers and use water in general will determine our indoor humidity levels. A shower will raise the humidity levels about as much as four hours of breathing.

To test our humidity level in the absence of a humidity gauge (advisable), we can watch the moisture levels on the surface of a glass of ice water. If little or no moisture forms immediately on the outside surface of the glass, our house is too dry. If we see moisture build up or mold on the ceilings, our house is likely too humid.

Changing our humidity is quite easy if it is too dry. A shower, humidifier or a room full of people will increase the humidity quite quickly. If the air is too moist, opening up all the windows (assuming it is dryer outside) is the simplest method. In a humid outside environment, we can reduce indoor plants, cook under an oven fan, and in general keep rotating the moist air out. Dehumidifiers are now available for extreme environments, but better to create our own dehumidifier by ventilating our home with fans and reducing moisture production.

Lung infections and most colds and flus respond well to higher humidity indoor environments. Humid air will allow the lungs to detoxify more efficiently. For this reason, humidifiers and steam rooms can be extremely helpful for lung infections and bronchial congestion. Eucalyptus oil, peppermint oil and/or camphor can be put in the water or steam tray to increase lung clearance.

Gargling and Swishing

Gargling and swishing with water daily with warm water to stimulate the gums is great for our oral health. Dental irrigation (e.g., Waterpik®) is also very good for this, as it shoots water into the gum line. Swishing vigorously also pulses water into the gum line, but this does not produce the focused 'power-washer' effect that an irrigation tool will have. Swishing has other benefits, however. Vigorous and extended swishing will exercise key jaw and auricular muscles, stimulating blood flow to the brain. Vigorous swishing will also stimulate the lymphatic system.

Should we feel a sore throat coming on, an immediate gargle with warm salt water is suggested. This is antimicrobial and soothing to irritated mucosal membranes. Gargling every 30-60 minutes is suggested for severe sore throats.

Therapeutic Water Consumption

Therapeutic water consumption is accomplished by drinking approximately ½ ounce of filtered tap, spring, ionized, or well water per pound of body weight each day, give or take activity level, diet and environment. Fresh food diets can supply 15-25 ounces of this. Add 16 ounces for hot summer days or one-hour workouts. Caffeinated drinks should be subtracted, as they are diuretic. Drinking warm or room-temperature water assimilates quickly. Cold water requires the body to heat the water first.

The best filtration systems are ceramic, ozone, UV, carbon or ionization. Reverse osmosis is not recommended but may be required for certain contaminants. If RO water is used, mineral supplements and shaking the water before drinking are recommended. Distilled water should only be consumed under the supervision of a health professional.

Copper and Silver Cups

Drinking with copper cups is an ancient Ayurvedic custom. A copper cup leaches copper into the water, which assists the body's detoxification processes. Silver cups are also sometimes used. These leach silver ions into the water. Silver is antimicrobial. The custom is to leave the water in the cup overnight (covered) to yield the highest therapeutic effect.

~ Six ~
Sustainable Sea Nutrition

This may seem an odd chapter to put in a book about water. The relationship between maintaining our planet's waters and our choice of foods and nutrition is direct, however. Progressively, humanity is treating the life within its oceans, rivers and seaways with almost total disregard as we forage for our foods. In first world countries at least, we have a great range of choice over our diets. This chapter is about helping us make better choices.

Endangered Fish

According to the Food and Agriculture Organization of the United Nations, almost three-quarters (69%) of the world's fish stocks are in danger of extinction or being massively overfished. Over the past five decades, the worldwide fish catch has increased from a little over 18 million tons in 1950 to over 143 million tons in 2006. Just over the 14 years from 1992 to 2006, the worldwide fish catch grew from 82 million tons to 143 million tons, close to a doubling of fish being removed from the world's seas and waterways.

Out of 2006's 143 million tons, only 110 million tons supplied human uses. This means that nearly 30% of the fish caught throughout the world does not even feed humans: Most of the remainder is used for fishmeal for animals. Another report showed that in 2006, 57% of fishmeal and 87% of fish oil was used for aquaculture. Another 12% of worldwide fish catch comes from recreational fishing.

As fish and fish oil sales grow around the world, fish stocks are running seriously low. Many major fisheries (regions with large fish populations) around the world are in trouble and many fish species are in decline or close to extinction. Some estimates have given many fisheries around the world only a few years of current and increased demand before they become extinct.

Aquaculture fish farms continue to be an environmentally viable alternative, although many problems exist with the growing number of aquaculture farms. Ocean experts have now established that contaminant levels of toxins like PCBs, viruses, and genetic manipulation are slowly finding their way into the wild marine environment, damaging natural fish stocks.

The bycatch problem has also become a critical issue for marine life. Sharks, porpoises, turtles and other beautiful ocean species are being endangered through accidental netting. *The problem is worse than is being reported,"* said Dr. Wallace "J" Nichols, who is also the director of the environmental group Ocean Revolution. *"Many fishing regions around the world have little or no system for reporting their catches."*

The thirst for fish and fish oils has been fueled by studies showing docosahexaenoic acid's (DHA) various health benefits.

Because DHA is easily extracted from fish, fish have become the central targets for the increasing demand for fish oil. Primarily because of DHA, most health professionals are now suggesting all of us have several fish meals each week. The pressure on the fish catch and the associated bycatch has only increased with this increased demand for fish and fish oil—a more concentrated form of DHA. This has led to independent projections that a critical worldwide fish shortage will exist in the coming years.

The Truth about DHA

The twenty-two-carbon chain, six-double-bond arrangement of DHA is either stored or converted to twenty-carbon, five-double-bond *eicosapentaenoic acid* (EPA) in the body of both humans and fish. *Alpha-linolenic acid* or ALA from flax, canola, walnuts, pumpkin seeds, and chia seeds readily converts to DHA in the body at levels ranging from 5-15%. Those with compromised livers may have reduced conversion rates due to an insufficiency of an enzyme called delta-6-desaturase. This, however, is often due to a lack of vitamin B6, which is essential in the conversion process. It is also often due to putting extreme pressure on the liver by the overconsumption of alcohol, smoking and other foods that burden the liver such as fried foods.

For those who cannot get enough ALA in their diet, or with compromised livers, DHA supplementation may be an appropriate strategy.

DHA has been touted as cardiovascular-protective. This has been shown in many studies. Because fish oil has both EPA and DHA, the assumption has been that both EPA and DHA were necessary to gain these benefits. Newer research indicates otherwise.

Typical crude fish oil will supply approximately 18% EPA and 12% DHA, subject to seasonal and species differences.

Surprisingly, fish do not produce DHA. Fish obtain their DHA by eating algae or eating marine life that feed on microalgae. Today some of these DHA-producing microalgae are being cultivated to produce high quality DHA oil. Two of highest DHA-producing microorganisms are *Crypthecodinium cohnii,* and *Schizochytrium* spp. Oil from these species is increasingly available in supplement form and in food formulations. This provides a pure form of DHA. Better yet, microalgae production is environmentally sustainable and puts no pressure on fish populations.

The same or more heart-healthy benefits available in fish oil are available in DHA-algae. Algal DHA will typically supply a standardized 35% DHA. EPA is short-lived within the body, while DHA is either stored or used by cells, and easily converts to EPA as needed. Microalgae DHA is also more heart-healthy than fish-derived EPA/DHA. In a randomized, placebo-controlled 2006 study published in the *Journal of the American College of Nutrition,* 116 coronary artery disease patients took either 1000mg algal-DHA alone or fish oil with 1252mg DHA+EPA for eight weeks. The DHA group experienced average triglyceride reductions of 21.8%, while the DHA+EPA group experienced 18.3% triglyceride reduction (Schwellenbach *et al.* 2006).

While fish stocks are being depleted throughout the world because of our unsustainable need for fish and fish oils, DHA-algae is grown sustainably in tanks, and more growing capacity can be added easily with virtually no environmental cost. Algal DHA is not only more environmentally sustainable: It is also a pure form of DHA, without the saturated fats found in fish; and without the risk of toxins such as PCB and mercury now found in many fish.

Shellfish and Bycatch

Shellfish are also an environmental concern. As Chris LaRock, Emergency Response Officer from Environment Canada put it, *"Chronic non-point source pollution from urbanization is increasingly endangering marine stocks, as bottom-feeders accumulate these toxins."* Filtering eaters such as shrimp, scallops, clams, oysters, and mussels have become increasingly toxic as a result. In addition, many shellfish species are now restricted for harvest because of low populations and bycatch problems. According to Dr. Nichols, most of us are not aware of shellfish trawling techniques: *"These shellfish are being caught by literally scraping huge areas of the ocean floor, damaging or killing coral, sea turtles, sponges, rays and other sea life. 50-90% of the shrimp hauls have accidental bycatch. It is like clear-cutting a forest to gather a few mushrooms."*

Shellfish aquaculture is another environmental concern, according to researchers and government officials like Dr. Nichols and Mr. LaRock. Traditional shellfish aquaculture is installed in coastal areas by clearing the seafloor of important plants like mangroves and fish habitats to isolate the shellfish. According to ocean experts, this practice is severely endangering precious coastal habitats.

Meanwhile, *glucosamine sulfate* derived from shellfish is partially responsible for mass shellfish extinction—along with shellfish eating of course. Anyway, marine-obtained glucosamine sulfate's absorption and efficacy is debatable. A sustainable alternative of shellfish-derived glucosamine is *glucosamine hydrochloride* derived from the fungi *Aspergillus niger*. Since it is not bound to potassium, the HCL version apparently has 83% active glucosamine versus 50.7% for sulfate. Meanwhile, research has shown glucosamine HCL to be readily assimilated. For those glucosamine fans, HCL is a more sustainable source.

Sea mussels have been increasingly threatened from over-harvesting, prompting some regulatory bodies to restrict both wild-craft mussel harvesting and aquaculture—which draws seeds from wild mussel stocks. New Maine state regulations, for example, limit blue mussel seed removal to four seed mussel conservation areas, because of depletion fears. Aquaculture mussels, typically grown in shoreline pools, have been plagued with various difficulties over the years. Seasonal die-offs due to water constriction and contamination multiplied by rock-attachment issues have threatened these unnatural aquaculture mussel populations. Meanwhile wild mussel populations are in danger from dredging, drag-netting, water pollution and the red tide toxin PSP, which has resulted in a good number of reported illnesses.

Shark Shortages

We may have a mortal fear of sharks, but sharks are an important part of the ecosystem of the oceans. Without sharks, other populations would expand too quickly, throwing off the balance. In other words, sharks help manage the marine environment.

Unfortunately, worldwide shark populations are becoming alarmingly reduced. A 2008 report by the World Conservation Union, a group of environmental scientists, showed that shark populations have decreased by more than 50% over the past four decades. Populations of some sharks, including the tiger shark, the bull shark, the scalloped hammerhead shark and the dusky shark, have decreased by more than 95% since the 1970s.

Shark fishing is unregulated in most waters. This means that it is open season on sharks. The shark fin trade continues to grow as a result. Shark fin soup is now considered a delicacy in some parts of the Orient. The gruesome practices of hunting sharks, cutting off their fins and dumping them back into the water is opposed by many—even fishing proponents. This along with shark cage feeding leaves little wonder why shark bites are more frequent.

Luckily, shark cartilage sales continue to lose ground as research has illustrated the lack of significant benefit to cancer patients. The title to a 2005 *Health News* article sums it up: *"Shark Cartilage Cancer 'Cure' Shows Dangers of Pseudoscience."* While shark cartilage's chondroitin sulfate has shown limited usefulness in osteoarthritis research, its large molecular structure limits its absorption across the intestinal wall. With absorption rates at less than 15% and joint absorption in question, this controversial material should be abandoned as a health supplement.

Healthy Water Botanicals

Nutrients from the ocean's plant kingdom are typically not as sensitive to over-harvesting and bycatch. They also have an impeccable record of health benefits in nutritional research. Most marine botanicals are either cultivated in tanks or sustainably wildcrafted—as in the case of kelp, with its stationary seasonal blooms forcing self-regulation. Because they rely upon photosynthesis rather than feeding, they grow prolifically. They can also easily be grown in controlled environments such as human-made lakes and tanks. Because they do not filter water as shellfish do, algae cause little toxicity concern.

There are some 70,000 known algae, and they are divided into three general types: *Chlorophyta* or green algae, *Phaeophyta* or brown algae, and red marine algae or *Rhodophyta*. These range from single-celled microalgae to giant broad-leafed kelps.

In terms of environmental food economics, sea vegetables trump all other food sources. While an acre of beef production yields about 20 pounds of useable protein and an acre of soybeans yields about 400 pounds, typical seaweeds like nori can yield 800 pounds per acre of tidal zone, and spirulina can yield a whopping 21,000 lbs of useable protein per acre of cultivation.

Spirulina and Chlorella

Spirulina and chlorella are leading microalgae foods. The market for these algae has been flourishing for over three decades, with a number of successful companies harvesting and freeze-drying algae in food-safety controlled environments. The largest spirulina producers cultivate spirulina in large fertilized ponds—many now organic. Spirulina is a good source of carotenoids, vitamins and minerals. It is also an economical source of protein as mentioned above. Spirulina nutritional content is impressive, containing all the essential and most non-essential amino acids, with 55-65% protein by weight. It also has a variety of minerals, vitamins and phytonutrients such as zeaxanthin, myxoxanthophyll and lutein. A number of clinical studies have indicated lower levels of inflammation, brain damage from stroke, and anti-cancer effects from spirulina consumption.

Chlorella pyrensoidosa, or simply chlorella, is also cultured in outdoor ponds. With over 800 published studies verifying its safety and efficacy for a number of health issues, chlorella enjoys a strong consumer-base among healthy consumers. Chlorella's ability to detoxify heavy metals and other toxins make it a favorite of health practitioners. Chlorella is a great source of dietary fiber, and it is one of the few foods that binds to mercury: A combination of chlorella and cilantro has shown clinical success in reducing mercury toxicity.

Chlorella's phytonutrients include C.G.F (chlorella growth factor), beta-carotene, and various vitamins. It is also a complete protein (40%-60%+ by weight) with every essential and non-essential amino acid. Clinical studies have shown that chlorella contributes to increased cell growth; stimulates T-cell and B-cell activities; increases macrophage function; and contributes to the improvement of fibromyalgia, hypertension and ulcerative colitis symptoms (Merchant and Andre 2001). Its cell wall is tough; so many producers have developed ways of pulverizing or crushing the cell wall, allowing assimilation of its nutrients. Apparently, the polysaccharides and fiber from its broken cell walls give chlorella its unique ability to bind to toxins (McCauley 2005).

Aphanizomenon flos-aquae

Aphanizomenon flos-aquae or simply 'AFA,' is an alga that grows on the pristine volcanic waters of the Klamath Lake of Oregon. The species does grow on other bodies of water, but the Klamath Lake has been known as the cleanest and most sustainable source. Commercial AFA harvesting began in the early 1980s. Although contamination was once a concern, today companies are micro-filtering AFA for potential contaminants. A number of commercial supplements and nutraceutical foods include AFA in their formulations. Unlike chlorella, AFA's nutrients are readily available because of its soft cell wall. The rich volcanic lakebed of Klamath Lake renders it an available source of all the essential and non-essential amino acids, making it, along with spirulina and chlorella, a complete food. AFA is 60% protein by weight and is packed with many vitamins and other phytonutrients. AFA also has 58 minerals at ppm levels and high chlorophyll content.

Astaxanthin

Another amazing green microalga is *Haematococcus pluvialis*, the highest known natural source of astaxanthin. Astaxanthin is an oxygenated carotenoid with significant antioxidant properties. It is thought to have hundreds of times the antioxidant value of vitamin E. Recent studies have shown astaxanthin to be effective for reducing inflammation and stimulating the immune system. Studies have also shown anti-tumor effects, as well as effectiveness in preventing and treating retinal oxidative damage and macular degeneration (Guerin 2003). The antioxidant effects and cancer inhibitory action of astaxanthin has been shown to be greater than beta-carotene. Reports from marathoners and tri-athletes indicate it increases recovery rates after exercise. Astaxanthin is now an ingredient in multivitamins and wellness formulations.

Vegetables of the Sea

There are about 1,500 species of sea vegetables, many of which flourish in the cold waters of the North Pacific and Atlantic oceans. Well known sea vegetables include nori, wakame, dulse, kombu, Irish moss, sea palm, and several species of *Laminaria*. While not particularly correct, most sea vegetables are commonly referred to as kelps. Wild sea veggies are harvested periodically and regrowth is managed carefully—easy to do since the kelp beds are stationary. Out of necessity, kelp farmers have a sustainable supply, and most areas have more than enough to supply market growth. Overharvesting, in fact, is quite difficult because the beds are visible and again, stationary. Careful harvesting is a requirement for harvesters that want to guarantee future harvests.

Sea vegetables like kelp have an impressive array of vitamins—more than most land-based vegetables, with A, B1, B2, B5, B12, C, B6, B3, folic acid, E, K, and a steroid vitamin D precursor. Nori and dulse have beta-carotene levels as high as 50,000 IU per 100 grams, for example. Certified organic kelps are showing 60 minerals at ppm levels. They are also good sources of calcium and magnesium. The brown algae also contain all the essential aminos and are high in protein by weight. Nori has 30% protein by weight and the others average about 9%. *Laminaria* algae also produce the sugar substitute mannitol.

Sea veggies also contain a number of beneficial polysaccharides and polyphenols. A sulfated polysaccharide called fucoidan has been shown to have anti-tumor, anticoagulant and anti-angiogenic properties. Studies show it also down-regulates Th2 (inhibiting allergic response), inhibits beta-amyloid formation (potential cause of Alzheimer's), inhibits proteinuria in Heymann nephritis, and decreases artery platelet deposits (Kuznetsova *et al.* 2004; Nagaoka *et al.* 2000; Berteau and Mulloy 2003).

Red Marine Algae

Red marine algae have become exciting nutraceuticals with confirmed health benefits. Attracting significant interest is *Dumontiae*, a larger-leaf *Rhodophyta* typically harvested in colder oceans by either wildcrafting or rope farming. *"Rope farming is highly-sustainable,"* Bob "Desert" Nichols has said. Mr. Nichols practically single-handedly developed the first commercial market for red marine algae in the mid 1990s. *Dumontiae* and other *Rhodophytes* have been confirmed to inhibit the growth of several viruses, notably herpes simplex I and II, and HIV. Most studies have pointed to their heparin-like sulfated polysaccharide content for antiviral effects, blocking both DNA and retroviral replication (Neushul 1990). *"We worked a lot with AIDS groups,"* said Mr. Nichols. *"Word of mouth got out and we were able to help many AIDS and HIV sufferers."*

Now other *Rhodophytes* are being studied for antiviral effects. Michael Neushul, PhD from University of California Santa Barbara's Biology Department has reported antiviral properties among all of the thirty-nine California red marine algae varieties he tested. Sulfated polysaccharides such as carrageenan are thought to have antiviral constituents, as well as dextran sulfate and other red alga heparinoids. Retrovirus inhibition, as mentioned above, and murine leukemia inhibition properties have also been shown (Neushul 1990; Gonzales *et al.* 1987; Straus *et al.* 1984).

Red algae have a number of food uses as well. Gelatinous polysaccharides agar, carrageenan and funoran all come from red algae and are used extensively in the food business as stabilizers. Agar contains calcium, iodine, bromine and other trace minerals. Some red algae also produce sorbitol—used as a sugar substitute.

Other nutrient-rich algae include *Dunaliella* sp., a potent source of lutein, beta-carotene and zeaxanthin. Also *Porthyridium* sp., one of the few *Rhodophyta* microalgae, and *Gigartina*—noted for varied nutraceutical and nutritional properties—should be considered.

Whole Sea Salt

Salt is one of those ionic elements the body needs in nature's doses, and within a matrix of its natural molecular structure. Like sugar, we have abandoned the natural version, opting for an ultra-processed and foreign white refined version.

Refined table salts start innocently enough: they are collected from seawater (much of America's salt comes from the not-so-pristine waters of the South San Francisco Bay—noted as one of the most polluted bays in America) or harvested from underground salt mines. After water flushing, table salt manufacturers will typically treat and precipitate out unwanted elements using chemical agents such as barium, sulfuric acid and chlorine. The resulting brine is vacuum-evaporated, and anti-caking chemicals such as tricalcium phosphate, silica dioxide, sodium ferrocyanide, ferric ammonium citrate and/or sodium silico-aluminate may be added, depending upon the manufacturer. Many salt manufacturers also add iodine and dextrose; and many foreign manufacturers add fluoride. The result is 'purified' salt—around 99% sodium chloride: A miracle of industrial modification.

Humans have treasured unrefined whole salts for their health-giving, anti-microbial, and culinary properties for thousands of years. And for good reason. Natural whole salt chipped from mines or solar-evaporated from water is not simply sodium chloride. Whole salt may contain up to 80 minerals and trace elements: Important minerals such as potassium, which primarily resides inside the cell membrane to balance sodium levels on the outside of the cell membrane; as well as boron, silica and zinc—all essential to healthy bones, muscles, nerves and enzyme metabolism. Even healthy traces of mercury, arsenic, and cadmium are found in natural whole salt. As we've discussed, over the past few years research has begun to link mineral and trace element deficiencies to a host of ailments, including arthritis, cardiovascular disease, asthma, and a number of autoimmune disorders.

While whole salt's levels of macrominerals like calcium, magnesium and potassium may not reach daily recommended allowance levels, whole salt contains a balanced spectrum of the trace elements missing from many modern diets. Whole salt is also alkalizing; helping provide a neutralizing environment. There is reason to believe that the crystalline structure of whole salt also renders its mineral ions more easily absorbed. Whole salt's potential ability to assist in detoxification is also gaining attention. Some holistic doctors are reporting success with whole salts used adjunctively as anti-microbial/anti-parasitic agents. Some have noted that whole salts help improve immunity and metabolism among their patients.

But isn't sodium unhealthy? Higher table salt consumption has been implicated in hypertension, edema, ulcers, and osteoporosis. Low-sodium diets can also be dangerous, however. A 1998 study led by Michael Alderman, M.D. showed higher mortality rates among lower sodium users within a population of 11,348 participants. In other words, too much or too little sodium may stress the body. Although peer-reviewed research is scant on whole salts, holistic doctors have observed reductions in blood pressure among patients using whole salts.

What about iodine? Is not white salt our primary source of iodine? It should not be and does not have to be. For a narrow diet devoid in dairy, berries like strawberries, sea vegetables and land vegetables, there can be an iodine deficiency. Many studies have related regional goiter levels to low-iodine levels. Other studies— like a 35,999-person study (Trowbridge *et al.* 1975) done among 10 states in the U.S.—found no relationship between goiter and low-iodine consumption. In fact, this study showed higher goiter levels among higher iodine excretion levels. Higher goiter levels have also been seen amongst adequate iodine diets, and some research has related malabsorption to be the causal issue. As such, it appears that both low- and high-iodine consumption can be problematic.

In a low-iodine diet, white iodized salt may be a reasonable source, however as in any isolated supplement program, we should point out that iodine absorption and utilization is dependent upon full-spectrum nutrition. For example, the body requires minerals like selenium to properly process iodine into T3 and T4, and selenium is typically present in whole salts. It should also be noted that a mere 1.6g of iodized salt will result in approximately 122µg of iodine, while absorbing diets under 100µg of iodine appear to be adequate for goiter prevention, while excess iodine diets have been linked to chronic high volume thyroid disorders. Getting enough iodine is not difficult, however. Most prepared foods in the western world have generous amounts of iodized salt in them.

While the term 'sea salt' conjures the ocean, experts agree that practically all harvested salt is 'sea salt'—salt mines are simply ancient seabeds. The term 'sea salt' is also a source of confusion for consumers looking for natural, whole salt. Beware of salts labeled "sea salt" or "natural sea salt." Refined salt can be called "sea salt."

Unrefined seashore-evaporated whole salts are different beasts altogether. They contain the full spectrum of minerals from their environment—assuming their environment is clean. There are traditional, hand-harvested whole sea salts from the French coast of Brittany, for example. This artisan salt is unique because the natural evaporation clay-base is thought to add beneficial elements to the body while drawing out toxins. Boasting a mere 82% sodium chloride level (with 12%+ moisture), this salt contains a number of macro and trace minerals, based on independent analysis.

Although a traditional source of salt for thousands of years, mined whole salt (or rock salt) has recently been gaining attention in the natural health community. These ancient underground whole salts are pressurized into complex crystalline form over millions of years of volcanic and tectonic plate movement.

One such salt cache lies within the famous Himalayan/Pakistan salt range—the oldest working salt mine in Asia—said to be 200-250 million years old. Still harvested by local traditional miners, its crystallized rock salt is labeled and distributed after importation into the U.S. One independent lab assay shows over 80 elements—albeit many in minute (trace) quantities—with sodium chloride levels over 97%. The larger, pinkish salt crystal rocks from this mine are also used as negative ion lamps. As they are heated, they expel healthy negative ions into the indoor air.

This mineral-rich pink rock salt is also found in the United States. A 155-million-year old volcanic ash-covered salt mine near Redmond, Utah is the site of some of the earth's purest salt crystals. A company laboratory assay report shows around 97% sodium chloride with 74 minerals and trace elements within the remaining 3% from this salt.

Minerals and trace elements often found in whole salts

calcium	magnesium	silicon	phosphorus
sulfur	chloride	potassium	chromium
manganese	iron	cobalt	nickel
copper	zinc	lithium	beryllium
fluoride	sodium	scandium	vanadium

gallium	germanium	arsenic	selenium
bromine	strontium	rubidium	molybdenum
rhodium	silver	cadmium	indium
tin	antimony	iodine	cesium
barium	lanthan	neodymium	gold
platinum	mercury	lead	uranium
actinium	thorium	wolfram	osmium
rubidium	ytterbium	zirconium	technetium
rhodium	palladium	tellurium	cerium
praseodymium	neodymium	promethium	samarium
europium	gadolinium	terbium	dysprosium
holmium	erbium	thulium	lutetium
hafnium	tantalum	bismuth	polonium
Francium	radium	neptunium	protactinium

Note again that most of these elements exist within whole salts in extremely tiny (trace) levels. Many if not all of these trace elements are required by the body's enzymes for metabolism, however. To put it mildly, trace elements are essential for good health. Water researcher Dr. Batmanghelidj suggests that we should consume a half-teaspoon of salt for every 64 ounces of water to maintain our body's sodium-water balance. Better make that a whole salt.

Some chefs say that whole salts also add a new taste dimension to a meal due to this trace mineral content—with each type of salt lending its own unique flavor. Some whole salts have won culinary awards for their distinct taste. Quite a package deal: a great source of minerals and trace elements with better tasting meals.

Calcium from the Sea

As mentioned, calcium is critical to numerous biochemical and metabolic activities within the body. While most of it is contained in the bones and teeth, it is also vital for nerve cells, artery wall cells, muscle tissues and many organs. It is necessary for muscle contraction, and is critical to the flexibility of the blood vessel walls.

While we might think bones are fairly stable and permanent, they actually undergo constant recycling and remodeling: an exchange of minerals like calcium, boron and strontium into bone, and then a resorption—or drawing out—of these elements. In a young body, there is more formation than resorption as the body's bones develop and grow. As the body ages, the bones resorb more than they form. They also begin to grow more porous and shrink and fuse in places. Consumption of calcium should grow as our body ages to replace the calcium we lose. Recommended allowance for calcium for a three year old is 500 milligrams a day, while those for a 51 year old are 1200 milligrams a day.

However, calcium alone cannot guarantee bone formation. Boron, strontium, selenium, zinc and vitamin D are all necessary for bone formation. Therefore, it is important we have balanced mineral supplementation. This means getting calcium from natural sources with a balance of the other elements—along with adequate sunlight to produce vitamin D.

One of the key minerals for calcium-bone absorption is strontium. Eclipsed in the media by calcium and magnesium, our strontium requirement is not well known. The reality is that strontium is a component of bone, and without it, calcium cannot properly build bone mass. Recent research using a pharmaceutical combination of strontium and renelic acid (called strontium renelate) has determined that strontium together with calcium and vitamin D stimulates bone mass building better than calcium and vitamin D alone (Marie 2006).

Coral calcium is also a good natural source of calcium, strontium, boron and various other trace elements. Lab assays of coral calcium show an almost ideal 2:1 calcium-to-magnesium ratio, together with more than 60 trace elements—including strontium.

Coral calcium is more sustainable than other marine calcium sources such as oyster shells, as long as dead coral is harvested. Harvesting live coral is not sustainable, as world coral populations are under pressure and on the decline. By far the most sustainable method for coral calcium is the gathering of dead coral sediment from the ocean floor. This 'sweeping' or vacuuming of dead coral provides for a healthier growing environment for the live coral heads growing around it. It is not unlike clearing dead brush to clear the way for the growth of new trees.

~ Seven ~

Living with Water

Water provides a unique means for therapy, stress-reduction and quality of life. The key is taking advantage of water's unique characteristics. This means getting in the water, being around water, and taking advantage of whatever bodies of water are nearby. Our bodies were intended to be around and within the water at least a portion of our lives. We should embrace those times.

Water Resonation

Our intuitive notion that water lends to higher states of relaxation and awareness is now a scientific fact. We know now that relaxation can be achieved simply by gazing into an aquarium, onto a lake or at the ocean, even from a distance. A number of studies have established that staring into an aquarium lowers stress levels and stimulates cognition. In one study, volunteers stared at an aquarium full of fish or a looping video of fish for eight minutes each for three times, one week apart. After each session, those staring into the aquarium had significantly lower pulse rates, lower muscle tension and increased skin temperature than those who watched a video of fish swimming around an aquarium (DeSchriver and Riddick 1990).

This study also discredited the notion that watching fish produces this relaxation response. It is the phenomenon of water movement that produces this response. This is the reason most people travel to the seashores, lakeshores and riverfronts when they want to relax and vacation. It is also the reason people covet living within view of the water. Being able to watch the motion of the water, and the reflection upon the surface of the water relaxes the body. Why? Because the water element within our body is harmonizing with the character of water. This is called *resonation*.

For example, a tuning fork set to A-440 will resonate at the 440-hertz frequency, transferring this frequency through the air until interfered with by a resonating object or instrument. A concert tuning fork will typically be tuned to the violin's third string. As a violin is tuned, the tuning fork and the violin's third string will resonate together. This occurs because of a facility within the violin's construction allowing it to become an acoustic resonator. An acoustic resonator is a point on an instrument or body that carries the vibration of a note for a period of time. In other words, it vibrates at the same frequency. On a violin, the string, the bridge, and the body of the violin all facilitate this resonating system. When the tuning fork is struck and the *A* note resonates through the concert hall, a violin tuned to the *A* note will resonate with the tuning fork, forming a harmonic between the violin and the tuning fork to tune by.

If another *A*-note tuning fork is held nearby the struck tuning fork, the second tuning fork will also begin to vibrate to the same note and frequency. The second tuning fork will become entrained to the first tuning fork. These two tuning forks are resonating together, with the second having been entrained to the first.

Resonators and entrainers appear throughout nature. A canyon resonates with the sounds of the wind, birds, moving trees, and animals. The canyon would be comparable to the body (or *bout*) of a guitar or violin, creating coherent resonance for those sound vibrations. An ocean beach or bay is a resonator of the waves marching in from distant storms. Nautilus shells and conch shells provide an interesting resonating mechanism. Most of us have "heard the ocean" by putting the ear up to one of these shells. The spiraling echo chamber provides a resonating cavity for the entrainment of these rhythmic sounds of wind and water.

The fact that we entrain and resonate with nature was confirmed by research from Oxford University's Laboratory of Physiology (Garcia-Lazaro *et al.* 2006). The researchers determined that natural sounds exhibit primarily 1/f spectra—which have gradual and gentle fluctuations in pitch and loudness. The researchers also found that human subjects tend to prefer melodies with 1/f distributions, as opposed to slower or faster distributions of fluctuations in loudness and pitch. The researchers then tested these sound fluctuations on the human auditory cortex. They found that the auditory cortex responds more positively to the 1/f distributions. The researchers wrote in their conclusion of this research that the *"auditory cortex is indeed tuned to the 1/f dynamics commonly found in the statistical distributions of natural soundscapes."*

The planet's natural waveforms impart this sort of coherency and resonance upon the body. The body needs a natural environment of air, sunshine, water, and natural food for sustenance.

Nature provides these elements. So there is a relationship of coherency between the body and its natural environment. This is expressed in measurable context when we consider the effect water has upon the body. The motion and character of natural, pure water resonates with the human body. Once the body is *in tune* with nature's waters, the body will be resonating with nature.

The movement of our bodies within water, the vision of moving water, or the interaction of water within our immediate environment also so happens to accompany our exposure to an increased level of negative ions. This of course relates back to the proven effects of negative ions we discussed earlier: Increased positive moods, increased cognition and many positive health effects.

To take advantage of this, we can simply spend time at the beach watching waves and playing in the shore break. We can sit next to the river watching the current. We can sit under a waterfall and rejoice the falling water. We can sit on the dock of a lake and become mesmerized by the rippled reflections on the water. Whatever body of water we prefer and are closest to will supply meditative beauty, wonder and relaxation to our inner being.

Swim Balancing

Humans must be taught to swim efficiently, but most of us will learn to swim instinctively. For this reason, parents don't have to do much to teach us to get comfortable in the water. A little standing by and assisting is usually all that is necessary. The floating aids can be helpful but they usually are not necessary. A little dog-paddling and we'll be off swimming into the deep end.

The younger the better when teaching children how to swim and be comfortable in the water. Given the choice, a child will often learn to swim before learning to walk. The buoyancy factor is more favorable when we are younger, and when we swim within salt water. This has to do with a combination of density, surface tension and resistance. Should a child learn when older, a fear of the water can set in, and together with additional weight density (the percentage of body water is reduced and replaced with more tissue as we age), we increase resistance and lose buoyancy.

Resistance and buoyancy loss can also increase immediately should we (or our child) panic.

Yes, panicking in the water leads to an immediate loss of buoyancy. This has been established in many years of lifeguard training, as drowning subjects that begin to struggle and panic will almost immediately lose their buoyancy. On the other hand, should a confident person relax in the water, the body will begin to float higher, possibly up to the surface. This also has to do with the utilization of the body's oxygen: The conversion of gaseous oxygen into energy and waste products heavier than oxygen.

In other words, as we harmonize our consciousness with the water around us, our body will come into balance with the motion of the water. This results in an equalization between our body's waters and those we may be swimming within.

As we swim, our internal waters interact with the wave motion of the water we are propelling through. This sensation leads to a release of tension associated with the stressors of the "solid" world. Any swimmer will tell you that following a nice swim, the body becomes more relaxed, tension is released and the mind is calmed. This is created by a combination of heightened levels of hormones and neurotransmitters such as endorphins and dopamine, along with a rebalancing of the vestibular organ system of the inner ear.

Swimming for 10-30 minutes each day is a great way to release tension and achieve cardiovascular health. In order to produce optimal effects, swimming different strokes and at varying speeds is suggested. A fast sprint for a period followed by a relaxed pace produces a combination of increased circulation, endorphins, oxygen debt and detoxification. The backstroke should be alternated with the crawl (freestyle) to balance muscle groups.

Therapeutic Surfing

There is an expression among the surfing community: *"Only a surfer knows the feeling."*

Humans have been surfing for many centuries at least. When the Polynesians surfed centuries ago, they did so with relish. They were experienced in the water, and knew how to navigate the tides, the waves and the wind. They certainly achieved the rush of elation as they handed down the knowledge of surfing to their sons and daughters over many generations. Hawaiians are still some of the most gifted and natural surfers in the world.

What causes the surfer's euphoria? While the production of hormones and neurotransmitters can explain part of the biochemical response, there is something about the force and power of an ocean wave breaking in such a precise way—allowing the surfer to harmonize with it utilizing a board and the motion of the body. There seems to be something about fitting into the crest of an overhead wave lifting and throwing overhead, creating the spiraling *"barrel"* or *"tube"* that all surfers aspire to. Most surfers will agree that *"pulling into a barrel"* of a wave captures the essence of water's power and beauty. Time seems to stand still for the surfer as he or she becomes locked in to the wave's majestic spiraling eye during a tube ride.

The evidence this euphoria is real becomes apparent when we see surfers paddling out into deep, cold ocean waters to face numbed feet and hands and the risk of visitation from big-toothed or jelly creatures of the depths. Just to achieve this euphoria, surfers will journey thousands of miles to places where rock-lined coastlines invite pitching crests over knife-like coral reefs. Much of the world's most exciting surfing takes place while vaulting over and tucking into thin walls of water breaking over sharp coral heads lying only inches from the water's surface.

Once in the water on a board, a surfer will sit for hours in a harsh ocean environment only to catch ten fifteen-second rides on a good day. Most surfers admit they are addicted. They feel depressed without waves. They will feel anxious and edgy without their saltwater fix. Why? While negative ions and neurotransmitters might explain some of this, there is something deeper going on. Some sort of resonation is taking place between the surfer and the waves.

Music provides a very similar effect.

Prior to its entry into the tubular (barrel-like) ear canal, sound is a longitudinal wave. These waveforms simply undulate through air molecules without actually moving this medium. We might compare this to the movement of tension through a spring. The spring does not go anywhere, but the tension travels through the spring as it undulates. This is often referred to as a transfer of motion through particulate matter without the actual particles moving. While symbolically correct, this would not be consistent with the waveform view of reality. While we might picture molecules floating around the air like tiny balloons, each of these molecules are really polar clouds of standing electromagnetic waveforms, as we showed earlier. As we pan out, we find the entire physical environment pulsing with resonating and interfering waveforms.

Remembering our discussion of resonation and entrainment, longitudinal sound waves move through nature's matrix waveforms through interaction. The specific method of interaction takes place through interference and conductance. As the wave pulse connects with an air molecular combination of waveforms, it is transduced through the molecule and its localized electromagnetic environment. The pulse is then handed off so to speak to neighboring molecules and their localized environment (which we might call a *microenvironment*). This pass-through effect creates a channel through which the existing waveform structure pulses, allowing a particular waveform to be conducted from one molecule to another. This conductance can be measured through pressure gradients, because the waveform interference modulates the density of waveforms within each microenvironment.

This microenvironment is somewhat symbolic because the localized environment around each molecule is continuous in a homogenous atmosphere. Still this local environment is important. For example, an air molecule bubbling within a liquid environment will not conduct sound in the same way that an air molecule might within the atmosphere of air. Its electromagnetic surroundings are completely different.

This microenvironmental modulation of air pressure through resonating wave interaction is just enough to vibrate the eardrum.

We can see a similar effect as we watch a boat moving through the water. The boat's movement creates waves, which interact and ripple through the existing ripples on the water. The new ripples interfere with the existing ripples, and a new waveform is created from this interference pattern. If the existing ripples are small as on a lake, the boat's movement might create a bow wave. If the existing ripples are rather large—like large ocean swells—then the boat will be surrounded by larger waves and the boat's waves will create a different resulting waveform pattern—noticeably different from the bow wave created on the lake. The wave signature of the boat's movement is specific in each case, but the resulting effect on the water's surface will be different in each circumstance. At the end of the day, the specific waveform created by the boat will not only be specific to the type of boat and its speed, but to the existing waveforms in the water. Even after the boat is gone, we will still be able to probably identify the size and speed of the boat by looking at the waves it created. The boat's waves will have changed the existing water surface. If the boat were a large supertanker, we would see very long, slow waves with large amplitudes. If the boat were a ski boat, the resulting waves would be shorter, faster and smaller.

This illustrates the movement of sound in many respects. Just as the boat is identified by its effect upon the water surface, the information within sound is determined through its effect upon the air pressure motion existing within the air. The motion existing within the air microenvironment will often determine the intensity of the sound. On a very windy day, our voice may be severely dampened, when compared to a still day, for example. If there larger sounds in the microenvironment—say a train passes by—our voices will be muted and even possibly transfigured. We may have to shout loudly to communicate in these conditions. Just as the wave motion within the water affects the resulting waveforms created by the boat, sound information is carried via interference with other waveforms moving through air.

A plethora of clinical observations has confirmed these points. Data from instrumentation including EEG, EKG, otoacoustical instruments, and various biofeedback devices have confirmed in different respects that different parts of the body are oscillating at different frequencies—and these different oscillations interact with each other. This means they create informational interference patterns. As we have examined brain waves, sound waves, sensual nerve input, visual spectrum and neurotransmitter frequencies together with hormone secretion, we arrive at the conclusion that endocrine gland activities are integrated with these various waveforms pulsing throughout the body.

We also see similar effects from the availability of negative ions. We know that waves and waterfalls both generate increased levels of negative ions. The generation of increased endorphins, serotonin and other physical effects is associated with this production of negative ions. These are only symptoms of a larger resonation.

Furthermore, the whole body appears to resonate to a central theme. We might compare this to listening to a large crowd at a sporting event on the television or radio. Because we are removed from the crowd, we can hear an overall hum of the stadium crowd. Although each individual audience member may be screaming or clapping uniquely, the noise of the entire stadium crowd may be represented by a single note or sound. Most of us have imitated or heard someone imitate the sound of an entire crowd in one tonal sound with uncanny accuracy. This overall sound arises from resonation.

The clinical research documenting the usefulness for resonation therapy (music therapy) is impressive. Music therapy has been identified as a valid complementary and alternative medicine by the National Institutes of Health and many hospitals other organizations. Music therapy has been used with success in cases of cancer, schizophrenia, dementia, cardiovascular diseases, somatic issues, anxiety, pain, post-surgery recovery, eating disorders, depression, multiple sclerosis, deafness tinnitus, and a host of other physical, emotional, and psychological issues. Music therapy during prenatal care and during labor has been shown to be a valuable addition to other therapies like breathing exercises and specific exercises.

In hospitals, music therapy is often used to help alleviate pain and increase post-surgical healing. It is often used in conjunction with anesthesia and pain medication. Music therapy has been shown to be dramatically effective in elevating mood, alleviating depression, inducing sleep and in general, decreasing hospital stays (Hillecke *et al.* 2005). Most of these effects have been observed in rigorous clinical conditions. One review of the research, published in the *Annals of the New York Academy of Sciences in 2005* (Thaut 2005) has called for *"a paradigm shift to move music therapy from an adjunct modality to a central treatment modality in rehabilitation and therapy."* Because of the credibility such statements render, music therapy is now covered under many states' Medicaid programs, and many insurance companies around the U.S. are starting to cover music therapy sessions.

There are a number of measurable physiological responses now shown by a growing library of research on music therapy. In one example, Wachiuli *et al.* (2007) found in a controlled study of 40 volunteers that subjects who engaged in recreational music-making using drumming experienced improved moods, lower stress-related cytokine interleukin-10 levels, and higher natural killer cell activity compared with the control group. These markers, of course, translate to better immune system response, suggesting greater disease prevention.

Surfing also has been shown to achieve similar states of increased immune function, increased moods and lower stress. A one-hour surf session will undoubtedly stimulate the production of endorphins, serotonin and dopamine. It will likely also stimulate thyroid hormones, adrenal hormones and a variety of neurotransmitters. The mechanisms for this have not been well researched, but we can draw from research from aquariums, swimming and stress-tanks that floating and moving within water resonates with the body's metabolism. Adding to that, the flow of water around our bodies in the form of spiraling waves resonates with a deeper element within our bodies, much as music resonates deep within. This is the perfect example of waveform coherence.

Over recent years, surfing has been applied to veterans suffering from post-traumatic stress syndrome with great success (Shafer 2009). Children with disabilities, including autism have shown great improvement in moods, focus and motivation following surfing (Pope 2009). These and other clinical applications illustrate the effects of *surfing therapy*.

While learning to surf is very difficult and requires many years of training and instruction, we can quickly and easily experience this resonance between our bodies and the ocean's waves. This is accomplished simply by grabbing a boogie board and "belly-boarding" some small shore break waves. It is quite easy to learn to belly-board, although it is recommended to go out with someone more experienced. As long as the novice stays away from the hard-surfaced surfboards and those spots where experienced surfers congregate, the experience can be safe and quite rewarding. Many waters will require a wetsuit to stay warm during the session, but where there are surfable waves, there are usually surf shops ready to rent out wetsuits and belly-boards very inexpensively. It is one of the cheapest "thrills" one will discover, and it will surely produce the resonation therapy described here.

Other Water Sports

Many other water sports can produce this state of euphoria and resonation. These range from sailing, river-rafting, kayaking, water-skiing, wake-boarding, water aerobics and other sorts of creative recreational activities. Many of these also utilize the dynamics of waves to produce effects similar to surfing.

All can be good, depending upon how we utilize the sport and our equipment, and how we treat the water. While jet-skiing, water-skiing and wake-boarding can be extremely fun, we should also consider the water environment. Jet skis and ski-boats leak fuel into the water and/or pollute the atmosphere with carbon emissions. These can create a negative effect upon our planet and its waters. Moderation and wisdom should be applied. For example, a sailing boat offers an incredible means for resonation with the wind and waves, while driving or riding on a speedboat will be smelly, loud and abrasive as it bounces over the water.

Indoor Chlorinated Pools and Spas

While chlorinated swimming pools can be a great means for exercise and recreation, it should also be noted that swimming in heavily chlorinated indoor pools can have negative health effects, and should be approached with a little caution. Several studies have compared allergy and asthma incidence with the frequency of indoor swimming pool use as children. In one study, indoor swimming pool use as children was associated with increased risks of hay fever as adults (Kohlhammer *et al.* 2006).

The connection between indoor pool use and bronchial diseases was further illustrated in a 2007 (Nickmilder *et al.*) study. This showed that asthma and other bronchial issues increase substantially for those who used indoor pools with greater frequency as children.

In 2004, Williams *et al.* illustrated that indoor pools with one parts per million of chlorine concentration caused 60% of the 41 swimmers (half with a history of exercise-induced asthma) to suffer from airway constriction. Meanwhile only 20% suffered from the same airway constriction in a pool with .5 parts per million—which is still sufficient for removal of microorganisms.

This is not to say we should not use our local swimming pool. The point is to be wise about its use. Indoor pool operators should open windows to increase fresh air ventilation. Pool operators should reduce the chlorine levels of indoor pools to minimum safe levels. Our use of indoor pools should be minimized to our time spent in the water, and we should alternate our time next to the water with periods of fresh air or sitting next to an open door or window. Outdoor chlorinated pools are certainly healthier.

The Future of Our Water

Face it: Pure water in the future will be harder and harder to find. As glaciers melt and we burn more fossil fuels and continue to dump chemicals into our waters, finding good sources of water will become increasingly difficult. *We must change our ways as individuals.* We must each individually change our habits with regard to what we buy, what we dump, and how we use the waters around us.

This means taking action:

We should discontinue buying toxic chemicals that will be used in our water, put down our sinks or put in our laundry. This means phosphate detergents, chlorine-based soaps, and petroleum- or ammonia-containing cleaners. This means when we have a toilet clog, we don't buy the first chemical-based clog remover. This means that we look for the words "biodegradable" in all of the products we use around the home. This means that we buy products that are made with natural ingredients.

This also means that we retain our forests and our soils. This means that we stop using gobs of virgin-tree toilet paper every time we want to poop. For example, if each person in the U.S. replaced only *one* toilet paper roll with a 100% recycled roll per year (or better yet, used one less roll), we would save 150,000 *acres* of trees!

Trees and forests are critical to the planet's recycling of carbon. The more carbon we dump into the atmosphere and the fewer plants available to absorb it, the hotter the planet will be. This is rearranging the glaciers and the water levels. The very waters that have kept the human race alive for millions of years will soon *decimate* the human race. Why? Because we do not care. Because we'd rather drive around in our SUVs than keep the human race alive.

Should we replant some of the forests we have decimated, cut carbon emissions immediately, and discontinue our massive use of synthetic chemistry, the planet may begin to slowly revitalize and detoxify itself. We may be able to break the planet's fever, but we will have to act fast: Each and every one of us.

As we consider our options, we are reminded of Rachel Carson's approach to the spraying of pesticides: *"Spray to the limit of your capacity..."* meaning spray as little as possible. As we weigh the benefits versus the costs of either producing chemicals or succumbing to massive infestations of insects, we need to have a plan. In the case of agriculture, it might have made sense in 1962 when chemicals were not as widespread and we knew little of the bioaccumulation we have discovered over recent years. Today our massive chemicals are disrupting our environment with synthetic toxicity in so many ways. In the meantime, we have developed many natural-based and organic solutions, which achieve the same results: There are many natural methods of reducing insects, and we must employ these methods immediately. These include vinegars, sulfur, castor oil, predatory insects, and many others. Organic farming is not only viable, but many organic farms produce better yields with more nutrients than their synthetic neighbors growing the same foods do. Many organic crops have proven to be stronger and less drought resistant than their conventional cousins are. Organic plants have stronger immune systems, giving them more resistance to fungi and other diseases. This applies to the human body as well. Organic foods are healthier and better for our immune systems.

The last five decades of synthetic chemical bombardment has revealed that we simply cannot continue on our present course. As a society and as individuals, we have made choices based upon personal luxury and profits rather than the long-term costs to the environment and our future survival. This arrogant consciousness must stop if we want our race to survive. We can only change the progression towards our own destruction if each and every one of us makes some radical changes in our lifestyle. It starts with our purchasing organically grown foods. If we purchase more organics, the larger agribusinesses will need to convert to organic.

Another change we can make is to buy as much food as possible from our local farmer's markets. Farmer's markets provide fresh food with minimal packaging, and employ the least amount of carbon for distribution purposes. Buying from farmer's markets or local community sustainable associations also supports organic food production.

This will be a tough one, but we must cut our plastic use. It is nearly impossible in today's society to rid our homes from plastic. As far as plastic-wrapped foods, the only thing we can do for now is try to purchase more fresh foods and demand from our manufacturers that they use recyclable containers. As consumers, we can gradually force this change.

So many consumer goods are available used. We throw so many working goods away. Buying used items recycles goods that might end up in landfills that leach into our groundwaters. Older things are also typically outgassed so they have less of a concentration of toxic materials to pollute our homes and bodies. Many older items are made with less plastics and more natural materials and fibers, although this is not always the case. Shopping "used" is a tremendous way to reduce our impact on the planet. By buying used furniture, cars and used appliances to the greatest extent, we can reduce our burden on the planet while our manufacturers are forced to produce goods more environmentally.

We now have the technology to achieve a massive conversion to sustainable energy production. Using geothermal, wind and solar systems, we can reduce coal-, nuclear- and petroleum-based electricity. Utilizing electric, fuel-cell, or (soon) solar-powered automobiles can dramatically reduce carbon-based travel. We have the technology—we just need the will. And we need to vote with our wallets.

As far as home furnishings, we can try to purchase natural fibers and natural woods as much as possible, also avoiding pressed woods with formaldehyde to the greatest extent. As for preserving our forests, a trip to New Zealand will illustrate how forests can be sustainably managed.

We can also build our houses from natural materials such as clay and straw-bale. Many natural buildings are still standing after hundreds of years.

There are so many options today for living in harmony with the planet. Once we make these changes, we will not only lift the burden of chemicals from the earth and its waters: We will also remove these chemicals from our own tissues. We will clear our bodies of those chemicals that cause cancer, cardiovascular disease, autoimmune disorders and so many other ailments.

The biggest reward is that if we are successful in removing synthetic chemistry from our planet, we will once again find the pure water that once populated the planet.

Water Conservation Strategies

Caring for our water also means conserving it. Western society, especially in America, consumes water luxuriously, as though there were unlimited quantities of it. In other words, we waste water. Consider this: The average American uses about 160 gallons of water per day, while more than half of the world's population uses about 25 gallons per day. America by far uses the most water of all countries in the world per capita. Meanwhile, many parts of our country, not to speak of many parts of the world, are running out of water.

There is a lot we can do to cut back our water usage:

The faucet should stay off when water is not necessary. This means not leaving the faucet on while washing dishes, hands, food, equipment, cars and otherwise. To wash the car, rinse once quickly, then fill a bucket with water and biodegradable soap. Scrub the car completely, rinse once again, and towel off to prevent spots. Detachable hose sprayers help reduce water when showering.

Wash dishes by hand as soon as they are used. This cuts back on the scrubbing and soaking required and reduces the amount of water used for the dishwasher. This is also more sanitary, as it preempts microorganism colonization. Energy Star-rated dishwashers use less water than a sink full of dirty dishes, however. Only use a dishwasher when it is a full load.

Mulch plants and trees thoroughly to reduce watering and evaporation. Plant drought-resistant plants. Water sparingly. Most plants need far less water than we feed them. Indoor plants typically only need watering once a week. Outdoor plants may need a little more in the summer, but can use far less in the winter. Water lawns and plants rarely and deeply so the roots are watered. Best to water during the early morning or early evening to decrease evaporation and maximize root absorption. Catchment water can be used for watering. A barrel under the house gutters can be siphoned out with a hose. Use drip irrigation. This utilizes far less water than watering with a hose.

Water should only sparingly be used to clean porches or sidewalks. Most of the time, a broom will work just fine.

The toilet is a great water waster. Flushing after every urination is a waste of water. After every two or three urinations is fine. Men can urinate outside in the yard if there is an area of complete privacy from neighbors and family. (Keep in mind that in most places including the United States, urinating in public is illegal).

A low-flow toilet is a good idea. A low-flow toilet can cut total household water use by over 25%. If you don't have a low-flow toilet, then displace some of the filling basin by immersing a bottle or bag filled with water into the basin. This will reduce the amount of water that flushes out. A float booster can also be added, which reduces the amount of water filling the basin.

Water can leak from any indoor or outdoor line. Check all lines periodically, especially if watering with a drip system.

Eat less meat. A pound of grains or beans requires about 25 gallons of water to produce. A pound of beef requires over 5,200 gallons.

Use less electricity, and go solar or wind if possible. Fossil fuel electric plants use 1,100-2,200 gallons of water per Btu. This translates to 8-16 gallons of water to keep a 60-watt light bulb on for 12 hours.

There are many other ways to conserve water. We will find more ways by being conscious of our water use. We simply have to understand that fresh water is not an inexhaustible resource. We have to consider water like a bank account: The more we draw out, the less there will be for later and for others.

~ ~

Water is a beautiful gift. We simply have to be respectful of it and appreciative for it. This requires some humility. Water can shows us this humility: It always seeks the lowest point. In that humble mood only, can we truly *'go with the flow.'*

References and Bibliography

Abdou AM, Higashiguchi S, Horie K, Kim M, Hatta H, Yokogoshi H. Relaxation and immunity enhancement effects of gamma-aminobutyric acid GABA. *Biofactors.* 2006;26(3):201-8.

Ackerman D. *A Natural History of the Senses.* New York: Vintage, 1991.

Airola P. *How to Get Well.* Phoenix, AZ: Health Plus, 1974.

Aissa J, Jurgens P, Litime M, Béhar I, Benveniste J. Electronic transmission of the cholinergic signal. *FASEB Jnl.* 1995;9:A683.

Aissa J, Litime M, Attias E, Allal A, Benveniste J. Transfer of molecular signals via electronic circuitry. *FASEB Jnl.* 1993;7:A602.

Aissa J, Litime MH, Attis E., Benveniste J. Molecular signalling at high dilution or by means of electronic circuitry. *J Immunol.* 1993;150:A146.

Aissa J, Nathan N, Arnoux B, Benveniste J. Biochemical and cellular effects of heparin-protamine injection in rabbits are partially inhibited by a PAF-acether receptor antagonist. *Eur J Pharmacol.* 1996 Apr 29;302(1-3):123-8.

American Conference of Governmental Industrial Hygienists. *Threshold limit values for chemical substances and physical agents in the work environment.* Cincinnati, OH: ACGIH, 1986.

Anderson M., Grissom C. Increasing the Heavy Atom Effect of Xenon by Adsorption to Zeolites: Photolysis of 2,3-Diazabicyclo[2.2.2]oct-2-ene. *J. Am. Chem. Soc.* 1996;118:9552-9556.

Anderson RC, Anderson JH. Acute toxic effects of fragrance products. *Arch Environ Health.* 1998 Mar-Apr;53(2):138-46.

Anderson RC, Anderson JH. Respiratory toxicity of fabric softener emissions. *J Toxicol Environ Health.* 2000 May 26;60(2):121-36.

Anderson RC, Anderson JH. Respiratory toxicity of mattress emissions in mice. *Arch Environ Health.* 2000 Jan-Feb;55(1):38-43.

Anderson RC, Anderson JH. Toxic effects of air freshener emissions. *Arch Environ Health.* 1997 Nov-Dec;52(6):433-41.

Andreucci VE, Russo D, Cianciaruso B, Andreucci M. Some sodium, potassium and water changes in the elderly and their treatment. *Nephrol Dial Transplant.* 1996;11 Suppl 9:9-17.

Asimov I. *The Chemicals of Life.* New York: Signet, 1954.

Askeland D. *The Science and Engineering of Materials.* Boston: PWS, 1994.

Aspect A, Grangier P, Roger G. Experimental Realization of Einstein-Podolsky-Rosen-Bohm Gedankenexperiment: A New Violation of Bell's Inequalities. *Physical Review Letters.* 1982;49(2):91-94.

Asplund R, Aberg HE. Oral dryness, nocturia and the menopause. *Maturitas.* 2005 Feb 14;50(2):86-90.

Bach E. *Heal Thyself.* Walden: Saffron CW Daniel, 1931-2003.

Baker SM. *Detoxification and Healing.* Chicago: Contemporary Books, 2004.

Balch P, Balch J. *Prescription for Nutritional Healing.* New York: Avery, 2000.

Ballentine R. *Diet & Nutrition: A holistic approach.* Honesdale, PA: Himalayan Int., 1978.

Ballentine RM. *Radical Healing.* New York: Harmony Books, 1999.

Barber CF. The use of music and colour theory as a behaviour modifier. *Br J Nurs.* 1999 Apr 8-21;8(7):443-8.

Barber, N.L., 2009, Summary of estimated water use in the United States in 2005: *U.S. Geological Survey Fact Sheet* 2009–3098, 2 p.

Barker A. *Scientific Method in Ptolemy's Harmonics.* Cambridge: Cambridge University Press, 2000.

Baron RA. Effects of negative ions on cognitive performance. *J Appl Psychol.* 1987 Feb;72(1):131-7.

Baron RA. Effects of negative ions on interpersonal attraction: evidence for intensification. *J Pers Soc Psychol.* 1987 Mar;52(3):547-53.

Basnyat B, Sleggs J, Spinger M. Seizures and delirium in a trekker: the consequences of excessive water drinking? *Wilderness Environ. Med.* 2000;11:69-70.

Bastide M, Daurat V, Doucet-Jaboeuf M, Pélegrin A, Dorfman P. Immunomodulator activity of very low doses of thymulin in mice, *Int J Immunotherapy.* 1987;3:191-200.

Bastide M, Doucet-Jaboeuf M, Daurat V. Activity and chronopharmacology of very low doses of physiological immune inducers. *Immun Today.* 1985;6:234-235.

Bastide M. Immunological examples on ultra high dilution research. In: Endler P, Schulte J (eds.): *Ultra High Dilution. Physiology and Physics.* Dordrech: Kluwer Academic Publishers, 1994:27-34.

Bates M. *The Forest and the Sea.* Alexandria, VA: Time-Life, 1980.

Batmanghelidj F. *Your Body's Many Cries for Water.* 2nd Ed. Vienna, VA: Global Health, 1997.

Beaulieu A, Fessele K. Agent Orange: management of patients exposed in Vietnam. *Clin J Oncol Nurs.* 2003 May-Jun;7(3):320-3.

Beauvais F, Bidet B, Descours B, Hieblot C, Burtin C, Benveniste J. Regulation of human basophil activation. I. Dissociation of cationic dye binding from histamine release in activated human basophils. *J Allergy Clin Immunol.* 1991 May;87(5):1020-8.

Beauvais F, Burtin C, Benveniste J. Voltage-dependent ion channels on human basophils: do they exist? *Immunol Lett.* 1995 May;46(1-2):81-3.

Beauvais F, Echasserieau K, Burtin C, Benveniste J. Regulation of human basophil activation; the role of Na+ and Ca2+ in IL-3-induced potentiation of IgE-mediated histamine release from human basophils. *Clin Exp Immunol.* 1994 Jan;95(1):191-4.

Beauvais F, Shimahara T, Inoue I, Hieblot C, Burtin C, Benveniste J. Regulation of human basophil activation. II. Histamine release is potentiated by K+ efflux and inhibited by Na+ influx. . *J Immunol.* 1992 Jan 1;148(1):149-54.

Becker R. *The Body Electric.* New York: Morrow, Inc., 1985.

Beecher GR. Phytonutrients' role in metabolism: effects on resistance to degenerative processes. *Nutr Rev.* 1999 Sep;57(9 Pt 2):S3-6.

Ben-Dou I. Effect of negative ionisation of inspired air on the response of asthmetic children to exercice and inhaled histamine. *Thorax* 1983:38;584-588.

Bennett JA. Dehydration: hazards and benefits. *Geriatr Nurs.* 2000 Mar-Apr;21(2):84-8.

Benveniste J, Aïssa J, Guillonnet D. A simple and fast method for in vivo demonstration of electromagnetic molecular signaling (EMS) via high dilution or computer recording. *FASEB Jnl.* 1999;13:A163.

Benveniste J, Aïssa J, Guillonnet D. Digital biology : Specificity of the digitized molecular signal. *FASEB Jnl.* 1998;12:A412.

Benveniste J, Aïssa J, Guillonnet D. The molecular signal is not functional in the absence of "informed" water. *FASEB Jnl.* 1999;13:A163.

Benveniste J, Aissa J, Litime MH, Tsaegaca GT, Thomas Y. Transfer of the molecular signal by electronic amplification. *FASEB J.* 1994;8:A398.

Benveniste J, Arnoux B, Hadji L. Highly dilute antigen increases coronary flow of isolated heart from immunized guinea-pigs. *FASEB J.* 1992;6:A1610.

Benveniste J, Davenas E, Ducot B, Spira A. Basophil achromasia by dilute ligand: a reappraisal. *FASEB Jnl.* 1991;5:A1008.

Benveniste J, Ducot B, Spira A. Memory of water revisited. *Nature.* 1994 Aug 4;370(6488):322.

Benveniste J, Guillonnet D. QED and digital biology. *Riv Biol.* 2004 Jan-Apr;97(1):169-72.

Benveniste J, Jurgens P, Aïssa J. Digital recording/transmission of the cholinergic signal. *FASEB Jnl.* 1996;10:A1479.

Benveniste J, Jurgens P, Hsueh W, Aïssa J. Transatlantic transfer of digitized antigen signal by telephone link. *Jnl Aller Clin Immun.* 1997;99:S175.

Benveniste J, Kahhak L, Guillonnet D. Specific remote detection of bacteria using an electromagnetic / digital procedure. *FASEB Jnl.* 1999;13:A852.

Benveniste J. Benveniste on Nature investigation. *Science.* 1988 Aug 26;241(4869):1028.

Benveniste J. Benveniste on the Benveniste affair. *Nature.* 1988 Oct 27;335(6193):759.

Benveniste J. Diagnosis of allergic diseases by basophil count and in vitro degranulation using manual and automated tests. *Nouv Presse Med.* 1981 Jan 24;10(3):165-9.

Benveniste J. Meta-analysis of homoeopathy trials. *Lancet.* 1998 Jan 31;351(9099):367.

Bernardi D, Dini FL, Azzarelli A, Giaconi A, Volterrani C, Lunardi M. Sudden cardiac death rate in an area characterized by high incidence of coronary artery disease and low hardness of drinking water. *Angiology.* 1995;46:145-149.

Berteau O and Mulloy B. 2003. Sulfated fucans, fresh perspectives: structures, functions, and biological properties of sulfated fucans and an overview of enzymes active toward this class of polysaccharide. *Glycobiology.* Jun;13(6):29R-40R.

Bertin G. *Spiral Structure in Galaxies: A Density Wave Theory.* Cambridge: MIT Press, 1996.

Bierman DJ. Does Consciousness Collapse the Wave-Packet? *Mind and Matter.* 1993;1(1):45-57.

Bittman BB, Berk LS, Felten DL, Westengard J, Simonton OC, Pappas J, Ninehouser M. Composite effects of group drumming music therapy on modulation of neuroendocrine-immune parameters in normal subjects. *Altern Ther Health Med.* 2001 Jan;7(1):38-47.

Bjerregaard C. Plato and the Greeks on Music as an Element in Education. *The Word.* 1913 Feb.

Boucher RC. Evidence for airway surface dehydration as the initiating event in CF airway disease. *J Intern Med.* 2007 Jan;261(1):5-16.

Bourre JM. Effects of nutrients (in food) on the structure and function of the nervous system: update on dietary requirements for brain. Part 1: micronutrients. *J Nutr Health Aging.* 2006 Sep-Oct;10(5):377-85.

Braunstein G, Labat C, Brunelleschi S, Benveniste J, Marsac J, Brink C. Evidence that the histamine sensitivity and responsiveness of guinea-pig isolated trachea are modulated by epithelial prostaglandin E2 production. *Br J Pharmacol.* 1988 Sep;95(1):300-8.

Brody J. *Jane Brody's Nutrition Book.* New York: WW Norton, 1981.

Brown V. *The Amateur Naturalists Handbook.* Englewood Cliffs, NJ: Prentice-Hall, 1980.

Brownstein D. *Salt: Your Way to Health.* West Bloomfield, MI: Medical Alternatives, 2006.

Bruseth S, Tveiten D. Homeopathy—the past or a part of future medicine? *Tidsskr Nor Laegeforen.* 1991 Dec 10;111(30):3692-4.

Busch A. Hydrotherapy improves pain, knee strength, and quality of life in women with fibromyalgia. *Aust J Physiother.* 2007;53(1):64.

Cahill RT. A New Light-Speed Anisotropy Experiment: Absolute Motion and Gravitational Waves Detected. *Progress in Physics.* 2006; (4).

Cai L, Mu LN, Lu H, Lu QY, You NC, Yu SZ, Le AD, Zhao J, Zhou XF, Marshall J, Heber D, Zhang ZF. Dietary selenium intake and genetic polymorphisms of the GSTP1 and p53 genes on the risk of esophageal squamous cell carcinoma. *Cancer Epidemiol Biomarkers Prev.* 2006 Feb;15(2):294-300.

Caldwell MM, Bornman JF, Ballare CL, Flint SD, Kulandaivelu G. Terrestrial ecosystems, increased solar ultraviolet radiation, and interactions with other climate change factors. *Photochem Photobiol Sci.* 2007 Mar;6(3):252-66.

Capitani D, Yethiraj A, Burnell EE. Memory effects across surfactant mesophases. *Langmuir.* 2007 Mar 13;23(6):3036-48.

Caple G, Sands DC, Layton G, Zucker V, Snider R. Biogenic ice nucleation—could it be metabolically initiated? *Journal of Theoretical Biology.* 1986;119:37-45.

Carson R. *Silent Spring.* Houghton Mifflin: Mariner Books, 1962.

CDC. Hyponatremic seizures among infants fed with commercial bottled drinking water - Wisconsin, 1993. *MMWR.* 1994;43:641-643.

Cengel YA, *Heat Transfer: A Practical Approach.* Boston: McGraw-Hill, 1998.

Chaney M, Ross M. *Nutrition.* New York: Houghton Mifflin, 1971.

Chast F. Homeopathy confronted with clinical research. *Ann Pharm Fr.* 2005 Jun;63(3):217-27.

Chilton F, Tucker L. *Win the War Within.* New York: Rodale, 2006.

Christopher J. *School of Natural Healing.* Springville UT: Christopher Publ, 1976.

Citro M, Smith CW, Scott-Morley A, Pongratz W, Endler PC. Transfer of information from molecules by means of electronic amplification. In P.C. Endler, J. Schulte (eds.): *Ultra High Dilution. Physiology and Physics.* Dordrecht: Kluwer Academic Publishers. 1994:209-214.

Cochran ES, Vidale JE, Tanaka S. Earth Tides Can Trigger Shallow Thrust Fault Earthquakes. *Science* 2004 Nov 12;306(5699);1164-1166.

Conely J. Music and the Military. *Air University Review.* 1972 Mar-Ap.

Contreras D, Steriade M. Cellular basis of EEG slow rhythms: a study of dynamic corticothalamic relationships. *J Neurosci.* 1995 Jan;15(1 Pt 2):604-22.

Cook J, The Therapeutic Use of Music. *Nursing Forum.* 1981;20:3:253-66.

Cooper K. *The Aerobics Program for Total Well-Being.* New York: Evans, 1980.

Couzy F, Kastenmayer P, Vigo M, Clough J, Munoz-Box R, Barclay DV. Calcium bioavailability from a calcium- and sulfate-rich mineral water, compared with milk, in young adult women. *Am J Clin Nutr.* 1995 Dec;62(6):1239-44.

Craciunescu CN, Wu R, Zeisel SH. Diethanolamine alters neurogenesis and induces apoptosis in fetal mouse hippocampus. *FASEB J.* 2006 Aug;20(10):1635-40.

Crick F. *Life Itself: Its Origin and Nature.* New York: Simon and Schuster, 1981.

Curtis *et al.* and Steel, K. Too Many Elderly Are Taking Dangerous Drugs. *Arch Internal Med.* 2004;164:1621-1625, 1603-1604.

Dantas F, Rampes H. Do homeopathic medicines provoke adverse effects? A systematic review. *Br Homeopath J.* 2000 Jul;89 Suppl 1:S35-8.

Darrow K. *The Renaissance of Physics.* New York: Macmillan, 1936.

Davenas E, Beauvais F, Amara J, Oberbaum M, Robinzon B, Miadonna B, Tedeschi A, Pomeranz B, Fortner P, Belon P, Sainte-Laudy J, Poitevin B, Benveniste J. Human basophil degranulation triggered by very dilute antiserum against IgE. *Nature.* 1988;333:816-818.

Davenas E, Poitevin B, Benveniste J. Effect on mouse peritoneal macrophages of orally administered very high dilutions of silica. *European Journal of Pharmacology.* 1987;135:313-319.

DaVinci L. (Dickens E. ed.) *The Da Vinci Notebooks.* London: Profile, 2005.

Davis-Berman J, Berman DS. The wilderness therapy program: an empirical study of its effects with adolescents in an outpatient setting. *Journal of Contemporary Psychotherapy.* 1989;19 (4):271-281.

Dean E, Mihalasky J, Ostrander S, Schroeder L. *Executive ESP.* Englewood Cliffs, NJ: Prentice-Hall, 1974.

Dean E. Infrared measurements of healer-treated water. In: Roll W, Beloff J, White R (Eds.): *Research in parapsychology 1982.* Metuchen, NJ: Scarecrow Press, 1983:100-101.

Del Giudice E, Preparata G, Vitiello G. Water as a free electric dipole laser. *Phys Rev Lett.* 1988;61:1085-1088.

Del Giudice E. Is the 'memory of water' a physical impossibility?. In P.C. Endler, J. Schulte (eds.): *Ultra High Dilution. Physiology and Physics.* Dordrecht: Kluwer Academic Publishers, 1994:117-120.

PURE WATER

Delyukov A, Didyk L. The effects of extra-low-frequency atmospheric pressure oscillations on human mental activity. *Int J Biometeorol.* 1999 Jul;43(1):31-7.

DeSchriver MM, Riddick CC. Effects of watching aquariums on elders' stress. *Anthrozoos* 4(1):44-48.

DeSchriver MM, Riddick CC. Effects of Watching Aquariums on Elders' Stress. *Anthrozoos: A Multidisciplinary Journal of The Interactions of People & Animals.* 1990;4(1):44-48

Deutsche Gesellschaft für Ernährung. Drink distilled water? *Med. Mo. Pharm.* 1993;16:146.

Devaraj TL. *Speaking of Ayurvedic Remedies for Common Diseases.* New Delhi: Sterling, 1985.

Donato F, Monarca S, Premi S., and Gelatti, U. Drinking water hardness and chronic degenerative diseases. Part III. Tumors, urolithiasis, fetal malformations, deterioration of the cognitive function in the aged and atopic eczema. *Ann. Ig.* 2003;15:57-70.

Dotolo Institute. *The Study of Colon Hydrotherapy.* Pinellas Park, FL: Dotolo, 2003.

Dunne B, Jahn R, Nelson R. Precognitive Remote Perception. *Princeton Engineering Anomalies Research Laboratory Report.* Princeton. 1983 Aug.

Dunne BJ, Jahn RG. Consciousness, information, and living systems. *Cell Mol Biol* 2005 Dec 14;51(7):703-14.

Durlach J, Bara M, Guiet-Bara A. Magnesium level in drinking water: its importance in cardiovascular risk. In: Itokawa Y, Durlach J: *Magnesium in Health and Disease.* London: J.Libbey, 1989:173-182.

Edmonds CJ, Burford D. Should children drink more water?: the effects of drinking water on cognition in children. *Appetite.* 2009 Jun;52(3):776-9.

Edris AE. Pharmaceutical and therapeutic potentials of essential oils and their individual volatile constituents: a review. *Phytother Res.* 2007 Apr;21(4):308-23.

Edwards R, Ibison M, Jessel-Kenyon J, Taylor R. Measurements of human bioluminescence. *Acup Elect Res, Intl Jnl,* 1990;15:85-94.

Einstein In Need Of Update? Calculations Show The Speed Of Light Might Change. *Science Daily.* 2001 Feb 12. www.sciencedaily.com/releases/ 2001/02/010212075309.htm. Accessed: 2007 Oct.

Eisenberg MJ. Magnesium deficiency and sudden death. *Am. Heart J.* 1992;124:544-549.

Electromagnetic fields: the biological evidence. *Science.* 1990;249:1378-1381.

Elwood PC. Epidemiology and trace elements. *Clin Endocrinol Metab.* 1985 Aug;14(3):617-28.

Emoto M (Thayne D, transl). *The Hidden Messages in Water.* Hillsboro, OR: Beyond Words, 2004.

Endler P, Pongratz W, van Wijk R, Waltl K, Hilgers H, Brandmaier R. Transmission of hormone information by non-molecular means. *FASEB Jnl.* 1994;8:A400.

Endler PC, Pongratz W, Kastberger G, Wiegant F, Schulte J. The effect of highly diluted agitated thyroxine on the climbing activity of frogs, *J Vet Hum Tox.* 1994;36:56-59.

Endler PC, Pongratz W, Smith CW, Schulte J. Non-molecular information transfer from thyroxine to frogs with regard to 'homoeopathic' toxicology, *J Vet Hum Tox.* 1995:37:259-260.

Endler PC, Pongratz W, Van Wijk R, Kastberger G, Haidvogl M. Effects of highly diluted sucussed thyroxine on metamorphosis of highland frogs, *Berlin J Res Hom.* 1991;1:151-160.

Endler PC, Pongratz W, Van Wijk R, Waltl K, Hilgers H, Brandmaier R. Transmission of hormone information by non-molecular means, *FASEB J.* 1994;8:A400.

Endler PC, Pongratz W, Van Wijk R, Wiegant F, Waltl K, Gehrer M, Hilgers H. A zoological example on ultra high dilution research. In: Endler PC, Schulte J (eds.): *Ultra High Dilution. Physiology and Physics.* Dordrecht: Kluwer Academic Publishers. 1994:39-68.

Endler PC, Pongratz W. *On effects of agitated highly diluted thyroxine (E-30).* Comprehensive report, available at the Institute for Zoology. University of Graz, Universitätsplatz 2, A-8010 Graz, 1994.

Endler PC, Schulte, J. *Ultra High Dilution. Physiology and Physics.* Dordrecht: Kluwer Academic Publ, 1994.

Enright JT. Water Dowsing: the Scheunen Experiments. *Naturwissenschaften.* 1995;82:360-369.

Environmental Protection Agency. *EPA Asbestos Materials Bans: Clarification.* 1999 May 18.

Environmental Working Group. *Human Toxome Project.* 2007. http://www.ewg.org/sites/humantoxome/. Accessed: 2007 Sep.

EPA. *A Brief Guide to Mold, Moisture and Your Home.* Environmental Protection Agency, Office of Air and Radiation/Indoor Environments Division. EPA 2002;402-K-02-003.

Ernst E. A systematic review of systematic reviews of homeopathy. *Br J Clin Pharmacol.* 2002 Dec;54(6):577-82.

Eschenhagen T, Zimmermann WH. Engineering myocardial tissue. *Circ Res.* 2005 Dec 9;97(12):1220-31.

European Union (1980) Council Directive 80/778/EEC of 15 July 1980 relating to the European Union Council Directive 98/83/EC of 3 November 1998 on the quality of water intended for human consumption. *Off. J. Eur. Commun.* 1998;L330:32-54.

Evans, M.S., Reid, K.H., Sharp, J.B. Dimethyl sulfoxide (DMSO) blocks conduction in peripheral nerve C fibers: A possible mechanism of analgesia. *Neurosci Lett.* 1993;150:145-148.

Fawell J, Nieuwenhuijsen MJ. Contaminants in drinking water. *Br Med Bull.* 2003;68:199-208.

Ferry M. Strategies for ensuring good hydration in the elderly. *Nutr Rev.* 2005 Jun;63(6 Pt 2):S22-9.

Fischer JL, Mihelc EM, Pollok KE, Smith ML. Chemotherapeutic selectivity conferred by selenium: a role for p53-dependent DNA repair. *Mol Cancer Ther.* 2007 Jan;6(1):355-61.

French SD, Cameron M, Walker BF, Beggars JW, Esterman AJ: Superficial heat or cold for low back pain. The Cochrane Database of Systematic Reviews 2006, Issue 1. Art. No.: CD004750.pub2. DOI: 10.1002/14651858.CD000530.pub2.

Frey A. Electromagnetic field interactions with biological systems. *FASEB Jnl.* 1993;7:272-28.

Galaev, YM. The Measuring of Ether-Drift Velocity and Kinematic Ether Viscosity within Optical Wave Bands. *Spacetime & Substance.* 2002;3(5):207-224.

Garcia-Lazaro JA, Ahmed B, Schnupp JW. Tuning to natural stimulus dynamics in primary auditory cortex. *Curr Biol.* 2006 Feb 7;16(3):264-71.

Garzon P, Eisenberg MJ. Variation in the mineral content of commercially available bottled waters: implication for health and disease. *Am. J. Med.* 1998;105:125-130.

Gehr P, Im Hof V, Geiser M, Schurch S. The mucociliary system of the lung—role of surfactants. *Schweiz Med Wochenschr.* 2000 May 13;130(19):691-8.

Geldreich EE, Taylor RH, Blannon JC, Reasoner DJ. Bacterial colonization of point-of-use water treatment devices. *J AWWA.* 1985;77:72-80.

Gerber R. *Vibrational Healing.* Sante Fe: Bear, 1988.

Gerbes AL, Gülberg V, Ginès P, Decaux G, Gross P, Gandjini H, Djian J; VPA Study Group. Therapy of hyponatremia in cirrhosis with a vasopressin receptor antagonist: a randomized double-blind multicenter trial. *Gastroenterology.* 2003 Apr;124(4):933-9.

Gittleman AL. *Guess What Came to Dinner.* New York: Avery, 2001.

Goedsche K, Forster M, Kroegel C, Uhlemann C. Repeated Cold Stimulations (Hydrotherapy according to Kneipp) in Patients with COPD. *Forsch Komplementarmed.* 2007 Jun;14(3):158-66.

Golub E. *The Limits of Medicine.* New York: Times Books, 1994.

Golubev IM, Zimin VP. On the standard of total hardness in drinking water. *Gig. Sanit.* 1994;(3):22-23.

Gomes A, Fernandes E, Lima JL. Fluorescence probes used for detection of reactive oxygen species. *J Biochem Biophys Methods.* 2005 Dec 31;65(2-3):45-80.

Gonzales, *et al.* 1987. Polysaccharides as antiviral agents: antiviral activity of carrageenan, *Antimicrobial Agents and Chemotherapy.* 31:1388-1393.

Grad B, Dean E. Independent confirmation of infrared healer effects. In: White R, Broughton R (Eds.): *Research in parapsychology 1983.* Metuchen, NJ: Scarecrow Press, 1984:81-83.

Grad B. A Telekinetic Effect on Plant Growth. *Intl Jnl Parapsy.* 1964;6:473.

Grad B. The 'Laying on of Hands': Implications for Psychotherapy, Gentling, and the Placebo Effect. *Jnl Amer Soc for Psych Res.* 1967 Oct;61(4):286-305.

Grad, B. A telekinetic effect on plant growth: II. Experiments involving treatment of saline in stoppered bottles. *Internl J Parapsychol.* 1964;6:473-478, 484-488.

Grady D, Herrington D, Bittner V, Blumenthal R, Davidson M, Hlatky M, Hsia J, Hulley S, Herd A, Khan S, Newby LK, Waters D, Vittinghoff E, Wenger N. Cardiovascular disease outcomes during 6.8 years of hormone therapy: Heart and Estrogen/progestin Replacement Study follow-up (HERS II). *JAMA.* 2002 Jul 3;288(1):49-57.

Grandjean AC, Grandjean NR. Dehydration and cognitive performance. *J Am Coll Nutr.* 2007 Oct;26(5 Suppl):549S-554S.

Gray-Davison F. *Ayurvedic Healing.* New York: Keats, 2002.

Greene Lab Scientists Investigating Viral Disease Incidence and Bee Colony Collapse Disorder. At the Frontline: *Columbia University Mailman School of Public Health.* 2007; May:2:2.

Grissom C. Magnetic field effects in biology: A survey of possible mechanisms with emphasis on radical pair recombination. *Chem. Rev.* 1995;95:3-24.

Groneberg DA, Wahn U, Hamelmann E. Probiotic-induced suppression of allergic sensitization and airway inflammation is associated with an increase of T regulatory-dependent mechanisms in a murine model of asthma. *Clin Exp Allergy.* 2007 Apr;37(4):498-505.

Guerin M, *et al.* 2003. Haematococcus astaxanthin: applications for human health and nutrition. *Trends Biotechnol.* May;21(5):210-6.

Haas M, Cooperstein R, Peterson D. Disentangling manual muscle testing and Applied Kinesiology: critique and reinterpretation of a literature review. Chiropr Osteopat. 2007 Aug 23;15:11.

Hadji L, Arnoux B, Benveniste J. Effect of dilute histamine on coronary flow of guinea-pig isolated heart. Inhibition by a magnetic field. *FASEB Jnl.* 1991;5:A1583.

Hadji L, Arnoux B, Benveniste J. Effect of dilute histamine on coronary flow of guinea-pig isolated heart. *FASEB J.* 1991;5:A1583.

Hagins WA, Robinson WE, Yoshikami S. Ionic aspects of excitation in rod outer segments. *Ciba Found Symp.* 1975;(31):169-89.

Hagins WA, Yoshikami S. Proceedings: A role for Ca2+ in excitation of retinal rods and cones. *Exp Eye Res.* 1974 Mar;18(3):299-305.

Halpern S. *Tuning the Human Instrument.* Palo Alto, CA: Spectrum Research Institute, 1978.

Hamel P. *Through Music to the Self: How to Appreciate and Experience Music.* Boulder: Shambala, 1979.

Hammitt WE. The relation between being away and privacy in urban forest recreation environments. *Enrironment and Behaviour.* 2000;32 (4):521-540.

Handwerk B. Are Earthquakes Encouraged by High Tides? *National Geographic News.* 2004 Oct 22.

Hans J. *The Structure and Dynamics of Waves and Vibrations.* New York:.Schocken and Co., 1975.

Hantusch B, Knittelfelder R, Wallmann J, Krieger S, Szalai K, Untersmayr E, Vogel M, Stadler BM, Scheiner O, Boltz-Nitulescu G, Jensen-Jarolim E. Internal images: human anti-idiotypic Fab antibodies mimic the IgE epitopes of grass pollen allergen Phl p 5a. *Mol Immunol.* 2006 Jul;43(14):2180-7.

Haring BS, Van Delft W. Changes in the mineral composition of food as a result of cooking in "hard" and "soft" waters. *Arch. Environ. Health.* 1981;36:33-35.

Harkins T, Grissom C. Magnetic Field Effects on B12 Ethanolamine Ammonia Lyase: Evidence for a Radical Mechanism. *Science.* 1994;263:958-960.

Harkins T, Grissom C. The Magnetic Field Dependent Step in B12 Ethanolamine Ammonia Lyase is Radical-Pair Recombination. *J. Am. Chem. Soc.* 1995;117:566-567.

Heaney RP, Dowell MS. Absorbability of the calcium in a high-calcium mineral water. *Osteoporos Int.* 1994 Nov;4(6):323-4.

Heaney RP. Absorbability and utility of calcium in mineral waters. *Am J Clin Nutr.* 2006 Aug;84(2):371-4.

Hectorne KJ, Fransway AF. Diazolidinyl urea: incidence of sensitivity, patterns of cross-reactivity and clinical relevance. *Contact Dermatitis.* 1994 Jan;30(1):16-9.

Hendel B, Ferreira P. *Water & Salt: The Essence of Life.* Gaithersburg: Natural Resources, 2003.

Heyers D, Manns M, Luksch H, Gu¨ntu¨rku¨n O, Mouritsen H. A Visual Pathway Links Brain Structures Active during Magnetic Compass Orientation in Migratory Birds. *PLoS One.* 2007;2(9):e937. 2007.

Hillecke T, Nickel A, Bolay HV. Scientific perspectives on music therapy. *Ann N Y Acad Sci.* 2005 Dec;1060:271-82.

Holmquist G. Susumo Ohno left us January 13, 2000, at the age of 71. *Cytogenet and Cell Genet.* 2000;88:171-172.

Holte K, Klarskov B, Christensen DS, Lund C, Nielsen KG, Bie P, Kehlet H. Liberal versus restrictive fluid administration to improve recovery after laparoscopic cholecystectomy: a randomized, double-blind study. *Ann Surg.* 2004 Nov;240(5):892-9.

Hope M. *The Psychology of Healing.* Longmead UK: Element Books, 1989.

Hopps HC, Feder GL. Chemical qualities of water that contribute to human health in a positive way. *Sci. Total Environ.* 1986;54:207-216.

Hoskin M.(ed.). *The Cambridge Illustrated History of Astronomy.* Cambridge: Cambridge Press, 1997.

Huang D, Ou B, Prior RL. The chemistry behind antioxidant capacity assays. J Agric Food Chem. 2005 Mar 23;53(6):1841-56.

Huffman C. Archytas of Tarentum: *Pythagorean, philosopher and Mathematician King.* Cambridge: Cambridge University Press, 2005.

Inbar O, Dotan R, Dlin RA, Neuman I, Bar-Or O. Breathing dry or humid air and exercise-induced asthma during swimming. *Eur J Appl Physiol Occup Physiol.* 1980;44(1):43-50.

Iwami O, Watanabe T, Moon CS, Nakatsuka H, Ikeda M. Motor neuron disease on the Kii Peninsula of Japan: excess manganese intake from food coupled with low magnesium in drinking water as a risk factor. *Sci. Total Environ.* 1994;149:121-135.

Izbicki G, Chavko R, Banauch GI, Weiden MD, Berger KI, Aldrich TK, Hall C, Kelly KJ, Prezant DJ. World trade center "sarcoid-like" granulomatous pulmonary disease in New York City fire department rescue workers. *Chest.* 2007 May;131(5):1414-23.

Jacqmin H, Commenges D, Letenneur L, Barberger-Gateau P, Dartigues JF. Components of drinking water and risk of cognitive impairment in the elderly. *Am. J. Epidemiol.* 1994;139, 48-57.

Jagetia GC, Aggarwal BB. "Spicing up" of the immune system by curcumin. *J Clin Immunol.* 2007 Jan;27(1):19-35.

Jahn H, Döring WK, Krampe H, Sieg S, Werner C, Poser W, Brunner E, Ehrenreich H. Preserved vasopressin response to osmostimulation despite decreased basal vasopressin levels in long-term abstinent alcoholics. *Alcohol Clin Exp Res.* 2004 Dec;28(12):1925-30.

Jahn R, Dunne, B. *Margins of Reality: the Role of Consciousness in the Physical World.* New York: Harcourt Brace Jovanovich, 1987.

Jahn RG, Dunne BJ, Nelson RG, Dobyns YH, Bradish GJ. Correlations of random binary sequences with pre-stated operator intention: a review of a 12-year program. *Explore* (NY). 2007 May-Jun;3(3):244-53, 341-3.

Jahn RG, Dunne BJ. The PEAR proposition. Explore (NY). 2007 May-Jun;3(3):205-26, 340-1.

Jahn RG, Dunne BJ. The pertinence of the Princeton Engineering Anomalies (PEAR) Laboratory to the pursuit of global health. Epilogue. *Explore* (NY). 2007 May-Jun;3(3):339.

Janssen S, Solomon G, Schettler T. Chemical Contaminants and Human Disease: A Summary of Evidence. *The Collaborative on Health and the Environment*. 2006. http://www.healthandenvironment.org. Accessed: 2007 Jul.

Jaroff L. The End of Homeopathy? *Time*. 2005;Oct 4.

Jarvis DC. *Folk Medicine*. Greenwich, CN: Fawcett, 1958.

Jasiński D, Pilecki O, Robak-Kontna K, Zbikowska-Bojko M. Analysis of type 1 diabetes mellitus symptoms at admission to hospital. *Endokrynol Diabetol Chor Przemiany Materii Wieku Rozw*. 2003;9(2):83-7.

Jeebhay MF, Quirce S. Occupational asthma in the developing and industrialised world: a review. *Int J Tuberc Lung Dis*. 2007 Feb;11(2):122-33.

Jensen B. *Nature Has a Remedy*. Los Angeles: Keats, 2001.

Jhon MS. *The Water Puzzle and the Hexagonal Key*. Uplifting, 2004.

Johnston RE. Pheromones, the vomeronasal system, and communication. From hormonal responses to individual recognition. *Ann N Y Acad Sci*. 1998 Nov 30;855:333-48.

Jonas WB, Kaptchuk TJ, Linde K. A critical overview of homeopathy. *Ann Intern Med*. 2003 Mar 4;138(5):393-9.

Jorgenson J. Therapeutic use of companion animals in health care. *Image J Nurs Sch*. 1997;29(3):249-54.

Jutte R, Riley D. A review of the use and role of low potencies in homeopathy. *Complement Ther Med*. 2005 Dec;13(4):291-6.

Kahhak L, Roche A, Dubray C, Arnoux C, Benveniste J. Decrease of ciliary beat frequency by platelet activating factor: protective effect of ketotifen. *Inflamm Res*. 1996 May;45(5):234-8.

Kamoi K, Ishibashi M, Yamaji T. Thirst and plasma levels of vasopressin, angiotensin II and atrial natriuretic peptide in patients with non-insulin-dependent diabetes mellitus. *Diabetes Res Clin Pract*. 1991 Mar;11(3):195-202.

Kandel E, Siegelbaum S, Schwartz J. *Synaptic transmission. Principles of Neural Science*. New York: Elsevier, 1991.

Kaplan R. The psychological benefits of nearby nature. In: Relf, D. (ed) *The Role of Horticulture in Human Well-Being and Social Development: A National Symposium*. Portland: Timber Press. 1992:125-133.

Kaplan S. A model of person - environment compatibility. *Environment and Behaviour* 1983;15:311-332.

Kaplan S. The restorative environment: nature and human experience. In: Relf, D. (ed) *The Role of Horticulture in Human Well-Being and Social Development: A National Symposium*. Portland: Timber Press. 1992:134-142.

Kaptchuk TJ. The placebo effect in alternative medicine: can the performance of a healing ritual have clinical significance? *Ann Intern Med*. 2002 Jun 4;136(11):817-25.

Karis TE, Jhon MS. Flow-induced anisotropy in the susceptibility of a particle suspension. *Proc Natl Acad Sci USA*. 1986 Jul;83(14):4973-4977.

Karnstedt J. Ions and Consciousness. *Whole Self*. 1991 Spring.

Kataoka M, Tsumura H, Kaku N, Torisu T. Toxic effects of povidone-iodine on synovial cell and articular cartilage. *Clin Rheumatol*. 2006 Sep;25(5):632-8.

Kavelaars J, Tamsma JT, Meinders AE. Hypernatremia in a non insulin dependent (type 2) diabetic patient with central diabetes insipidus. *Neth J Med*. 2001 Mar;58(3):150-4.

Keet E. Beauty or Bust. *Alternative Medicine*. 2007 Jan.

Kelder P. *Ancient Secret of the Fountain of Youth: Book 1*. New York: Doubleday, 1998.

Kenney WL, Chiu P. Influence of age on thirst and fluid intake. *Med Sci Sports Exerc*. 2001 Sep;33(9):1524-32.

Kim LS, Axelrod LJ, Howard P, Buratovich N, Waters RF. Efficacy of methylsulfonylmethane (MSM) in osteoarthritis pain of the knee: a pilot clinical trial. *Osteoarthritis Cartilage*. 2006 Mar;14(3):286-94.

Klatz RM, Goldman RM, Cebula C. *Infection Protection*. New York: HarperResource, 2002.

Kleffmann J. Daytime Sources of Nitrous Acid (HONO) in the Atmospheric Boundary Layer. *Chemphyschem*. 2007 Apr 10;8(8):1137-1144.

Klein R, Landau MG. *Healing: The Body Betrayed*. Minneapolis: DCI:Chronimed, 1992.

Kloss J. *Back to Eden*. Twin Oaks, WI: Lotus Press, 1939-1999.

Kohlhammer Y, Döring A, Schäfer T, Wichmann HE, Heinrich J; KORA Study Group. Swimming pool attendance and hay fever rates later in life. *Allergy*. 2006 Nov;61(11):1305-9.

Kondratyuk VA. On the health significance of microelements in low-mineral water. *Gig. Sanit*. 1989;(2):81-82.

Kosenko E, Kaminsky Y, Stavrovskaya I, Sirota T, Kondrashova MN. The stimulatory effect of negative air ions and hydrogen peroxide on the activity of superoxide dismutase. *FEBS Lett*. 1997 Jun 30;410(2-3):309-12.

Krueger AP, Reed EJ. Biological impact of small air ions. *Science*. 1976 Sep 24;193(4259):1209-13.

Kugler JP, Hustead T. Hyponatremia and hypernatremia in the elderly. *Am Fam Physician*. 2000 Jun 15;61(12):3623-30.

Kung HC, Hoyert DL, Xu J, Murphy SL. Deaths: Final Data for 2005. *National Vital Statistics Reports*. 2008;56(10). http://www.cdc.gov/nchs/data/ nvsr/nvsr56/nvsr56_10.pdf. Accessed: 2008 Jun.

Kurz R. Clinical medicine versus homeopathy. *Padiatr Padol*. 1992;27(2):37-41.

Kuznetsova TA, *et al*. 2004. Biological activity of fucoidans from brown algae and the prospects of their use in medicine. *Antibiot Khimioter*. 49(5):24-30.

Lad V. Ayurveda: *The Science of Self-Healing*. Twin Lakes, WI: Lotus Press.

Lafrenière, G. The material universe is made purely out of Aether. *Matter is made of Waves*. 2002. http://www.glafreniere.com/matter.htm. Accessed: 2007 Jun.

Lafrenière, G. The material Universe is made purely out of Aether. Matter is made of Waves. 2002. http://www.glafreniere.com/matter.htm. Accessed: 2007 Jun.

LaKind JS, McKenna EA, Hubner RP, Tardiff RG. A Review of the Comparative Mammalian Toxicity of Ethylene Glycol and Propylene Glycol. *Crit Rev Tox*. 1999:29(4);331-365.

Lakin-Thomas PL. Transcriptional feedback oscillators: maybe, maybe not. *J Biol Rhythms*. 2006 Apr;21(2):83-92.

Lappe FM. *Diet for a Small Planet*. New York: Ballantine, 1971.

Lappe JM, Travers-Gustafson D, Davies KM, Recker RR, Heaney RP. Vitamin D and calcium supplementation reduces cancer risk: results of a randomized trial. *Am J Clin Nutr*. 2007 Jun;85(6):1586-91.

Lattin GL, Moore CJ, Moore SL, Weisberg SB, Zellers A. Density of Plastic Particles found in zooplankton trawls from Coastal Waters of California to the North Pacific Central Gyre. Proceedings of the *Plastic Debris Rivers to Sea Conference*. 2005 Sept 8.

Lattin GL, Moore CJ, Zellers AF, Moore SL, Weisberg SB. A comparison of neustonic plastic and zooplankton at different depths near the southern California shore. *Mar Pollut Bull*. 2004 Aug;49(4):291-4.

LaValle JB. *The Cox-2 Connection*. Rochester, VT: Healing Arts, 2001.

Lean G. US study links more than 200 diseases to pollution. London Independent. 2004 Nov 14.

Leape L. Lucian Leape on patient safety in U.S. hospitals. Interview by Peter I Buerhaus. *J Nurs Scholarsh*. 2004;36(4):366-70.

Leder D. Spooky actions at a distance: physics, psi, and distant healing. *J Altern Complement Med*. 2005 Oct;11(5):923-30.

Lee MY, Dordick JS. Enzyme activation for nonaqueous media. *Curr Opin Biotechnol*. 2002 Aug;13(4):376-84.

Lefort J, Sedivy P, Desquand S, Randon J, Coeffier E, Maridonneau-Parini I, Floch A, Benveniste J, Vargaftig BB. Pharmacological profile of 48740 R.P., a PAF-acether antagonist. *Eur J Pharmacol*. 1988 Jun 10;150(3):257-68.

Lennihan B. Homeopathy: natural mind-body healing. *J Psychosoc Nurs Ment Health Serv*. 2004 Jul;42(7):30-40.

Levin AI, Novikov JV, Plitman SI, Noarov JA, Lastochkina KO. Effect of water of varying degrees of hardness on the cardiovascular system. *Gig. Sanit*. 1981;(10):16-19.

Lewis A. Rescue remedy. *Nurs Times*. 1999 May 26-Jun 1;95(21):27.

Li Q, Gandhi OP. Calculation of magnetic field-induced current densities for humans from EAS countertop activation/deactivation devices that use ferromagnetic cores. *Phys Med Biol*. 2005 Jan 21;50(2):373-85.

Lin PW, Chan WC, Ng BF, Lam LC. Efficacy of aromatherapy (Lavandula angustifolia) as an intervention for agitated behaviours in Chinese older persons with dementia: a cross-over randomized trial. *Int J Geriatr Psychiatry*. 2007 May;22(5):405-10.

Linde K, Clausius N, Ramirez G, Melchart D, Eitel F, Hedges LV, Jonas WB. Are the clinical effects of homeopathy placebo effects? A meta-analysis of placebo-controlled trials. *Lancet*. 1997 Sep 20;350(9081):834-43.

Lipski E. *Digestive Wellness*. Los Angeles, CA: Keats, 2000.

Litime M, Aïssa J, Benveniste J. Antigen signaling at high dilution. *FASEB Jnl*. 1993;7:A602.

Livanova L, Levshina I, Nozdracheva L, Elbakidze MG, Airapetiants MG. The protective action of negative air ions in acute stress in rats with different typological behavioral characteristics. *Zh Vyssh Nerv Deiat Im I P Pavlova*. 1998 May-Jun;48(3):554-7.

Lloyd JU. *American Materia Medica, Therapeutics and Pharmacognosy*. Portland, OR: Eclectic Medical Publications, 1989-1983.

Lockie, L.M., Norcross, B. A clinical study on the effects of dimethyl sulfoxide in 103 patients with acute and chronic musculoskeletal injures and inflammation. *Ann NY Acad Sci*. 1967;141:599-602.

Lorenz I, Schneider EM, Stolz P, Brack A, Strube J. Sensitive flow cytometric method to test basophil activation influenced by homeopathic histamine dilutions. *Forsch Komplementarmed Klass Naturheilkd*. 2003 Dec;10(6):316-24.

Lovejoy S, Pecknold S, Schertzer D. Stratified multifractal magnetization and surface geomagnetic fields—I. Spectral analysis and modeling. *Geophysical Journal International*. 2001;145(1);112-126.

Mack GW, Weseman CA, Langhans GW, Scherzer H, Gillen CM, Nadel ER. Body fluid balance in dehydrated healthy older men: thirst and renal osmoregulation. *J Appl Physiol*. 1994 Apr;76(4):1615-23.

Maier R, Greter SE, Maier N. Effects of pulsed electromagnetic fields on cognitive processes - a pilot study on pulsed field interference with cognitive regeneration. *Acta Neurol Scand*. 2004 Jul;110(1):46-52.

Manz F. Hydration and disease. *J Am Coll Nutr*. 2007 Oct;26(5 Suppl):535S-541S.

Marie PJ. Strontium ranelate: a physiological approach for optimizing bone formation and resorption. *Bone*. 2006 Feb;38(2 Suppl 1):S10-4.

Mathie RT. The research evidence base for homeopathy: a fresh assessment of the literature. *Homeopathy*. 2003 Apr;92(2):84-91.

Matsumoto, J. Clinical trials of dimethyl sulfoxide in rheumatoid arthritis patients in Japan. *Ann NY Acad Sci*. 1967;141:560-568.

Mattix KD, Winchester PD, Scherer LR. Incidence of abdominal wall defects is related to surface water atrazine and nitrate levels. *J Pediatr Surg*. 2007 Jun;42(6):947-9.

Matutinovic Z, Galic M. Relative magnetic hearing threshold. *Laryngol Rhinol Otol*. 1982 Jan;61(1):38-41.

Mayaux MJ, Guihard-Moscato ML, Schwartz D, Benveniste J, Coquin Y, Crapanne JB, Poiterin B, Rodary M, Chevrel JP, Mollet M. Controlled clinical trial of homoeopathy in postoperative ileus. *Lancet*. 1988 Mar 5;1(8584):528-9.

McAloon Dyke M, Davis KM, Clark BA, Fish LC, Elahi D, Minaker KL. Effects of hypertonicity on water intake in the elderly: an age-related failure. *Geriatr Nephrol Urol*. 1997;7(1):11-6.

McCarty MF, Barroso-Aranda J, Contreras F. Regular thermal therapy may promote insulin sensitivity while boosting expression of endothelial nitric oxide synthase—effects comparable to those of exercise training. *Med Hypotheses*. 2009 Jul;73(1):103-5.

McCauley B. *Achieving Great Health*. Lansing, MI: Spartan, 2005.

McConnaughey E. *Sea Vegetables*. Happy Camp, CA: Naturegraph, 1985.

McDougall J, McDougall M. *The McDougal Plan*. Clinton, NJ: New Win, 1983.

McTaggart L. *The Field*. New York: Quill, 2003.

Mee L. Reviving Dead Zones. *Sci Amer*. 2006 Nov.

Melles Z, Kiss SA. Influence of the magnesium content of drinking water and of magnesium therapy on the occurrence of preeclampsia. *Magnes. Res*. 1992;5:277-279.

Merchant RE and Andre CA. 2001. A review of recent clinical trials of the nutritional supplement Chlorella pyrenoidosa in the treatment of fibromyalgia, hypertension, and ulcerative colitis. *Altern Ther Health Med*. May-Jun;7(3):79-91.

Merrell WC, Shalts E. Homeopathy. *Med Clin North Am*. 2002 Jan;86(1):47-62.

Milgrom LR. Is homeopathy possible? *J R Soc Health*. 2006 Sep;126(5):211-8.

Miller GT. *Living in the Environment*. Belmont, CA: Wadsworth, 1996.

Mocchegiani E, Giacconi R, Cipriano C, Costarelli L, Muti E, Tesei S, Giuli C, Papa R, Marcellini F, Mariani E, Rink L, Herbein G, Varin A, Fulop T, Monti D, Jajte J, Dedoussis G, Gonos ES, Trougakos IP, Malavolta M. Zinc, metallothioneins, and longevity—effect of zinc supplementation: zincage study. Ann N Y Acad Sci. 2007 Nov;1119:129-46.

Modern Biology. Austin: Harcourt Brace, 1993.

Mohan JE, Ziska LH, Schlesinger WH, Thomas RB, Sicher RC, George K, Clark JS. Biomass and toxicity responses of poison ivy (Toxicodendron radicans) to elevated atmospheric CO2. *Proc Natl Acad Sci U S A*. 2006 Jun 13;103(24):9086-9.

Monarca S, Donato F, Zerbini I, Calderon RL, Craun GF. Review of epidemiological studies on drinking water hardness and cardiovascular diseases. *Eur J Cardiovasc Prev Rehabil*. 2006 Aug;13(4):495-506.

Monarca S. Zerbini I, Simonati C, Gelatti U. Drinking water hardness and chronic degenerative diseases. Part II. Cardiovascular diseases. *Ann. Ig*. 2003;15:41-56.

Montanes P, Goldblum MC, Boller F. The naming impairment of living and nonliving items in Alzheimer's disease. *J Int Neuropsychol Soc*. 1995 Jan;1(1):39-48.

Moore CJ, Moore SL, Leecaster MK, Weisberg SB. A comparison of plastic and plankton in the north Pacific central gyre. *Mar Pollut Bull*. 2001 Dec;42(12):1297-300.

Moore CJ, Moore SL, Weisberg SB, Lattin GL, Zellers AF. A comparison of neustonic plastic and zooplankton abundance in southern California's coastal waters. *Mar Pollut Bull*. 2002 Oct;44(10):1035-8. PubMed PMID: 12474963.

Moore CJ. Synthetic polymers in the marine environment: a rapidly increasing, long-term threat. *Environ Res*. 2008 Oct;108(2):131-9.

Moorhead KJ, Morgan HC. *Spirulina: Nature's Superfood*. Kailua-Kona, HI: Nutrex, 1995.

Morell V. Minds of their Own. *Nat Geo*. 2008 Mar:36-61.

Morton C. *Velocity Alters Electric Field*. www.amasci.com/ freenrg/ morton1.html. Accessed 2007 July.

Moshe M. Method and apparatus for predicting the occurrence of an earthquake by identifying electromagnetic precursors. US Patent Issued on May 28, 1996. Number 5521508.

Muhlack S, Lemmer W, Klotz P, Muller T, Lehmann E, Klieser E. Anxiolytic effect of rescue remedy for psychiatric patients: a double-blind, placebo-controlled, randomized trial. *J Clin Psychopharmacol*. 2006 Oct;26(5):541-2.

Municino A, Nicolino A, Milanese M, Gronda E, Andreuzzi B, Oliva F, Chiarella F, Cardio-HKT Study Group. Hydrotherapy in advanced heart failure: the cardio-HKT pilot study. *Monaldi Arch Chest Dis*. 2006 Dec;66(4):247-54.

Murchie G. *The Seven Mysteries of Life*. Boston: Houghton Mifflin Company, 1978.

Murphy R. *Organon Philosophy Workbook*. Blacksburg, VA: HANA, 1994.

Murray M and Pizzorno J. *Encyclopedia of Natural Medicine*. 2nd Edition. Roseville, CA: Prima Publishing, 1998.

Muzzarelli L, Force M, Sebold M. Aromatherapy and reducing preprocedural anxiety: A controlled prospective study. *Gastroenterol Nurs*. 2006 Nov-Dec;29(6):466-71.

Nadkarni AK, Nadkarni KM. *Indian Materia Medica*. (Vols 1 and 2). Bombay, India: Popular Pradashan, 1908, 1976.

Nagaoka M, *et al*. 2000. Anti-ulcer effects and biological activities of polysaccharides from marine algae. *Biofactors*. 12(1-4):267-74.

Nakatani K, Yau KW. Calcium and light adaptation in retinal rods and cones. *Nature*. 1988 Jul 7;334(6177):69-71.

Napoli N, Thompson J, Civitelli R, Armamento-Villareal R. Effects of dietary calcium compared with calcium supplements on estrogen metabolism and bone mineral density. *Am J Clin Nutr*. 2007;85(5):1428-1433.

Nardi G, Donato F, Monarca S, Gelatti U. Drinking water hardness and chronic degenerative diseases. I. Analysis of epidemiological research. *Ann Ig*. 2003 Jan-Feb;15(1):35-40.

Natarajan E, Grissom C. The Origin of Magnetic Field Dependent Recombination in Alkylcobalamin Radical Pairs. *Photochem Photobiol*. 1996;64:286-295.

Navarro Silvera SA, Rohan TE. Trace elements and cancer risk: a review of the epidemiologic evidence. *Cancer Causes Control*. 2007 Feb;18(1):7-27.

Nelson RD, Jahn RG, Dunne BJ, Dobyns YH, Bradish GJ. FieldREG II: consciousness field effects: replications and explorations. *Explore* (NY). 2007 May-Jun;3(3):279-93, 344.

Neumann von J. (1955): Mathematical Foundations of Quantum Mechanics.Princeton: Princeton University Press. Translated by R. Beyer from Mathematische Grundlagen der Quantenmechanik, Springer, Berlin, 1932.

Neushul. 1990. Antiviral carbohydrates from marine red algae. Hydrobiologia. 204/205:99-104.

Newton PE. The Effect of Sound on Plant Grwoth. JAES. 1971 Mar;19(3):202-205.

Nickmilder M, Bernard A. Ecological association between childhood asthma and availability of indoor chlorinated swimming pools in Europe. *Occup Environ Med*. 2007 Jan;64(1):37-46.

Niculescu MD, Wu R, Guo Z, da Costa KA, Zeisel SH. Diethanolamine alters proliferation and choline metabolism in mouse neural precursor cells. *Toxicol Sci*. 2007 Apr;96(2):321-6.

O'Dwyer JJ. *College Physics*. Pacific Grove, CA: Brooks/Cole, 1990.

Oehme FW (ed.). *Toxicity of heavy metals in the environment. Part 1*. New York: M.Dekker, 1979.

Oh CK, Lücker PW, Wetzelsberger N, Kuhlmann F. The determination of magnesium, calcium, sodium and potassium in assorted foods with special attention to the loss of electrolytes after various forms of food preparations. *Mag.-Bull*. 1986;8:297-302.

Okayama Y, Begishvili TB, Church MK. Comparison of mechanisms of IL-3 induced histamine release and IL-3 priming effect on human basophils. *Clin Exp Allergy*. 1993 Nov;23(11):901-10.

Ole D. Rughede, On the Theory and Physics of the Aether. *Progress in Physics*. 2006; (1).

One Hundred Million Americans See Medical Mistakes Directly Touching Them as Patients, Friends, Relatives. *National Patient Safety Foundation. Press Release*. 1997 Oct 9. http://npsf.org/pr/pressrel/ final-sur.htm. Accessed: 2007 Mar.

Ostrander S, Schroeder L, Ostrander N. *Super-Learning*. New York: Delta, 1979.

Ozone Hole Healing Gradually. *Associated Press*. 2005 Sept 16, 03:18 pm ET.

Pacione M. Urban environmental quality and human wellbeing-a social geographical perspective. *Landscape and Urban Planning* 2003;986:1-12.

Palmqvist C, Wardlaw AJ, Bradding P. Chemokines and their receptors as potential targets for the treatment of asthma. *Br J Pharmacol*. 2007 Apr 30.

Palumbo A. Gravitational and geomagnetic tidal source of earthquake triggering. *Italian Physical Society*. 1989 Nov;12(6).

Parcell S. Sulfur in human nutrition and applications in medicine. *Altern Med Rev*. 2002 Feb;7(1):22-44.

Pardo A, Nevo K, Vigiser D, Lazarov A. The effect of physical and chemical properties of swimming pool water and its close environment on the development of contact dermatitis in hydrotherapists. *Am J Ind Med.* 2007 Feb;50(2):122-6.

Pavlovic M. *Einstein's Theory of Relativity - Scientific Theory or Illusion?* http://www.milanrpalovic.freeservers. com. Accessed 2007 Oct.

Payment P, Franco E, Richardson L, Siemiatyck, J. Gastrointestinal health effects associated with the consumption of drinking water produced by point-of-use domestic reverse-osmosis filtration units. *Appl. Environ. Microbiol.* 1991;57:945-948.

Payment, P. Bacterial colonization of reverse-osmosis water filtration units. *Can. J. Microbiol.* 1989;35:1065-1067.

PDR. *Physicians' Desk Reference.* Montvale, NJ: Thomson, 2003.

Percy, E.C., Carson, J.D. The use of DMSO in tennis elbow and rotator cuff tendinitis: A double-blind study. Med Sci Sports Exercise. 1981;13:215-219.

Petiot JF, Sainte-Laudy J, Benveniste J. Interpretation of results on a human basophil degranulation test. *Ann Biol Clin (Paris).* 1981;39(6):355-9.

Pflege Z. *Physics.* 2000 Feb;53(2):111-2.

Piluso LG, Moffatt-Smith C. Disinfection using ultraviolet radiation as an antimicrobial agent: a review and synthesis of mechanisms and concerns. PDA J Pharm Sci Technol. 2006 Jan-Feb;60(1):1-16.

Pinto JT, Sinha R, Papp K, Facompre ND, Desai D, El-Bayoumy K. Differential effects of naturally occurring and synthetic organoselenium compounds on biomarkers in androgen responsive and androgen independent human prostate carcinoma cells. *Int J Cancer.* 2007 Apr 1;120(7):1410-7.

Piper PW. Yeast superoxide dismutase mutants reveal a pro-oxidant action of weak organic acid food preservatives. *Free Radic Biol Med.* 1999 Dec;27(11-12):1219-27.

Poitevin B, Davenas E, Benveniste J. In vitro immunological degranulation of human basophils is modulated by lung histamine and Apis mellifica. *Br J Clin Pharmacol.* 1988 Apr;25(4):439-44.

Pongratz W, Endler PC, Poitevin B, Kartnig T. Effect of extremely diluted plant hormone on cell culture, *Proc. 1995 AAAS Ann. Meeting,* Atlanta, 1995.

Pope J. Surfing helps calm autistic children. *Las Vegas Sun.* 2009 June 20.

Preisinger E, Quittan M. Thermo- and hydrotherapy. *Wien Med Wochenschr.* 1994;144(20-21):520-6.

Protheroe WM, Captiotti ER, Newsom GH. *Exploring the Universe.* Columbus, OH: Merrill, 1989,

PubMed PMID: 10466018. Der Marderosian A. Understanding homeopathy. *J Am Pharm Assoc.* 1996 May;NS36(5):317-21.

Rachmanin Y, Filippova AV, Michailova R, Belyaeva N, Lamentova T, Robbins DJ, Sly MR. Serum zinc and demineralized water. *Am J Cli. Nutr.* 1981;34:962-963.

Raloff J. Ill Winds. *Science News:* 2001;160(14):218.

Ramello A, Vitale C, Marangella M. Epidemiology of nephrolithiasis. *J Nephrol.* 2000 Nov-Dec;13 Suppl 3:S45-50.

Rappoport J. Both sides of the pharmaceutical death coin. *Townsend Letter for Doctors and Patients.* 2006 Oct.

Reger D, Goode S, Mercer E. *Chemistry: Principles & Practice.* Fort Worth, TX: Harcourt Brace, 1993.

Reilly D, Taylor M, Beattie N, Campbell J, McSharry C, Aitchison T, Carter R, Stevenson R. Is evidence for homoeopathy reproducible? *Lancet,* 1994;344:1601-1606.

Reilly D. The puzzle of homeopathy. *J Altern Complement Med.* 2001;7 Suppl 1:S103-9.

Reilly T, Stevenson I. An investigation of the effects of negative air ions on responses to submaximal exercise at different times of day. *J Hum Ergol.* 1993 Jun;22(1):1-9.

Reilly T, Taylor M, McSharry C, Aitchison T. Is homoeopathy a placebo response? Controlled trial of homoeopathic potency, with pollen in hayfever as model. *Lancet.* 1986;II:881-886.

Reiter RJ, Garcia JJ, Pie J. Oxidative toxicity in models of neurodegeneration: responses to melatonin. *Restor Neurol Neurosci.* 1998 Jun;12(2-3):135-42.

Retallack D. *The Sound of Music and Plants.* Marina Del Rey, CA: Devorss, 1973.

Rodriguez GJ, Cordina SM, Vazquez G, Suri MF, Kirmani JF, Ezzeddine MA, Qureshi AI. The hydration influence on the risk of stroke (THIRST) study. *Neurocrit Care.* 2009;10(2):187-94.

Rosenlund M, Picciotto S, Forastiere F, Stafoggia M, Perucci CA. Traffic-related air pollution in relation to incidence and prognosis of coronary heart disease. *Epidemiology.* 2008 Jan;19(1):121-8.

Rubenowitz E, Molin I, Axelsson G, Rylander R. (2000) Magnesium in drinking water in relation to morbidity and mortality from acute myocardial infarction. Epidemiology. 2000;11:416-421.

Sainte-Laudy J, Belon P. Analysis of immunosuppressive activity of serial dilutions of histamine on human basophil activation by flow cytometry. *Inflam Rsrch.* 1996 Suppl. 1:S33-S34.

Sakugawa H, Cape JN. Harmful effects of atmospheric nitrous acid on the physiological status of

Sanders R. Slow brain waves play key role in coordinating complex activity. UC Berkeley News. 2006 Sep 14.

Sarah Janssen S, Solomon G, Schettler T. Chemical Contaminants and Human Disease:A Summary of Evidence. The Collaborative on Health and the Environment. 2006. http://www.healthand-environment.org. Accessed: 2007 Jul.

Sauvant M, Pepin D. Drinking water and cardiovascular disease. *Food Chem Toxicol.* 2002;40:1311-1325.

Schmidt H, Quantum processes predicted? *New Sci.* 1969 Oct 16.

Schmitt B, Frölich L. Creative therapy options for patients with dementia—a systematic review. *Fortschr Neurol Psychiatr.* 2007 Dec;75(12):699-707.

Schols JM, De Groot CP, van der Cammen TJ, Olde Rikkert MG. Preventing and treating dehydration in the elderly during periods of illness and warm weather. *J Nutr Health Aging.* 2009 Feb;13(2):150-7.

Schumann K, Elsenhans B, Reichl F, Pfob H, Wurster K. Does intake of highly demineralized water damage the rat gastrointestinal tract? *Vet Hum Toxicol.* 1993;35:28-31.

Schwartz S, De Mattei R, Brame E, Spottiswoode S. Infrared spectra alteration in water proximate to the palms of therapeutic practitioners. In: Wiener D, Nelson R (Eds.): *Research in parapsychology 1986.* Metuchen, NJ: Scarecrow Press, 1987:24-29.

Schwellenbach LJ, Olson KL. McConnell KJ, Stolepart RS, Nash JD, Merenich JA. The triglyceride-lowering effects of a modest dose of docosahexaenoic acid alone versus in combination with low dose eicosapentaenoic acid in patients with coronary artery disease and elevated triglycerides. *J Am Coll Nutr.* 2006;25(6):480-485.

Scopacasa F, Horowitz M, Wishart JM, Need AG, Morris HA, Wittert G, Nordin BE. Calcium supplementation suppresses bone resorption in early postmenopausal women. *Calcif Tissue Int.* 1998 Jan;62(1):8-12.

Scott VL, De Wolf AM, Kang Y, Altura BT, Virji MA, Cook DR, Altura BM. Ionized hypomagnesemia in patients undergoing orthotopic liver transplantation: a complication of citrate intoxication. *Liver Transpl Surg.* 1996 Sep;2(5):343-7.

Senekowitsch F, Endler P, Pongratz W, Smith C. Hormone effects by CD record/replay. *FASEB J.* 1995;9:A392.

Senior F. Fallout. *New York Magazine.* Fall: 2003.

Serra-Valls A. Electromagnetic Industrion and the Conservation of Momentum in the Spiral Paradox. *Cornell University Library.* http://arxiv.org/ftp/physics/papers/0012/0012009.pdf. Accessed: 2007 Jul.

Serway R. *Physics For Scientists & Engineers.* Philadelphia: Harcourt Brace, 1992.

Shafer S. Surf therapy for injured veterans. *The California Report.* 2009 Sept 2.

Shafik A. Role of warm-water bath in anorectal conditions. The "thermosphincteric reflex". *J Clin Gastroenterol.* 1993 Jun;16(4):304-8.

Shaikh ZH, Taylor HC, Maroo PV, Llerena LA. Syndrome of inappropriate antidiuretic hormone secretion associated with lisinopril. *Ann Pharmacother.* 2000 Feb;34(2):176-9.

Shang A, Huwiler-Müntener K, Nartey L, Juni P, Dorig S, Sterne JA, *et al.* Are the clinical effects of homoeopathy placebo effects? Comparative study of placebo-controlled trials of homoeopathy and allopathy. Lancet. 2005;366:726–32.

Shankar R. *My Music, My Life.* New York: Simon & Schuster, 1968.

Sherman G, Zeller L, Avriel A, Friger M, Harari M, Sukenik S. Intermittent balneotherapy at the Dead Sea area for patients with knee osteoarthritis. *Isr Med Assoc J.* 2009 Feb;11(2):88-93.

Shevelev IA, Kostelianetz NB, Kamenkovich VM, Sharaev GA. EEG alpha-wave in the visual cortex: check of the hypothesis of the scanning process. *Int J Psychophysiol.* 1991 Aug;11(2):195-201.

Shui-Yin Lo. Anomalous State of Ice. *Mod Phys Ltrs.* 1996;10(19):909-919.

Smith CW. Coherence in living biological systems. *Neural Network World.* 1994:4(3):379-388.

Smith MJ. "Effect of Magnetic Fields on Enzyme Reactivity" in Barnothy M.(ed.), *Biological Effects of Magnetic Fields.* New York: Plenum Press, 1969.

Smith MJ. *The Influence on Enzyme Growth By the 'Laying on of Hands: Dimensions of Healing.* Los Altos, California: Academy of Parapsychology and Medicine, 1973.

Smith T. *Homeopathic Medicine: A Doctor's Guide.* Rochester, VT: Healing Arts, 1989.

Smith-Sonneborn J. Age-correlated effects of caffeine on non-irradiated and UV-irradiated Paramecium Aurelia. *J Gerontol.* 1974 May;29(3):256-60.

Smith-Sonneborn J. DNA repair and longevity assurance in Paramecium tetraurelia. *Science.* 1979 Mar 16;203(4385):1115-7.

Soler M, Chandra S, Ruiz D, Davidson E, Hendrickson D, Christou G. A third isolated oxidation state for the Mn12 family of singl molecule magnets. *ChemComm;* 2000; Nov 22.

Soni MG, Carabin IG, Burdock GA. Safety assessment of esters of p-hydroxybenzoic acid (parabens). *Food Chem Toxicol.* 2005 Jul;43(7):985-1015.

Spanagel R, Rosenwasser AM, Schumann G, Sarkar DK. Alcohol consumption and the body's biological clock. *Alcohol Clin Exp Res.* 2005 Aug;29(8):1550-7.

REFERENCES AND BIBLIOGRAPHY

Speed Of Light May Not Be Constant, Physicist Suggests. Science Daily. 1999 Oct 6. www.sciencedaily.com/releases/1999/10/991005114024.htm. Accessed: 2007 Jun.

Spence A. *Basic Human Anatomy.* Menlo Park, CA: Benjamin/Commings, 1986.

Spillane M. Good Vibrations, A Sound 'Diet' for Plants. *The Growing Edge.* 1991 Spring.

Spiller G. *The Super Pyramid.* New York: HRS Press, 1993.

Steiner R. *Agriculture.* Kimberton, PA: Bio-Dynamic Farming, 1924-1993.

Sulman FG, Levy D, Lunkan L, Pfeifer Y, Tal E. New methods in the treatment of weather sensitivity. *Fortschr Med.* 1977 Mar 17;95(11):746-52.

Sulman FG. Migraine and headache due to weather and allied causes and its specific treatment. *Ups J Med Sci Suppl.* 1980;31:41-4.

Taoka S, Padmakumar R, Grissom C, Banerjee R. Magnetic Field Effects on Coenzyme B-12 Dependent Enzymes: Validation of Ethanolamine Ammonia Lyase Results and Extension to Human Methylmalonyl CoA Mutase. *Bioelectromagnetics.* 1997;18:506-513.

Taraban M, Leshina T, Anderson M, Grissom C. Magnetic Field Dependence and the Role of electron spin in Heme Enzymes: Horseradish Peroxidase. *J. Am. Chem. Soc.* 1997;119:5768-5769.

Teitelbaum J. From Fatigue to Fantastic. New York: Avery, 2001.

Thaut MH. The future of music in therapy and medicine. Ann N Y Acad Sci. 2005 Dec;1060:303-8.

Thomas Y, Litime H, Benveniste J. Modulation of human neutrophil activation by "electronic" phorbol myristate acetate (PMA). *FASEB Jnl.* 1996;10:A1479.

Thomas Y, Schiff M, Belkadi L, Jurgens P, Kahhak L, Benveniste J. Activation of human neutrophils by electronically transmitted phorbol-myristate acetate. *Med Hypoth.* 2000;54:33-39.

Thomas Y, Schiff M, Litime M, Belkadi L, Benveniste J. Direct transmission to cells of a molecular signal (phorbol myristate acetate, PMA) via an electronic device. *FASEB Jnl.* 1995;9:A227.

Thompson D. *On Growth and Form.* Cambridge: Cambridge University Press, 1992.

Tisler T, Zagorc-Koncan J. Aquatic toxicity of selected chemicals as a basic criterion for environmental classification. *Arh Hig Rada Toksikol.* 2003 Sep;54(3):207-13.

Tišler T, Zagorc-Koncan J. The 'whole-effluent' toxicity approach. *Internl J Environ Poll.* 2007, 31, 3-12.

Tisserand R. *The Art of Aromatherapy.* New York: Inner Traditions, 1979.

Tiwari M. Ayurveda: *A Life of Balance.* Rochester, VT: Healing Arts, 1995.

Trivedi B. Magnetic Map Found to Guide Animal Migration. *National Geographic Today.* 2001 Oct 12.

Trowbridge FL, Hand KE, Nichaman MZ. Findings relating to goiter and iodine in the Ten-State Nutrition Survey. *Am J Clin Nutr.* 1975 Jul;28(7):712-6.

Tsong T. Deciphering the language of cells. *Trends in Biochem Sci.* 1989;14:89-92.

Tubek S. Role of trace elements in primary arterial hypertension: is mineral water style or prophylaxis? *Biol Trace Elem Res.* 2006 Winter;114(1-3):1-5.

Udermann H, Fischer G. Studies on the influence of positive or negative small ions on the catechol amine content in the brain of the mouse following shorttime or prolonged exposure. *Zentralbl Bakteriol Mikrobiol Hyg.* 1982 Apr;176(1):72-8.

Ulrich RS. Aesthetic and affective response to natural environment. In Altman, I. and Wohlwill, J. F. (eds) *Human Behaviour and Environment: Advances in Theory and Research. Volume 6: Behaviour and the Natural Environment.* New York: Plenum Press: 1983:85-125.

Ulrich RS. Natural versus urban scenes: some psychophysiological effects. *Environment and Behaviour.* 1981:523-556.

Ulrich RS. Visual landscapes and psychological well being. *Landscape Research.* 1979;4:17-23.

Vallance A. Can biological activity be maintained at ultra-high dilution? An overview of homeopathy, evidence, and Bayesian philosophy. *J Altern Complement Med.* 1998 Spring;4(1):49-76.

van Wijk K, Haney M, Scales JA. 1D energy transport in a strongly scattering laboratory model. *Phys Rev E Stat Nonlin Soft Matter Phys.* 2004 Mar;69(3 Pt 2):036611.

van Wijk R, Wiegant FAC. *Cultured mammalian cells in homeopathy research: the similia principle in self-recovery.* Utrecht, University Utrecht Publisher, 1994.

Vescelius E. *Music and Health.* New York: Goodyear Book Shop, 1918.

Vieno N, Tuhkanen T, Kronberg L. Elimination of pharmaceuticals in sewage treatment plants in Finland. Water Res. 2007 Mar;41(5):1001-12.

Vieno NM, Härkki H, Tuhkanen T, Kronberg L. Occurrence of pharmaceuticals in river water and their elimination in a pilot-scale drinking water treatment plant. Environ Sci Technol. 2007 Jul 15;41(14):5077-84.

Wachiuli M, Koyama M, Utsuyama M, Bittman BB, Kitagawa M, Hirokawa K. Recreational music-making modulates natural killer cell activity, cytokines, and mood states in corporate employees. *Med Sci Monit.* 2007 Feb;13(2):CR57-70.

213

Walach H, Jonas WB, Ives J, van Wijk R, Weingartner O. Research on homeopathy: state of the art. *J Altern Complement Med.* 2005 Oct;11(5):813-29.

Walach H. Is homeopathy accessible to research? *Schweiz Rundsch Med Prax.* 1994 Dec 20;83(51-52):1439-47.

Watson L. *Beyond Supernature.* New York: Bantam, 1987.

Watson L. *Supernature.* New York: Bantam, 1973.

Wayne R. *Chemistry of the Atmospheres.* Oxford Press, 1991.

Wazna-Wesly JM, Meranda DL, Carey P, Shenker Y. Effect of atrial natriuretic hormone on vasopressin and thirst response to osmotic stimulation in human subjects. *J Lab Clin Med.* 1995 Jun;125(6):734-42.

Weatherley-Jones E, Thompson E, Thomas K. The placebo-controlled trial as a test of complementary and alternative medicine: observations from research experience of individualised homeopathic treatment. *Homeopathy.* 2004 Oct;93(4):186-9.

Weaver J, Astumian R. The response of living cells to very weak electric fields: the thermal noise limit. *Science.* 1990;247:459-462.

Wee K, Rogers T, Altan BS, Hackney SA, Hamm C. Engineering and medical applications of diatoms. *J Nanosci Nanotechnol.* 2005 Jan;5(1):88-91.

Weinberger P, Measures M. The effect of two audible sound frequencies on the germination and growth of a spring and winter wheat. *Can. J. Bot.* 1968;46(9):1151-1158.

Weiner MA. *Secrets of Fijian Medicine.* Berkeley, CA: Univ. of Calif., 1969.

Werbach M. *Nutritional Influences on Illness.* Tarzana, CA: Third Line Press, 1996.

West P. *Surf Your Biowaves.* London: Quantum, 1999.

Wheeler FJ. *The Bach Remedies Repertory.* New Canaan, CN: Keats, 1997.

Whittaker E. *History of the Theories of Aether and Electricity.* New York: Nelson LTD, 1953.

WHO. *Guidelines for Drinking-water Quality.* 2nd ed, vol. 2. Geneva: World Health Organization, 1996.

WHO. *Guidelines on health aspects of water desalination. ETS/80.4.* Geneva: World Health Organization, 1980.

WHO. Health effects of the removal of substances occurring naturally in drinking water, with special reference to demineralized and desalinated water. Report on a working group (Brussels, 20-23 March 1978). *EURO Reports and Studies.* 1979;16.

WHO. How trace elements in water contribute to health. *WHO Chronicle.* 1978;32:382-385.

Wilen J, Hornsten R, Sandstrom M, Bjerle P, Wiklund U, Stensson O, Lyskov E, Mild KH. Electromagnetic field exposure and health among RF plastic sealer operators. *Bioelectromagnetics.* 2004 Jan;25(1):5-15.

Wilkinson SM, Love SB, Westcombe AM, Gambles MA, Burgess CC, Cargill A, Young T, Maher EJ, Ramirez AJ. Effectiveness of aromatherapy massage in the management of anxiety and depression in patients with cancer: a multicenter randomized controlled trial. *J Clin Oncol.* 2007 Feb 10;25(5):532-9.

Williams A. Electron microscopic changes associated with water absorption in the jejunum. *Gut.* 1963;4:1-7.

Williams A. Increased Concentration of Chlorine in Swimming Pool Water Causes Exercise-Induced Bronchochonstriction (EIB). Presented at the American College of Sports Medicine 51st Annual Meeting, Indianapolis, June 2-5, 2004. *News release, American College of Sports Medicine.*

Wilson L. *Nutritional Balancing and Hair Mineral Analysis.* Prescott, AZ: LD Wilson Cons, 1998.

Winchester AM. *Biology and its Relation to Mankind.* New York: Van Nostrand Reinhold, 1969.

Wittenberg JS. *The Rebellious Body.* New York: Insight, 1996.

Wolf, M. Beyond the Point Particle - *A Wave Structure for the Electron. Galilean Electrodynamics.* 1995 Oct;6(5):83-91.

Worwood VA. *The Complete Book of Essential Oils & Aromatherapy.* San Rafael, CA: New World, 1991.

Yang CY, Cheng MF, Tsai SS, Hsieh YL. Calcium, magnesium, and nitrate in drinking water and gastric cancer mortality. *Jpn J Cancer Res.* 1998;89:124-130.

Yang CY, Chiu H, Chiu J, Tsai SS., Cheng MF. Calcium and magnesium in drinking water and risk of death from colon cancer. *Jpn J Cancer Res.* 1997;88:928-933

Yang CY, Chiu HF, Cheng MF, Hsu TY, Cheng MF, Wu TN. Calcium and magnesium in drinking water and the risk of death from breast cancer. *J Toxicol Environ Health.* 2000;60:231-241.

Yang CY, Chiu HF, Cheng MF, Tsai SS, Hung CF, Chiu HF. Rectal cancer mortality and total hardness levels in Taiwan's drinking water. *Environ Research.* 1999;80:311-316.

Yang CY, Chiu HF, Cheng MF, Tsai SS, Hung CF, Tseng YT. Pancreatic cancer mortality and total hardness levels in Taiwan's drinking water. *J Toxicol. Environ. Health.* 1999;56, 361-369.

Yang CY, Chiu HF, Cheng,MF, Tsai SS, Hung C, Lin M. Esophageal cancer mortality and total hardness levels in Taiwan's drinking water. *Environ Research.* 1999;A;81:302-308.

Yarows SA, Fusilier WB, Weder AB. Sodium concentration from water softeners. *Arch Intern Med.* 1997 Jan 27;157(2):218-22.

Yellen G. The voltage-gated potassium channels and their relatives. *Nature* 2002 Sept 5;419:35-42.

Yokoi S, Ikeya M, Yagi T, Nagai K. Mouse circadian rhythm before the Kobe earthquake in 1995. *Bioelectromagnetics.* 2003 May;24(4):289-91.

Youbicier-Simo BJ, Boudard F, Meckaouche M, Bastide M, Baylé JD. The effects of embryonic bursectomy and in ovo administration of highly diluted bursin on adrenocorticotropic and immune response of chicken, *Int. J. Immunother.* 1993;9:169-190.

Zaks A, Klibanov AM. The effect of water on enzyme action in organic media. *J Biol Chem.* 1988 Jun 15;263(17):8017-21.

Zamora JL. Chemical and microbiologic characteristics and toxicity of povidone-iodine solutions. *Am J Surg.* 1986 Mar;151(3):400-6.

Zhang C, Popp, F., Bischof, M.(eds.). *Electromagnetic standing waves as background of acupuncture system. Current Development in Biophysics - the Stage from an Ugly Duckling to a Beautiful Swan.* Hangzhou: Hangzhou University Press, 1996.

Zumiani G, Tasin L, Urbani F, Tinozzi CC, Carabelli A, Cristofolini M. [Clinico-statistical study on hydropinic and balneothermal therapy of psoriatic patients using the low mineral-content waters of the Comano springs]. *Minerva Med.* 1986 Apr 14;77(16):627-34.

Index